Venturing Forth:

Navigating Middle Age after Divorce

Contents

Prologue:
A Leap into the Unknown

"Grant me the serenity to accept the things
I cannot change, the courage to change the things I can
and the wisdom to know the difference."

- Reinhold Niebuhr

Four years had passed, a journey from feeling like I couldn't take the pain anymore to finally finding freedom from it. The pain had vanished. On a warm June day, I stood on the edge of a cliff in Polignano a Mare, Puglia, enthralled by the scene that lay before me. The cerulean sea shimmered, its waves gracefully dancing harmoniously with the gentle breeze. The colors and motion of the sea invoked a sense of tranquility and awe, providing a serene backdrop to the tumultuous journey that had brought me to this moment. With a charming Italian man wrapping his hands around me, a profound surge of gratitude overwhelmed me as if I had stumbled upon a surreal dream, an episode from a movie. As the gentle wind brushed against my face, memories from my past began to resurface, carrying me back to the beginning.

It was the summer of 2002 in Boston when I, a Taiwanese woman, and my ex-husband, Caetano, a charismatic Brazilian man, first crossed paths at Au Bon Pain in Cambridge, Harvard Square. Drawn to one another, we were entranced in a cross-cultural romance that ignited our spirits.

As two young exchange students, we spent a wonderful and unattached summer together. I was in Boston that year to visit the college, while he was there to search for his new path after graduating from college in Brazil. We spent the summer walking by the Charles River and picnicking at Boston Common. I even turned eighteen years old with him, and he took me to a small Chinese restaurant near his basement studio apartment to celebrate. We bid farewell to Boston after that lunch together. He headed to Barcelona, and I traveled back to Hawaii to finish my last year of high school, each continuing with our separate plans in life.

It wasn't until 2009, during the vibrant Carnival in Rio de Janeiro, that our paths again crossed. Gathered with my two friends to celebrate our master's degree graduation, thoughts of the Brazilian man I had known years ago in Boston resurfaced. I decided to reach out to him, and to my delight, he accepted the invitation without hesitation and showed up in the Christ Redeemer city of Rio de Janeiro from Sao Paulo, where he resided. The reunion quickly sparked a renewed excitement after a couple of sips of caipirinha at Ipanema Beach. Our connection was fueled by a shared longing for exploration and a determination to bridge our physical distance. The enchantment of our

Brazilian-Taiwanese union was irresistible, and we reveled in the romance of maintaining a long-distance relationship. Countless late-night conversations, text exchanges, and longing-filled video calls served as lifelines, keeping our hearts connected across oceans and time zones.

Fifteen years had passed since our initial journey down the conventional courtship path. We decided to take the next step after enduring a year of long-distance challenges, moving in together, first to Brazil, then to Taiwan, introducing one another to our families, and sharing nearly every waking moment. Our lives appeared inseparable, and the birth of our two precious daughters entered our world. However, our relationship failed to thrive despite conforming to societal expectations and achieving significant milestones.

With the passage of time, the once-harmonious foundation of our relationship began to fracture. Even the arrival of our daughters failed to solidify our bond. The attempt to change jobs and routines to salvage our failing marriage only seemed to exacerbate our struggles as our efforts to make things work appeared futile. Unbeknownst to either of us, darkness loomed, revealing itself through unspoken expectations and unaddressed differences. Our love, once vibrant, now crumbled beneath the weight of unresolved conflicts and festering resentments. What had initially been a beautiful connection had transformed into a battleground of lingering disagreements and unspoken grievances.

Throughout those tumultuous years in Taiwan, our once-tender words morphed into shards of abusive language, slicing deep into my spirit and causing me to doubt the genuineness of our relationship. The wounds from the emotional turmoil ran deep, casting dark shadows over my sense of self-worth and plunging me into a state of uncertainty and desolation. It became evident that we were no longer the same individuals we had been when we first encountered each other. As we reached rock bottom, the weight of toxicity transformed into a monster that devoured me, inviting depression into my life.

I vividly remember those days and nights when my younger daughter was just a few days old. The postpartum hormonal changes heightened the depression I was already grappling with, leaving me incapable of functioning without a constant stream of tears flowing down my face. The tears poured down relentlessly, akin to a rainfall that defied my desperate pleas for them to cease. They cascaded like an uncontrollable waterfall, persisting day after day. During those days, Caetano had never visited me and my newborn baby.

Though I questioned myself numerous times—"Is this the life I truly want?"—the doubts were often pushed aside. Leaving my marriage wasn't an option readily considered. I was solely focused on fixing and repairing what seemed broken. The weight of maintaining a "perfect" family for the sake of my children left little room for thoughts of change. I didn't want to be the mother who tore the family apart. Despite the constant internal battle, I carried the pain and wounds within me, determined to move forward without even considering the possibility of divorce. I refused to talk to anyone, refused to accept that I was in the middle of the storm. When you find yourself lost in the woods, it sometimes takes a while to realize that you are truly lost. And it takes courage to believe that you need to find solutions and emerge stronger from it.

The Beginning of the End

At the beginning of 2019, I began one last effort to salvage my crumbling marriage. Meticulously planning a romantic date night, I arranged for my parents and a nanny to care for my two young infant daughters. The younger one was only about six months old, while the older one was just under two years old. I booked a high-end hotel and made a reservation at a Michelin-starred restaurant in the heart of Taipei City, intending to rekindle the spark in our relationship. It had been far too long since we had enjoyed quality time together. I desperately wanted to fix our problems just one more time, so I poured significant effort into organizing this date night, hoping for a breakthrough.

By the end of the night, I was an exhausted mother craving restful sleep, a rare opportunity without any disturbances from my babies. That night, I eagerly looked forward to sleeping. However, Caetano expressed his desire for sex, and I declined, explaining that I was beyond exhausted and on the verge of falling asleep. My body couldn't hold out anymore; it wasn't a situation where I could even pretend to get over it. However, despite my explanations, it seemed as though all the effort I had put in and the quality time we had shared didn't matter. He insisted on forcing himself on me while I continued to plead for some space to rest. For the next twenty minutes, an influx of criticism ensued, inundating me for not complying with his sexual demands and not fulfilling my perceived role as a wife. I felt as though I was solely there to satisfy his physical needs. Above all, my well-being didn't matter to him at all. At 1:00

a.m., I reached my breaking point and expressed that I would leave the room if he couldn't stop. As I stood at the door, he said coldly, "I will make sure you regret this forever if you step out of this room." I opened the door and walked out. I knew I didn't have anything left. My cup was empty, my heart was broken, and my body had been torn apart. I guess I was so exhausted from all the dynamics that I couldn't even shed a single tear.

I sat alone in the hotel lobby for another thirty minutes, unsure of where to go and who to call at that time of night. Finally, I decided to grab my phone and call my grandmother, who lived nearby. I concocted a lie, saying, "Grandma, I'm sorry for calling you so late. I stayed out late partying and forgot the hotel key. Caetano had already fallen asleep and didn't hear me knocking on the door. Can I come over to your place for the night?" Even then, I tried to conceal the whole truth, suffering silently and alone.

At that juncture, we were already planning a move to Barcelona with our two young daughters, hopeful that a change of scenery would help mend our problems. However, following the events of that night at the hotel, it was the first time I honestly considered that this relationship had reached its breaking point. I mustered the courage to open up to Caetano and express my desire to part ways while still committing to co-parenting our children in Barcelona. As expected, it was not a successful conversation. Despite the weight on my shoulders and the ache in my heart, we made our way to Barcelona a few months later, concealing the burden I carried from the prying eyes of others.

Our move to Barcelona amplified my pain. As much as I desired the end of our relationship, I was uncertain about how to initiate it. In addition to applying for legal residence documentation, settling the kids down in a new environment, and making sure all the relocation processes were correctly done, the courage to take that decisive step eluded me, leaving me unsure about the best time for either him or me to move out of our shared apartment in Barcelona. In the midst of this unacknowledged plea, I continued to navigate my life in an unfamiliar place, feeling stuck in uncertainty and unsure of the future. Little did I know that our arrival would coincide with the onset of a global pandemic and the subsequent COVID lockdown. The walls of our new home felt suffocating, echoing our broken relationship. As the world grappled with uncertainty and isolation, I was trapped in a different kind of prison.

However, one fateful day, the local COVID restrictions were finally lifted, granting us the freedom to explore the neighborhood once again. With a sense of renewed hope, we decided to take our children to Tibidabo—a long-awaited outing and our first since the outbreak began. We embraced the moment with excitement and apprehension as we stood atop Tibidabo, overlooking the breathtaking Barcelona skyline. In front of our children, we maintained the facade that everything was fine, occupying ourselves with the beauty of the city we now called home.

After we settled back into our apartment, an unexpected wave of anger suddenly engulfed Caetano, igniting a heated argument. This particular day was different from our usual back-and-forth arguments. It escalated to screaming, to yelling, as if two adults were out of control in front of two kids. On the very same night, I nestled under a blanket next to my two young daughters, their innocent sleep a stark contrast to the turmoil within me. I feared waking them, so I stifled my cries, allowing only silent sobs to escape.

While I won't delve into the intricate details of our arguments or engage in assigning blame, I believe it's important to recognize that every story possesses multiple perspectives. It would be inappropriate and unfair for me to speak on behalf of Caetano. In the disintegration of a marriage like ours, it is true that both parties bear responsibility, and I humbly acknowledge that I had my own issues to confront and address. I do not seek to cast myself as a victim; rather, I am here to share the transformative events that transpired after that particular day, offering a glimpse into the magic that transpired.

Annie

"Annie liked your photo," an Instagram message popped up on my phone screen.

It was as though the Universe had intervened, delivering a small but profound sign. In that instant, I felt a strong urge to connect with Annie—an empathetic confidante and experienced single mother who may understand the intricacies of my circumstances.

I hadn't spoken to Annie in years; our interaction had been limited to maintaining a social network of friends, occasionally responding to each other's posts or dropping a comment here and there. Picking up my phone, I hesitated for a moment. I was never one to easily reveal my vulnerability or seek help from others, especially from a friend with whom I hadn't genuinely engaged in years.

Throughout the years, I had become skilled at wearing a mask of normalcy, adept at pretending that everything was fine and concealing my inner turmoil from those around me. I had mastered the art of hiding my pain, ensuring that no one caught a glimpse of the depths of my suffering. However, in that pivotal moment, as if the Universe was gently nudging me, reminding me of Annie's presence, and telling me I was not alone, I felt a powerful sign urging me to let go and share the heavy burden that weighed upon my heart. "Talk to her! It's okay. Go for it!" The voice of the Universe was beckoning me to open up and release the silent pain I had carried for far too long.

"Hi, Annie. I hope you're doing well. I have a very personal and sensitive question, and I was wondering if you could offer me some advice." With trembling fingers, I carefully composed the message, pausing briefly before finally pressing the Send button.

Annie responded promptly, "You can ask me anything."

"I understand that you're a single mother. I would like to know, how long did it take for you to consider separation? And what was life like for you after the separation? Did your child cry?" I asked Annie, seeking her personal insights and experiences.

Annie shared, "There were various factors involved in my marriage, but it took me approximately a year to decide to take action." She reassured me, "Don't worry about the children, and don't feel sorry for them in this regard. They are fortunate to have a mother like you." She continued, "I can tell you that life for most people improves after divorce. Some start dating again, while others see advancements in their careers. In my opinion, marriage is one of the most challenging relationships in life, especially when children are involved."

"I agree," I responded, patiently awaiting Annie's reply. As I waited, I reflected on my own feelings. "I'm reading your text message and looking at your life, trying to figure out how to navigate this path myself," I confessed to Annie, expressing my vulnerability and seeking her guidance.

"Well, it's been ten years for me now. Rebuilding a new life takes time. But I can assure you that children will adjust well. I neither encourage nor discourage separation; I simply share my experiences. Divorce can be challenging and messy, although some separations can be amicable. Unfortunately, that wasn't the case for me. No one truly understood what I was going through in my life, especially when I decided to leave my marriage," Annie shared, empathizing with my situation.

"I encourage myself every day. It requires a lot of strength and careful planning," she added. "Leave the house. The fact that your arguments have become louder and the acts are in front of the children is inappropriate. You need to find a safe place for your mind immediately. We're not just talking about a failing marriage; we're talking about your mental health in general." Annie's voice conveyed her worry through the phone screen. It felt as if she was right in front of me, gripping my shoulders tightly, shaking me to wake up from my situation. "Right now, instead of worrying about the children, you must prioritize your well-being! Listen to me, Hsin. If you're not okay, your children won't ever truly be okay either."

"In airplane emergency instructions, they always tell you to put on your own oxygen mask before assisting others, including children. It's the same principle here. You can't let guilt or concern for their dad's actions hold you back. By staying in this harmful situation, you're setting a poor example for your daughters on how they should be treated and how they should handle such situations in the future. Children are perceptive, and they see and sense everything happening," Annie continued to urge me.

"Trust me, your kids will feel worse if they see you allowing yourself to live a painful life just for their sake. So don't worry about the children. Instead, focus on removing yourself from this harmful situation. Take the kids with you because they need their mom's love and protection. Take the time to restructure your support system and surround yourself with love. Give yourself a chance to live the life you want, and permit yourself to get out of a life you are suffering. It's time to move out and move on!" I imagined Annie looking at me firmly, trying to convey that the situation was more severe than I thought.

"Kids want you to be happy, just like you want them to be," Annie had said. Her voice echoed in my mind as I read her words. "Move on! Take care of yourself. You will have their blessing."

That thirty-minute conversation with Annie that night marked a profound turning point in my life. Her wisdom, empathy, and shared experiences were key to unlocking the door. It was up to me to step forward and embrace the journey ahead. She reassured me that I wasn't alone, that there was a path to move forward on, and that I deserved a life free from toxicity and stress.

With Annie's support, I began to gather the strength and courage to envision a different future for myself and my children. Her words became my guiding light, helping me navigate the treacherous path of healing and liberation. They acted as a soothing balm to my wounded spirit, inspiring me to take the first steps toward reclaiming my self-worth and rebuilding a life based on love, respect, and empowerment.

I am filled with eternal gratitude as I contemplate that life-changing conversation with Annie. Through her, I discovered the power of shared experiences and the strength that lies within us all. Her words ignited a spark of hope within me, propelling me toward a brighter future. And with that, I courageously crossed the bridge, symbolizing the beginning of my transformation. It's remarkable how a seemingly insignificant Instagram notification turned out to be a gentle reminder from the Universe, guiding me and offering support along the way.

The tears that once streamed down my cheeks have ceased their flow. Behind the clouds of my troubled mind, a glimmer of sunshine emerges, attempting to pierce through. The fear that consumed me has now transformed into courage and determination.

I believe I lost approximately 15 kg during that period—losing sleep, appetite, and sexual desire. Uncontrollable weeping, intense headaches, and constant negative self-talk all contributed to weight loss. Ironically, the stress seemed to assist me in shedding the extra weight I had gained during pregnancy, which had stubbornly clung to my body for years. It's a peculiar way to lose weight, but I suppose I should be happy something positive emerged from it. (Haha!)

Embarking on a Journey of Mindful Living

As the breeze continued to brush across my face in Puglia, I reflected on the incredible distance I had traveled. No longer confined by the pain of the past, I embraced the power to shape the kind of life I desired. My marriage had taught me invaluable lessons about what I didn't want, serving as a guiding compass for the new chapter of my life.

After years of struggle, my divorce agreement was finally finalized. And that's probably why I feel more comfortable writing this book now, knowing that I have reached a significant milestone. While I won't dig into the details of the divorce drama, my children and I were essentially "locked" in Spain for years without the freedom to leave the country, even for me to visit my family in Taiwan. This restriction was partly due to the pandemic, but it was also a result of Caetano's refusal to grant mutual permission for travel. Although the process of divorcing proved to be more painful than anticipated, both financially and emotionally, instead of being achingly depressed, I have come to appreciate the resilience I have developed through countless struggles. In the midst of the challenges, I had only one choice—to build a new life. My primary focus was on healing and creating a nurturing environment for myself and my children.

Throughout these transformative years, I embarked on a journey of mindful living, which will be explained more deeply in Chapter 3. It all began with regular yoga practice, conscious eating, prioritizing adequate and quality sleep, practicing gratitude through journaling, cultivating positive thinking, decluttering relationships, and embracing a simple and sustainable lifestyle.

I have been dedicated to practicing hot yoga since my college years in Boston. However, I paused my yoga practice for a few years when I had my first daughter. With the demands of parenting and moving, yoga somehow got removed from my routine. It's a bit embarrassing to admit, because yoga provided a non-cardio workout that allowed me to break a sweat and achieve my weight loss goals. For a solid ten years, I committed myself to a weekly ninety-minute hot yoga routine, continuously striving to perfect my poses. (I later realized perfecting poses is not what yoga is about.)

It wasn't until I moved to a new apartment after the separation that I decided to reintroduce it into my life. I thought, "Why not try hot yoga?" as it was a familiar practice I had enjoyed. I started searching for hot yoga studios in Barcelona, and the first studio that popped up seemed perfect. Without hesitation, I quickly signed up and showed up for my first practice the following day. As I stepped onto the mat and settled into the familiar rhythm, I found comfort in those moments of stillness. It was during these moments that I could give myself ninety minutes of complete focus on refining my physical and mental well-being without overthinking and negative self-talk, reconnecting with myself on a deeper level.

With each practice, I gradually grasped the true essence of yoga, which is not solely about perfecting every single pose but rather about learning about myself as I am in each moment. It's about embracing self-acceptance and finding harmony within myself. At the end of each practice, during the final resting poses savasana, my yoga teacher consistently reminded us, "Keep practicing, keep breathing, and keep listening to yourself. Thank yourself for the effort you put in today. Namaste"

Through yoga, I gain knowledge and appreciation for exploring the significance of breath, meditation, energy, and the interconnectedness of the Universe. Through yoga, I commence my wellness journey. Through yoga, I practice self-care in calmness. Through yoga, the door opens for me to start searching for myself.

The Universe

The Universe! This word will make several appearances throughout this book, so it's worth taking a moment to address its meaning. The Universe, in a spiritual context, as I define it, refers to the vast and interconnected web of life. It is the idea that there is a greater power or energy that flows through everything and everyone, connecting us all. Recognizing this connection can bring a sense of meaning and purpose and a feeling of being part of something greater than ourselves. You can call it the "higher self" or "God." In this book, the concept of the Universe is not rooted in any specific religious belief, although I deeply respect diverse religious perspectives. The term Universe is mainly about exploring the interconnectedness of existence and our place within it.

During my final year at university in Boston, I had my first encounter with the term Universe while tuning into *The Oprah*

Winfrey Show. The memory of that moment remains vivid in my mind. I was fascinated as Oprah passionately discussed the importance of self-belief, emphasizing that our existence goes beyond physical bodies. She introduced the concept of the law of attraction and its power to guide us in manifesting our desires. This idea intrigued me, prompting me to purchase a book on the law of attraction and wholeheartedly embrace the practice of creating a vision board to attract and manifest my dreams.

In establishing a connection with the Universe and harnessing its power. It serves as a fundamental element, acting as a vibrational signal that reciprocates between you and the Universe. From a scientific perspective, all matter in the Universe is composed of molecules that possess energy. Atoms, which are the building blocks of matter, consist of subatomic particles like protons, neutrons, and electrons. These particles combine to form molecules, shaping the essence of all substances.

In this expansive and interconnected network of energy known as the Universe, vibrations are key. The law of vibrations asserts that everything in the Universe, including thoughts, emotions, and objects, is comprised of energy and emits vibrations at varying frequencies. These vibrations interact and magnetically attract similar energies, influencing our experiences and manifestations in significant ways.

We emit energy into the universal field by consciously directing our thoughts, intentions, and actions. As a result, we attract and engage with energies that align with our own, creating a harmonious resonance. This understanding grants us the power to shape our reality through intentional energy alignment. By aligning our energy with our desires and purpose, we manifest our aspirations and foster a profound connection with the world around us.

To effectively manifest your desires in accordance with the law of attraction, it is crucial to understand that sending out high vibrations to the Universe is only part of the equation. While it is vital to align your thoughts, emotions, and beliefs with what you want, it does not guarantee that your dreams will simply materialize without any effort on your part.

The manifestation process entails a harmonious blend of sending out positive vibrations and taking inspired action. On this transformative journey, I have inevitably encountered signs along the way, much like Santiago, the young Andalusian shepherd boy in Paulo Coelho's *The Alchemist*. Paying attention to these signs and following your inner guidance will guide you toward realizing your dreams.

As a woman approaching her forties, if I were to impart wisdom to my younger self in her twenties, I would emphasize the importance of understanding the law of attraction and the receptive nature of the Universe. However, I would also stress the significance of internal reflection and gaining clarity about our true desires to attract the right things into our lives.

Reflecting on the past fifteen years or so, I realize that I was intensely focused on manifesting everything I believed I wanted: a spouse, a family, a stable job, a home of my own, regular travel experiences, and children who would follow a conventional path of growing up, attending school, and eventually getting married. It is often ingrained in society to conform to external expectations and the desires imposed on us by others.

However, before my journey entirely transpired, the Universe had whispered to me on several occasions, signaling that what I was pursuing wasn't truly aligned with my deepest desires. However, I failed to perceive the signs and neglected to listen to my inner voice. It wasn't until the Universe screamed at me that various areas of my life, including my marriage, health, and parenting, began to crumble apart, inviting depression into my life. That was when I realized that I had nothing left to give. I felt that the cup that was supposed to hold the water was empty and that the glass itself was breaking apart, metaphorically speaking.

My wellness journey has brought transformative shifts to every aspect of my life, including single parenting, rebuilding my support system, and restructuring my career. In this book, my goal is to share my experiences, offering insights into how my mindfulness practices have influenced these areas of my life.

The original purpose of mindfulness is not to treat symptoms but to explore the inner depths of our being, leading to profound changes in our lives. Mindfulness is not about making our immune system better, improving marital relationships, or enhancing work performance (at least not directly and scientifically); instead, it is about getting closer to our purest nature.

Just like practicing sports skills, mindfulness requires finding a suitable methodology and continuing the practice to reap its greatest benefits. A mind that leads to tranquility requires a high level of focused attention and the integration of keen mindfulness awareness. Only when the sediment settles can we see the clarity of the pond water. When the distractions of the mind diminish, we can observe the workings of the mind more clearly.

According to Carol Ryff, psychological well-being consists of six key dimensions:

1. Self-acceptance: The ability to have a positive perception of oneself, accept one's strengths and weaknesses, and have a sense of self-worth.
2. Positive relations with others: Having meaningful and satisfying relationships with others, including friends, family, and social connections.
3. Autonomy: Feeling independent, self-reliant, and able to make choices that align with one's values and beliefs.
4. Environmental mastery: The capacity to effectively manage and adapt to one's environment, including challenges and opportunities.
5. Purpose in life: Having a clear sense of meaning, direction, and goals in life and feeling a sense of purpose and fulfillment.
6. Personal growth: The willingness and ability to continue growing, learning, and developing as an individual.

The six factors work together to contribute to an individual's overall psychological well-being and life satisfaction.

Reinhold Niebuhr, a theologian, said that the key to our happiness lies not in the events themselves but in our perception of them. The water temperature in the wells is usually around 18 degrees Celsius all year round. Drinking it on a summer day makes you feel cool, while drinking it on a winter day makes you feel warm. The water temperature never changes, but environmental factors have changed our perception of it. Calmness allows us to accept things we cannot change, courage empowers us to change the things we can, and wisdom helps us discern between the two.

Dating Mindfully

During this period, several wonderful things did happen to me in the shadow of all that sorrow. I had the fortunate opportunity to meet very kind people in Barcelona, each carrying their unique charm and valuable lessons for me to learn. Even luckier, I got to meet men from diverse corners of the globe. In their presence, I discovered the freedom to explore, engage in the intricate dance of romance, and deeply understand my desires.

Despite my desire to find a partner who genuinely cared and loved me, I was cautious about adventuring into another serious relationship. Consequently, I gradually discovered the realm of casual relationships, a world without boundaries. Within this space, I could explore different relationship styles, engage in intimate connections, and explore diverse cultures. It was a fantastical world where the boundaries of my imagination became the playground of my reality. Why not indulge in the pleasures of this extraordinary journey? Who was I to deny myself the richness of human connection and the exploration of passionate encounters?

When it came to dating, I didn't immediately transition from a traditional committed dating style to diving into casual relationships right after my divorce. Instead, I was falling back into familiar patterns, treating my first post-divorce date as if it were fifteen years ago. We exchanged introductions like we were conducting an interview as I sipped on my sparkling water while contemplating whether he was the right person to open up to. I caught myself searching for the "old-time checklist" to see if he met all the criteria for a potential partner. Recalling how I started calculating the appropriate time to respond to his messages and how many dates I should go on before considering intimacy is amusing. It felt as though I was following an outdated dating guidebook. However, unsurprisingly, that approach didn't lead to a successful connection.

Although I knew what I didn't want after the divorce, I wasn't exactly sure what I wanted, how far I could go, or if I was even ready to talk about "love" again. The painful experiences of my past relationships have created a fear and reluctance to open up to love again. Perhaps also due to my nature as a single mother, I am cautious about ensuring that my personal and family space is consciously and unconsciously guarded.

What I knew for sure was that after years of commitment, I needed a break and space to explore myself and prioritize self-care. I didn't want to juggle multiple dates simultaneously. Instead, I needed time to learn to be alone again and regain my independence. I realized finding a partner who aligned with my desires and values would be challenging without a clear understanding of my identity. Furthermore, it became clear that the "perfect partner" checklist I had once prioritized and worked so hard to fulfill was not bringing me the happiness I sought. It was a valuable learning lesson that urged me not to repeat the patterns of the past.

While I desire to cherish quality time with a special someone, it's crucial for me not to rush into a commitment. Instead, I want to focus on the time we can share without placing expectations on the future. This approach allows me the freedom to assess whether I genuinely want to integrate this person into my routine. One thing I learned from my marriage is that even with a husband sleeping next to me every night and being around me all the time, I still felt like the loneliest person in the world. Therefore, it became more important for me to stay present and create a beautiful story together, even if it was just for a day or a month, rather than obsessing over ensuring its longevity.

With an open heart and an adventurous spirit, I embarked on a journey of casual relationships, eager to continue this extraordinary tale. I consciously manifested my desires to the Universe, embracing a mindset of openness and a willingness to explore new experiences. With this newfound awareness, I sought connections with diverse types of men, exploring profiles and personalities I had never considered before. Each encounter held a sense of anticipation as I unraveled the layers of my own identity and allowed myself to be transfixed by the magic of human connection. As the chapters of my story ensued, I knew that the road ahead would be filled with experiences and personal growth.

While dating can be enjoyable, it is not always filled with constant happiness. It encompasses a range of emotions and can sometimes give rise to doubts. However, through the power of mindfulness, I learned to approach the dating journey with greater equanimity and self-awareness. This allowed me to fully embrace the spectrum of feelings that arose, whether it be excitement, joy, uncertainty, or even moments of doubt. I gained a deeper understanding of myself and my desires by staying present in each experience and observing my thoughts and emotions without judgment.

Mindfulness practice has played a crucial role in helping me navigate challenging situations with a sense of calmness. It has allowed me to perceive things and situations from a broader perspective, enabling me to detach myself from overwhelming emotions. Even when emotions arise, I have discovered the power of mindfulness techniques such as meditation, deep breathing, taking a walk, or enjoying nature. These practices aid in my quick recovery and grounding, serving as my anchor during the ups and downs. This became particularly important during moments when I struggled to reach a divorce agreement with Caetano. I consciously chose not to let that stress transfer to my romantic dates. Instead, I sought to use that connection as a way to ease my stress and temporarily escape the pain. It became an opportunity for me to find relief and create positive experiences amid arduous circumstances.

Essentially, mindfulness taught me to embrace the present moment, fully experience a range of emotions, and cultivate authentic and meaningful connections aligned with my personal journey. I realized these dating experiences were not solely focused on reaching an end goal or finding "the one." Instead, they became a journey of self-discovery, growth, and mutual learning. Each connection and interaction allowed me to remain attuned to my own needs and boundaries while respecting the unique experiences of others. Whenever doubts or insecurities arose, I learned to pause, take deep breaths, and bring myself back to the present moment. This allowed me to reconnect with my inner wisdom and make decisions that aligned with my values and intentions.

I learned to prioritize my well-being and dedicate time to understanding my desires and needs in a relationship. As I navigated the uncertain waters of post-divorce dating, numerous questions arose. When was the right time to start dating again? How often should a couple meet? How much effort should I invest in this new relationship? Were we open to seeing other people? How could I effectively communicate my needs when I was still in the process of figuring them out myself? Did this fall into the category of friends with benefits?

During the first six months after my separation from Caetano, I kept myself emotionally and socially closed off. I only made time to meet a few close friends for lunch and coffee and arrange playdates for the kids. I had implemented a strict sleeping, eating, and exercise routine. I wasn't in the mindset to actively go out and meet new people in bars or social settings. In fact, I was content being alone and enjoying my own company. I remember a friend jokingly suggesting that the only chance I had to start dating would be the Amazon delivery guy.

Throughout my dating journey, I experimented with various methods of meeting people, both online and offline. Unlike in my twenties, when Tinder and other dating apps didn't even exist, most of my experiences were through organic encounters. However, I recognized the need to let go of my long-held belief that online dating was strange or unsafe. It had been fifteen years since I last dated someone new, and I understood the importance of embracing new possibilities and approaches in my search for connection. I recognize that the online world offers a unique opportunity to connect with individuals I might not have encountered in my day-to-day life. It was a chance to broaden my horizons, engage in conversations with people from diverse backgrounds, and expand my understanding of what was possible in a relationship. Surprisingly, as an active Instagram user, I discovered that this photo-sharing platform had covertly transformed into a dating app of sorts, enabling me to connect with like-minded individuals who shared similar interests and passions.

Of course, I also kept an open mind when it came to meeting people through more traditional avenues, such as social events, the single-parent community, mutual friends, or chance encounters. I recognized the importance of face-to-face interactions and the serendipity often accompanying them. By combining both online and offline approaches, I aimed to create a dating experience that embraced a wide range of possibilities.

In my journey of casual relationships, I have embraced the idea of taking my time to truly understand someone and, equally importantly, to honor the space I need for myself. I encourage them to pursue their sources of joy and hope for the same understanding in return. I have learned not to become overly fixated on defining and labeling our connection with terms like "girlfriend" or "boyfriend." If our bond is strong and we enjoy each other's company, that is what truly matters. Let us focus on the present moment and the growth we can experience together again, even if it's only for a day or a month. And if the time comes for us to part ways, it is important to respect those feelings.

In this journey called life, it is not about trying to control one another but rather about sharing our joys and supporting each other's personal growth. If we encounter someone who brings happiness into our lives, we should feel free to move forward without holding onto resentment or hard feelings. After all, isn't that the essence of life—to share experiences, learn, and grow together or separately?

I recall the wise words of a spirited Colombian lady who once said, "For those positive experiences that somehow don't work out, move on with your life and let them cook on the side. The Universe will let it mature when the time comes." This perspective, with a sprinkle of humor, resonates deeply with me. It reminds me that not every connection is meant to be a lifelong commitment, and it's perfectly fine to let go of what doesn't align with my journey. Of course, when it comes to negative experiences, it's best to let them go far, far away immediately! Trusting in the impeccable timing of the Universe, I confidently release attachments and embrace the notion that everything happens for a reason, even if it involves a little bit of cosmic culinary magic.

Casual relationships may not be the right fit for everyone, as each individual's needs and preferences vary. When venturing into the dating journey after divorce, it's essential to acknowledge what didn't work in the past and approach this new chapter with an open mind. Embrace the opportunity to explore different paths and discover what truly resonates with your desires and aspirations. Maintain an optimistic outlook and remain open to the possibilities that await you. Remember, the Universe is abundant and has a way of presenting opportunities at the perfect time. Trust in the timing of your life and have faith that everything you desire will be granted to you when the moment is perfectly aligned.

Each dating experience has taught me profound lessons about others' unique personalities, upbringings, dreams, backgrounds, and careers. It's fascinating to witness each date's strong personalities and observe their entirely different perspectives on relationships. As a result, I find myself on a riveting journey with each of them, embracing their quirks and, of course, enjoying the variety in body types as well. *Wink. Of course, there are moments in these relationships where the balance may be disrupted. However, mindfulness has helped me learn to maintain a sense of composure, unlike my past tendencies to engage in emotional conflicts during my marriage. The practice of self-care and mindful living has greatly aided me in this regard. It has instilled within me a newfound confidence to distance myself from situations that lack peace and to walk away without the fear of losing something valuable.

For every new connection I forge, I try to establish clear boundaries while approaching it with an open mind. My approach is rooted in the belief that our time together should be about enjoying quality moments, prioritizing each other's happiness, and fostering open communication. We take things at a comfortable pace, maintaining a peaceful and respectful atmosphere. Through these experiences, I have come to appreciate the beauty of diversity in relationships. Each encounter presents an opportunity for growth, understanding, and broadening my perspectives. Through these unique connections, I continue to explore the depths of human connection.

As someone capable of holding onto pain without expressing it for years, I acknowledge that open communication has always been one of the most challenging aspects for me to learn. However, I also recognize that it is a necessary change. Being vulnerable, talking about my feelings, and communicating openly are by far the hardest things I have had to learn. At the beginning of my dating journey, I often remained silent, even when something made me uncomfortable. When those uncomfortable feelings arose, I would withdraw and avoid confronting the issue, choosing to hide instead of communicating openly. Perhaps this hesitancy in openly expressing my opinion stems from my Asian cultural background, where we weren't always encouraged to voice our thoughts and emotions freely (at least when I was young).

In a Taiwanese classroom, if a teacher asks, "Any questions?" you can rest assured that there will be little to no response. It's a cultural norm for students in Taiwan to be less expressive and hesitant when it comes to asking questions in a classroom setting. On the other hand, during my time as a student in the USA, I noticed a stark contrast. Professors and teachers would often have to allocate additional time at the end of the class to address the multitude of endless questions from curious students.

Culturally speaking, Taiwanese society tends to place greater emphasis on respect for authority and maintaining a sense of harmony within the group. This can sometimes lead to a reluctance to express individual opinions or ask questions openly. Children are often taught to listen attentively and absorb knowledge without interrupting the flow of the lesson.

While this cultural trait has its benefits, such as fostering discipline and attentiveness, it can also pose challenges when it comes to open communication and expressing personal thoughts and opinions. It took me time to recognize that in order to grow and learn, it is vital to overcome this cultural conditioning and embrace a more expressive and inquisitive mindset.

Through my journey of self-discovery and personal growth, I am learning to break free from these cultural barriers and be more assertive in expressing my thoughts and asking questions. It's a journey, right? Who knows, maybe one day I'll become an over-communicative expert!

It is important to note that this is not a dating book. As of the day I am writing this, I am still learning how to date! Rather, it is a source of courage and encouragement for you to try something new, welcome the unfamiliar, and venture into uncharted territory with an open heart. It invites you to step outside your comfort zone, take risks, and approach dating with curiosity and adventure.

If you are seeking an "Annie" in your life to guide you forward, to the woman reading this book and contemplating the uncertainties that lie ahead after a divorce, I assure you—everything will be alright. My purpose here is to be a beacon of hope, reminding you that setting on a new journey is not only possible but attainable. Through my personal experiences and reflections, I aim to share with you that you have the power to redefine your life and discover happiness, even in the aftermath of the challenges brought by divorce.

Within the pages of this book, you will find reassurance that you are not alone in your experiences and that a world of possibilities is waiting to be explored. It serves as a reminder that love and connection are not limited by past circumstances or societal expectations. By challenging conventional norms and forging your path, you have the power to rewrite your story and create fulfilling relationships that align with your authentic self.

Chapter 1:
The Healing Begins

"Awareness is the first step in healing."

- Dean Ornish

In 2020, the world was gripped by a pandemic, and Spain was no exception. As one of the countries most severely impacted, it faced significant challenges. On March 14, 2020, the Spanish government implemented a two-week lockdown in an attempt to control the spread of COVID-19. However, as the situation persisted, the lockdown was extended and ultimately lasted for a total of eleven weeks, until May 2020.

During this time, Spain grappled with the impact of a severe lockdown that imposed strict restrictions on its citizens. People were only allowed to leave their homes for essential purposes, resulting in streets that were once lively and bustling now becoming a ghost town eerily quiet without activity. Public spaces, which were typically filled with locals and tourists, were left empty and devoid of life. The city took on a surreal atmosphere as businesses closed their doors, and the vibrant energy that once characterized Barcelona was replaced by an unsettling stillness and uncertainty.

In the midst of the pandemic and the strict lockdown measures, my personal life was also in turmoil. My marriage had reached its breaking point, and discussions of separation had already taken place even before we decided to move to Barcelona just six months before the pandemic arrived. The decision to relocate to this city was made with the intention of co-parenting our children, but the process was more complex than I imagined and was on hold due to the pandemic.

Weeks turned into months, and with each passing day, the tension between Caetano and me grew more palpable. We were locked together in the same space, suffering from the complexities of our strained relationship. The environment we shared became increasingly stressful and toxic, taking a toll on the well-being of our entire family. It was an overwhelming experience, leaving me feeling adrift and lost in a city that still held so much unfamiliarity. The weight of the situation, coupled with the challenges posed by the pandemic, heightened the pain and confusion that consumed me. To get myself out of the situation a little bit, I decided to explore a quieter, lesser-known area of the city. It became my temporary escape, a way to find peace amidst the suffocating atmosphere surrounding us.

On a sunny morning in June, I adorned myself in a lovely blue linen dress. Its shoulder-length cut reached just above my elbows, and its knee-length hem gracefully brushed against my knees. As the weather grew warmer, I felt a sense of anticipation in the air. The streets of the Sarria neighborhood, especially the hilly side where I resided, were typically quieter than the bustling city. However, the impact of the pandemic had made them even more serene. Some shops and restaurants had shuttered their doors, bearing the weight of COVID-19's consequences. Despite the circumstances, I ventured out, making my way toward the Muntaner metro station. While standing at a red light, patiently waiting to cross the street, I took a moment to adjust my hair and ensure my face mask was properly secured. (That's right! We were still legally obliged to wear masks in all public spaces.)

Seconds later, the light shifted to green, signaling the time to move forward. With each step I took, my eyes locked with a man's gaze walking toward me. He gave me a wink, and without breaking our stride, we both continued on our way. In that split second, I felt a surge of excitement and thought, "Wow! That feels good." It was a fleeting moment, a mere blip in the chaos of my failing marriage, but it brought forth a rare and pleasant sensation.

I made my way to the metro station, heading to Casa Vicens, a modernist building situated in the Gracia neighborhood of Barcelona, considered the notable architect Antoni Gaudí's first major project. It was built in the 1880s as a summer house for the Vicens family.

The main reason for choosing Casa Vicens as my first exploration of Gaudí's architecture was because my yoga studio was conveniently located just around the corner. Every time I approached my regular practice, the building's exterior, with its natural forms, colorful ceramic tiles, and Oriental and

Neo-Moorish stylistic touches, never failed to catch my attention. I couldn't help but wonder who lived in such an enchanted and unique place.

As I stepped into Casa Vicens, I first noticed the flourishing garden surrounding the building, with palm trees and marigolds. It soon became apparent that some of this planting would have to be removed for construction work. As a result, Gaudí decided to immortalize the lost natural elements by incorporating them into the house's decorations.

The ironwork, painting, and ceramics on the exterior all hark back to the plants that once surrounded the house. At the entrance to the grounds is a sizable wrought-iron gate featuring palm leaves, referencing the trees that once towered over the building. Marigolds are featured in the ceramic tiling on the building's facade, resplendent in polychromatic hues.

The architect envisioned Casa Vicens as a place to escape the busy city and instead contemplate nature. Gaudí built the arched windows to allow the natural world to be visible from inside the house, creating continuity between the two. Natural motifs are also seen throughout the house. Gaudí used pressed cardboard to create three-dimensional models of ivy, fruit, and flowers for the interior decor. The bedrooms, corridors, and dining room are full of exuberant leafy decorations, while in the small lounge on the first floor, a painting on the domed roof gives the illusion of peering through a glass window into the sky. I wandered through the rooms, marveling at the exquisite details of the decor, from the ornate ceilings to the carefully crafted furniture. Every corner held surprises, offering a glimpse into the visionary mind of Gaudí. It was a sanctuary of art and architecture, where history and creativity intertwined, leaving an indelible impression on all who ventured within its walls.

Exiting the building, I discovered a small round table on the terrace of Casa Vicens' café. I ordered a cup of coffee, settled into the chair, and took a moment to remove my face mask, allowing myself to breathe freely. As I sat there, the warmth of the sun on my skin, I contemplated the intricacies of life in Barcelona. With so many challenges weighing on my mind, I struggled to envision my future at that moment. Questions swirled in my thoughts: Was moving to Barcelona the right decision? The feeling of loneliness enveloped me, intensifying the sense of solitude that accompanied my physical state. I could hear my voice whispering, "I want to end my marriage, but how? Is it the right decision?" I could envision the disapproving expressions on my traditional parents' faces, their words echoing in my ears, "Don't leave. It's your duty as a wife to keep the family together." The weight of societal expectations and the fear of putting my children's mental well-being at risk consumed my thoughts, creating a web of uncertainty and doubt.

It wasn't my first time engaging in such internal conversations; they had been recurring for years. Yet, as I rose from that café table, it felt eerily familiar. Ignoring the persistent signals, I prepared myself to return home as if it were just another ordinary day.

Approaching my apartment after the challenging five-block uphill walk from the metro station, I paused to catch my breath. That was when I noticed a man standing a few blocks away, engrossed in painting graffiti on a shop door. He stood there alone, with a small ladder by his side and scattered paint sprays on the ground. To my astonishment, it suddenly dawned on me that the man who had winked at me earlier was none other than the artist commissioned to create a mural on a wall right next to my home.

To this day, I cannot be certain if he was the same person, but the familiarity of his gaze and the warmth of his smile left an indelible impression on me. It was during our second encounter, as I traversed the street, that our eyes met once more. He stood confidently at the opposite end of the traffic light with his painting equipment in hand, facing my direction. As I approached, we locked eyes, and a smile passed between us in that brief instant. I reciprocated, a glimmer of genuine joy breaking through the clouds of my troubled thoughts. Without breaking my stride, I continued on my way home, carrying with me the uplifting memory of that simple act of kindness—a breath of fresh air amid the suffocating atmosphere that awaited me behind the doors of my clouded home, brimming with negativity and toxicity.

In that fleeting encounter, as our paths crossed twice that day, a stranger had the power to make me feel good, if only for a brief moment. It was as if the Universe was delivering a gentle reminder that during life's trials and tribulations, there are unexpected moments of joy that can touch our souls and uplift our spirits. Unfortunately, during that phase of my life, I was unable to hear my own voice and overlooked the signs from the Universe. I became consumed by sadness and pain, without taking the necessary steps to bring about change.

The mural, situated to the direct left of my apartment, greeted my gaze every time I stepped outside. Its vibrant presence commanded attention—a graffiti depiction of a modern woman donning trendy sunglasses, her hair neatly combed back. With her chin slightly lifted and a pair of stunning earrings, she radiated a confident and stylish aura. The artwork, rendered in striking shades of black, gray, and white, exuded a sense of contemporary allure. In the bottom left corner, the artist's signature adorned the piece, accompanied by a simple yet cheerful smiley face. Every time I passed by, it evoked a bittersweet feeling reminiscent of our brief encounter. It stirred within me a mix of cherished and positive emotions. This small light of joy stood in stark contrast to the emotions I faced at home, where I was confronted with the chaotic mess of my current situation, uncertain of what lay ahead.

A week after speaking to Annie on Instagram, I finally started taking action by first reaching out to my parents and asking them to wire me the savings that I had purposely left in Taiwan, just in case anything unexpected happened in Barcelona and I needed a backup (without telling my parents the reason so that they wouldn't worry about me). With the emergency funds in hand, I began searching for a new roof and a new school for my kids. Eventually, I found an apartment in a small town north of Barcelona, away from the touristy areas.

I remember those days when I discreetly packed my belongings, little by little, in preparation for the move to the new apartment. With each journey up and down the Sarria hills under the scorching summer sun, I carried the weight of oversized IKEA bags on my weary shoulders, trying my best to avoid any unnecessary conflict within the confines of our shared home. And, of course, breaking the news wasn't a smooth flow.

I vividly remember the moment I introduced the new apartment to my kids, trying to make it a special surprise without the presence of their father. I secretly wished they wouldn't be too affected by the changes because they were still young toddlers. I set up a large children's pool on our new terrace and arranged some bubble games for them to enjoy. It was my way of creating a welcoming and inviting atmosphere, hoping they would feel comfortable in our new home.

What Do I Want to Do Next?

It had been a month since we stepped foot into the new apartment, and there I stood, my body leaning against the balcony door, peering into the vast expanse of the night. The stillness enveloped me as my children slumbered peacefully, unaware of the tempest brewing within my soul. The journey I had embarked upon, navigating the treacherous terrain of challenges, had pushed me to the very limits of my existence. The atmosphere was far from ideal. My children were sensitive, often crying in the middle of the night, and my ex-husband's emotions ran high, leaving me questioning the lasting impact on our children. The unraveling of my marriage, the embrace of single parenthood, and the daunting task of forging a new life in Barcelona had all taken their toll, their weight pressing down upon my entire body.

Yet, there is a silver lining in the realm of single parenting—the resilience and power it instills within you. My children, in their innocent presence, became my guiding light, fueling my determination to overcome the challenges. I hoped that one day, through my growth and strength, I could serve as a role model for them, showing them that even in the face of adversity, we have the capacity to rise above and thrive. It would be a lifelong learning of small steps, just like the Spanish saying "paso a paso," meaning "step by step."

In that raw and unguarded moment, as I stood on the precipice of my balcony, I surrendered myself to the depths of my emotions. The realization washed over me like a gentle breeze, whispering in my ear, "I need to find my strength so that everything else around me can find its balance." I asked myself, "What do I want to do next?" Despite not having a clear answer, I knew I wanted to be a writer, to tell stories, and maybe one day I could write a book. So I began by creating a blog as a platform to practice writing, exploring various forms, such as ghostwriting, guest posts, and freelance writing to craft my skills.

As I write this book and reflect on my journey, I can't help but marvel at how the Universe has answered my wishes. It's incredible to realize that I am connected to the Universe, and it has taken my requests into consideration. In fact, it has gone above and beyond, granting me incredible stories and experiences that have shaped me into the person I am today. These experiences have become a boundless wellspring of inspiration from which I draw, and I am eager to share them with you.

In order to provide for myself and my family, I also took on the role of an international buying agent. Although unrelated to writing, this job allowed me to assist people in Taiwan by sourcing Spanish products. While I must admit that I wasn't entirely sure about the legality of this particular income source, I am one of those individuals who always waits for the traffic light to turn green before crossing the street, even at 2:00 a.m. Despite the unconventional nature of my role as a buyer, it was crucial for my survival.

Though I faced financial constraints during that time, I was determined to change my life. One notable thing that occurred was my newfound adventure in spiritual discipline. I embraced a simpler way of living, practicing mindful eating, and prioritizing getting enough sleep. When you have limited funds, a Chinese saying goes, "Put the money on the knife's edge," emphasizing the need for careful spending. Before my time in Barcelona, I indulged in fine dining and extravagant travel destinations and had a wardrobe filled with shoes or heels that caused me pain, excessive clothes, and bags I didn't use.

Looking back, I realize how wasteful I was in my consumption. It wasn't about indulging in premium products; it was about accumulating things without utilizing them, driven by an intention to impress others rather than a genuine passion or purpose. This realization made me understand that many of these behaviors were rooted in my desire for validation from society, to prove to myself and others that I was enough or even more than enough. It was not just about my marital issues; there were also several other aspects of my life that required attention and improvement.

Cooking has never been my greatest strength; the kitchen has never been my territory. I still remember when I was younger, my grandfather would always encourage me to stand next to my mom and aunts to learn cooking. He would tell me that by standing next to them every day, I would eventually learn one dish or one technique! He was right! I should have paid more attention to that. The process of shifting to a mindful eating lifestyle began because initially, I felt that vegetables were easier (and cheaper) to handle than meat. Personally, I didn't know how to choose good meat or even determine if the meat was still good after a short period in the fridge. I shifted toward a vegan and seafood cooking style to make my life easier and ensure a healthy lifestyle, occasionally incorporating meat. It wasn't until I discovered the book *How to Eat* by Thich Nhat Hanh that I truly understood how to combine mindfulness and food to create a new level of internal joy. According to Thich Nhat Hanh, the core of mindful eating is, "Don't chew your worries, your fear, or your anger. If you chew your planning and your anxiety, it's difficult to feel thankful for each piece of food. Just be present and chew your food."

The kids and I also started growing our food by planting small gardens on our terrace. We spent time getting our hands dirty and learning how plants grow and the importance of nurturing them. Gardening with the kids not only fostered a deeper connection with nature but also brought us closer as a family. It became a shared project where we celebrated every little sprout and rejoiced in the first harvest of our homegrown vegetables. They would draw on clay pots, while I was responsible for seed germination. It was a valuable learning experience for us all. As the Zen master Thich Nhat Hanh said, "Spend time with your food; every minute of your meal should be happy. Few people have the time and opportunity to sit down and enjoy a meal like that." We are very fortunate.

Despite our limitations and struggles, we truly appreciate having shelter, food, and the opportunity to live in the beautiful city of Barcelona.

One major shift I have made is adjusting my sleep schedule. In the past, I was always a night owl, reluctant to go to bed even when it was already 3:00 a.m. I would wake up early in the morning, go to the office, and function on less than five hours of sleep, working a minimum of sixty hours a week in a high-stress environment. I was constantly exhausted, but I convinced myself that it was fine and I would catch up on sleep over the weekend.

It wasn't until I became a mother that I realized the importance of getting enough sleep, especially during those early years with my kids when I fully experienced the challenges of sleep deprivation. Sleep is sacred and should not be taken for granted. I understood that to be productive and have a clear mind the next day, I needed to prioritize sleep. During my early days of the mindfulness journey, I delved into prioritizing self-care, gradually started going to bed earlier, and created a consistent sleep routine. By allowing myself sufficient rest, I noticed a remarkable improvement in my energy levels, focus, and overall mood. The change in my sleep habits has been a game-changer, contributing to a healthier and more balanced life.

Travel has always been a great passion of mine, and throughout my life, I have had the opportunity to live and explore six continents before the age of thirty-five. In fact, I have spent more time living outside my home country of Taiwan than in it. As a result, I have gained considerable experience in relocating internationally and adapting to different cultures. However, this time was different. Instead of just me, I was accompanied by two toddlers, one Shiba Inu dog, and a husband with whom I didn't have the best relationship. Unlike with previous moves, I didn't have a school lined up, a prearranged career waiting for me, or even a friend or family member residing in the new city. Other than two brief visits as a tourist, each lasting only a week, I arrived in Barcelona as a complete newcomer, like a blank sheet of paper without any guiding directions. And, no, I don't speak Spanish or Catalan.

I needed to start building a support system for myself and my kids. Lost in the depths of this profound loneliness, I clung to the faint glimmers of connection that remained, no matter how fragile and distant they seemed. Desperation drove me to reach out to mere acquaintances, sending messages to people I had crossed paths with only a handful of times.

In my twenties, making friends was an easy territory for me. I would meet people through school and work, slowly expanding my networks. However, this time was different. I didn't have these familiar sources to begin my life anew in Barcelona, and I knew I had to make an extra effort to reach out to people and play a proactive role in finding new connections.

I remember the first time I wrote a message in the kids' school parents' WhatsApp group, introducing myself as a single mother who was new to town and didn't speak Spanish or Catalan. I expressed my desire to find playdates for my children. To my surprise, I received multiple invitations for playdates almost instantly. On the following Friday, nearly the entire class of my older daughter joined us at our usual playground to show their support. Thinking back to that moment still gives me goosebumps, and I am immensely thankful for their kindness and generosity.

Some moms went the extra mile, reaching out to me privately and handing me second-hand school uniforms they no longer needed. On rainy days, they thoughtfully offered us a ride home instead of having us walk on the street and get soaked. These acts of kindness and support warmed my heart and made me feel welcome in a new community. It was during these moments that I realized the power of human connection and the beauty of finding friendship in unexpected places.

In my personal circle, my desperation led me to reach out to a handful of people I had only briefly encountered, many of whom I hadn't spoken to during the COVID-19 pandemic. One of them was Victoria, whom I met during a yoga class. She quickly became one of my closest friends in Barcelona. Victoria, an outspoken Lithuanian girl living in Barcelona for over a decade, has consistently impressed me with her ability to express her opinions openly and clearly without offending anyone. Whenever I witness her confident demeanor, I jokingly remind myself that I need to adopt at least 10 percent of her personality traits into my own.

We would have coffee and chit-chat in the neighborhood of Provença in the afternoon. We would walk around the city, talking non-stop about our lives and how we ended up in Barcelona. She would join me in some activities, such as visiting galleries, walking in the park, and even attending live concerts in less desirable neighborhoods that she wouldn't usually go to. She extended her invitation to her lovely apartment for lunch. She even went the extra mile and prepared a Burofax, which is a legal notice, with her boyfriend when I got scammed by a freelancer I was working with. She was right there for me! For a period of time, she was the only person I would receive texts from and my only emotional support system outside of the parenting world.

Elsa and Cristina were two more connections I made. They were two lovely Spanish girls with whom I shared a morning hike a week before the COVID lockdown began. They have taught me so much about Spanish culture. Elsa is now a mother, and we now spend time together every month, forming a close bond. Cristina, on the other hand, was kind enough to show me around her hometown of Valencia before starting her career in Italy.

Last but not least . . . there was *the artist.*

The Catalan Artist

Driven by curiosity, fueled by the desire to uncover more about the enigmatic artist whose signature adorned the bottom of his remarkable painting, I meticulously searched for clues, diligently scouring the Instagram account of the shop that had commissioned him. And there, I found his account. With a mix of excitement and apprehension, I tapped on the tags and delved into his public profile. As I scrolled through his Instagram feed, a kaleidoscope of graffiti, sketches, and storyboard snippets appeared before my eyes. However, alongside the excitement, a wave of uncertainty also washed over me. Was it a wise decision to reach out in this manner? I didn't want to come across as strange or desperate. After all, forging connections through a single wink, a brief smile, and Instagram interactions was uncharted territory for me, a far cry from the days of traditional friend-making.

With a deep breath, I clicked on the Follow button, hoping to capture his interest and potentially cultivate a friendship. In an earnest attempt to connect, I shared a photo of his artwork, making sure to tag him in the process, with the intention that he would appreciate my gesture of sharing. It felt as though I had orchestrated a serendipitous event, creating an opportunity to become his friend. To my delight, he sent me a message not too long after expressing gratitude for showcasing his work.

Despite the quirky thing I did, credit to my momentary creepiness, our story began to unfold, marking the start of an unexpected roller-coaster connection.

"Thank you," he said.

"You're welcome," I replied.

"Where are you from?" he asked.

"I'm from Taiwan, and I recently arrived in Barcelona. I separated from my husband and left the apartment where you saw me. I don't have any friends in the city yet, but I'm trying to make new connections. If you don't mind being my friend, we could meet for coffee when you're free," I responded, trying to address my situation without writing an essay.

"I'm sorry to hear about your marriage. Sure, we can arrange a time for coffee," he replied, acknowledging that he remembered who I was without saying more.

"My name is Hsin."

"I'm Xavier. Nice meeting you."

He followed me back!

On an early September afternoon, with the buzz of children starting their new school year, we settled into the rhythm of our daily lives. As I leisurely wandered through the charming labyrinth of narrow streets in the neighborhood of Raval, Barcelona, the air was infused with a vibrant mix of cultural diversity and artistic energy. My gaze wandered curiously in every direction, devoid of a specific destination. Unexpectedly, the sky transformed from a clear blue to a somber gray, and raindrops began to fall delicately, gradually evolving into a torrential downpour that swiftly drenched the streets.

"Oh my! Talk about perfect timing," I exclaimed, a sense of urgency gripping me as I frantically sought shelter from the relentless rain. With a quick scan of my surroundings, I hastened toward the arch-shaped entrance of Plaça de Vicenç Martorell, eager to find respite and dry myself off.

While waiting for the rain to subside, I instinctively pulled out my phone and posted an Instagram story about the unexpected downpour, hoping to pass the time. Meanwhile, I pondered the possibility of making a dash toward the Plaça de

Catalunya metro station, a mere five-minute walk away. It didn't sound too bad, did it?

Just as I was gearing up to sprint toward the metro station, I felt the familiar vibrations of my phone in my bag. I quickly retrieved it and noticed a notification from Instagram. To my surprise, it was him—Xavier.

"I live very close by. I could bring an umbrella to you," he kindly offered in a message. However, despite the rain pouring down around me, I hesitated and politely declined, explaining that I had already left the location. It was a spontaneous response, driven by a mix of not wanting to inconvenience him and perhaps a touch of self-restraint.

Yet a part of me started to indulge in a brief daydream of the romantic artist gallantly appearing with an umbrella, ready to rescue me from the downpour. Oh, how my imagination conjured up scenes of our third encounter, where he would save me from the rain in a serendipitous moment of romance. Alas, in reality, I was soaked and continued my day with nothing but a whimsical tale that only existed in the realm of my dreams.

Reflecting on my dating history, I realize that my "portfolio" has been rather dull. It mostly consists of white-collar, highly educated office men who strive tirelessly to climb the corporate ladder and accumulate wealth. The other half are those with grand entrepreneurial dreams. It's as if I subconsciously created a checklist based on my own background before becoming a writer. Perhaps it's because I, too, was once caught up in pursuing success and recognition in the corporate world, working tirelessly to become someone I didn't want to be.

So, with Xavier, my imagination took flight and blossomed, prompting me to reflect on the archetypal portrayal of artists in movies, TV shows, and books. Are they as sensitive, creative, interesting, and individualistic as they are often depicted? And above all, do they possess a natural inclination toward romance that sets them apart from others? These musings swirled in my mind, coloring my perceptions of Xavier and adding an extra layer of intrigue to our budding connection.

"Okay, snap out of it!" I mentally urged myself. Our connection was meant to be purely platonic. I had the responsibility of two kids and had recently gone through a separation. I needed to focus on rebuilding my life and ensuring a smooth transition into this new chapter of single parenting. Dating was not my priority. What I needed was a friend, not a romantic partner!

Moreover, I was sure that I didn't want to have any more children, and it seemed that Xavier, being single without kids, deserved the life he desired. Right then and there, I caught myself assuming and making decisions about someone I hardly knew. I took a deep breath, attempting to create enough reasons to clear my mind and find clarity.

Nice to Meet You

Weeks after the rainy day in Raval, we finally scheduled a late afternoon for our first official "nice-to-meet-you" encounter. Personally, I didn't perceive it as a typical romantic date, as my mind was more preoccupied with questions like, "Is this a good idea?" and, "What should I say?"

Xavier stood in the corner of the street block, donning a casual T-shirt and shorts, a small bag slung over his left shoulder. As I drew nearer, I noticed that familiar smile once more, but this time, I had the chance to experience it up close, accompanied by a warm and comforting hug.

"How are you feeling? Your work and kids, are they fine?" As we walked on this narrow side street to find a terrace nearby, he gently placed his left hand on my right shoulder and asked.

"I'm fine. Everything is fine. Work is going well, and the kids are doing fine," I replied, though the words tasted like a bitter lie on my tongue. In reality, I struggled to find the right words to convey my true emotions and vulnerabilities, especially to someone I had just met. How could I possibly unload the weight of my life onto a brand-new acquaintance? The last thing I wanted was to burden or scare away a potential friend. So we delicately avoided discussing the ongoing process of my divorce and the emotional turmoil my children were enduring. Deep down, I knew I was far from fine. Almost every night, tears streamed down my face as I sought comfort on my balcony, the only witness to my silent sobs.

As we settled into our seats, he took a sip of beer and rolled his tobacco, while I opted for a bottle of sparkling water. It was then that he began to share his story.

Xavier, a Spanish man born and raised in Catalonia, preferred to be called Catalan. I secretly admire his appearance while he speaks. His short hair, composed of strands of white and gray, perfectly complemented his beard that gracefully framed his jaw, chin, and upper and lower lips. His lips, though slightly dry, only added to his irresistible charm. I found it incredibly charming as he spoke to me in a gentle Spanish accent. The combination of a Spanish man with an accent, coupled with the idea of the artist's imagination I had formed before we even met, heightened the magnetic pull I felt. Whenever he shared his story, his gaze would lock onto mine, unwavering, giving me butterflies in my stomach.

Amidst the persistent rain, we found ourselves involved in an extraordinary four-hour conversation, engrossed in discussions and eagerly sharing our life stories and experiences. Time seemed to stand still as we reveled in each other's presence.

In my personal experience, I don't remember having a four-hour date just accompanied by sparkling water! I shared a little bit about my background, but we spent most of the time talking about Barcelona, Spanish, and the mural he had just completed.

One of my most memorable conversations with Xavier was when he casually mentioned that he had moved out of his mother's apartment and purchased his property about ten years ago. My mind quickly did the math, and I couldn't help but blurt out, "You mean you moved out at thirty years old?

Now, let me clarify: I wasn't passing any judgment. It was just a stark cultural difference between us. In Spain, it's pretty common for people to live with their families until a later age, for both economic and cultural reasons. Spanish people, much like those in Taiwan, place a strong emphasis on family. In fact, my father still lives with my grandparents, and it's considered a blessing to have multiple generations under one roof. However, personally, I've been living independently since my sophomore year in high school, either in dorms or rental properties. I guess I've always valued my privacy a little too much to imagine any other way. That's probably why my marriage didn't work. Just kidding, but it does make me wonder!

As we bid farewell, he made a heartfelt promise to take me on a unique tour of the city, where he would introduce me to more art that I could truly appreciate. The excitement lingered as we entered the metro station together, but we headed to different platforms, minutes later finding ourselves sitting across from each other on opposite sides, only divided by a platform and the passing trains. In that fleeting moment, I discreetly snapped a picture of him with my phone, capturing the magic of our encounter. Our destinations, though divergent, perfectly mirrored the contrasting chapters of our lives at that moment: he headed toward the bustling city center, his vibrant home, while I ventured away toward a serene and quieter corner.

About one week later, he generously devoted his time to accompanying me on an expedition throughout the city, unveiling its hidden treasures and enlightening me about the diverse backgrounds and distinctive artistic styles of various creators. It was yet another rainy day. While he patiently guided me through the neighborhoods of Raval, Poble Sec, and Sant Antoni, we wandered through narrow streets, with him explaining some of the famous graffiti, lesser-known landmarks, and how the art world works in Barcelona. I felt a sense of serendipity, as if the Universe was orchestrating my romantic daydreams that had flickered through my mind in Plaça de Vicenç Martorell, where my artist had come to my rescue with an umbrella. However, with its playful demeanor, the rain seemed to possess a mischievous sense of humor, persisting in its relentless downpour without a hint of mercy.

Up until this point, I remained uncertain about our feelings for each other and never mustered the courage to ask if he was the guy who winked at me while crossing the street. Our conversations covered a wide range of topics, yet there were also notable gaps in what we discussed. There was a certain enigmatic quality about Xavier, where at times he would open up and share his personal stories, ambitions, and even recent dating experiences. However, for the most part, he seemed somewhat disconnected, as if there were hidden depths waiting to be unveiled. It felt as though only time could truly reveal the essence of who he was.

After he graciously showed me around the neighborhood, even amidst the rain, the day seemed to take on a beautiful hue. As our time together came to a close, he gently pressed two polite kisses on my cheek and softly uttered, "We'll talk more."

"Yes, let's find time to meet again," I replied, hopeful for the future.

We had no more contact for the next few weeks.

Despite my efforts to reach out and set up another coffee meet-up, it became apparent that he was unavailable, and his responses were noticeably colder. The once-vibrant communication between us dwindled, leaving our friendship to fade into the realms of obscurity. I was confused and disappointed in the face of his sudden disinterest. Of course, during that time, my mental strength was incredibly fragile. I found myself questioning, "What is wrong with me?" "What problem do I have that I can't be his friend?" Generally, I have always been the one that people gravitate toward, eager to approach and engage in conversation. This experience felt foreign and unsettling, leaving me feeling uneasy.

However, I made a conscious decision to continue on my healing journey, not allowing myself to show any signs of distress. I convinced myself that he had concluded I wasn't the right fit to be his friend, which was outside my control. Weeks passed, and I was fully occupied with sorting out the different facets of my life.

"Hey! How are you? Would you like to go for a coffee tomorrow?" One October morning, out of the blue, I received a text message from Xavier that took me by surprise.

"Sure! Is 10:00 a.m. a good time?" I felt confused, but I still replied.

We both arrived promptly at the cafe and ordered two small cups of coffee with milk to go. As we leisurely walked along the serene Rambla del Raval, the October breeze gently caressed our faces, signaling the arrival of cooler weather and bidding farewell to the summer. Our eyes were drawn to Fernando Botero's iconic sculpture, *El Gato*, *The Cat*, and a nearby bench seemed to invite us to take a seat, setting the stage for our conversation.

"How have you been lately?" he asked, his voice filled with genuine concern as he poured a pack of sugar into his coffee.

"I'm fine. Everything is fine," I uttered, pausing for a moment of silence. "Errr, actually I'm not fine," I decided to open up, allowing myself to be more honest instead of pretending that everything in my world was functioning perfectly. For the first time, I let my vulnerability show and stopped pretending to be the strong woman who knew and did it all.

Xavier sat there, fully engaged and attentively listening to me as I poured out my problems for three straight hours. He gave me undivided attention with each sip of his coffee and the occasional puff of his tobacco. I shared my family issues, financial struggles, work challenges, concerns about my children, and the intricacies of my relationship history. It was a relief to finally let go of the facade of perfection and release it all. Throughout our conversation, Xavier remained quiet, creating a safe space for me to unload my burdens.

That became one of the most valuable three hours in my life, because I allowed myself to be vulnerable, to be myself. I will forever appreciate his generous gift of time during that day.

After sharing some of the most personal stories with Xavier, I started to wonder about his life and the reasons behind his disappearance. Was he simply the type of person who withdraws at times? Was it a common way of socializing in Barcelona? Or perhaps he had started seeing someone? Numerous thoughts raced through my mind as I tried to make sense of his absence and understand the dynamics of our evolving connection.

In addition to these questions, doubts about the nature of our relationship began to surface. Was Xavier a friend, or was there something more? The fact that he had vanished without any communication at all only added to my confusion. In my understanding, friendship was a continuous bond, so why the sudden absence? Although he had been attentive and caring during our recent conversation, the lingering uncertainty persisted in my mind, making it difficult to find clarity.

"And how about you? How have you been lately?" I inquired, hoping to find the answer to my confusion.

"I'm fine as well. I've been very busy with work lately," he continued, sharing his story. "I was also seeing this girl I met last year, but it looks like it won't work out."

"Oh, I'm sorry to hear that," I replied, my response tinged with a hint of unsurprise. During these months filled with a mixture of feelings and the artist's captivating story I had created in my imagination, I was unsure about where I stood with Xavier. However, one thing remained certain: my deep admiration for his work and character. There was an inherent romance in our interactions, devoid of any forced pretense. He represents to me the notion that simple can be special.

"I want to take you to this boutique shop that I know you will like," he said after three hours of conversation, his gaze and tone evoking butterflies in my stomach once again. It felt wonderful to have someone who genuinely thought about and cared for my interests.

"Oh, my romantic artist," I thought, secretly cherishing him.

As Xavier led me toward the shop, we unexpectedly bumped into a stylish, short-haired woman. She greeted me with brief eye contact, and they engaged in a conversation in Spanish for a minute, which I couldn't comprehend. It reminded me that I should prioritize improving my Spanish skills soon. After their exchange, they went their separate ways.

"That was the girl I mentioned, the one I was seeing but it didn't work out," Xavier explained, looking at me.

I thought, "Wow! In the sprawling city of Barcelona, in the early morning, did we just happen to run into each other?" Xavier and I were both taken aback by the coincidence. "Is everything going to be okay?" I asked.

"Yes, don't worry!" Xavier reassured me, putting my concerns to rest.

Xavier continued to guide me to the boutique shop, opening the door and exchanging greetings with the owner, who happened to be his friend. The interior of the shop was adorned with a stunning collection of mosaic lamps, each radiating vibrant colors that added to the shop's dreamy atmosphere and ambiance. Some lamps hung from the ceiling, while others were carefully displayed along the sides of the shop. While Xavier was conversing with the owner, I continued to venture further inside. My gaze was drawn to tribal masks adorning the walls and various percussion instruments scattered throughout the space.

Completely enthralled, I engrossed myself in the shop's dazzling displays, examining each piece with fascination. As I made my way toward the center, the air suddenly became alive with the harmonious melodies of percussion music, its upbeat rhythm filling the space. Turning my head, I discovered Xavier and the shop owner playing the percussion instruments, their synchronized performance adding to my admiration for Xavier. In that moment, a newfound attraction stirred within me—an acknowledgment of my sexual interest in him.

While I was confident in my readiness to move on from my previous relationship prior to meeting Xavier, there was still a lingering question in my mind about whether I was truly prepared for another romantic journey, whether it was with him or someone else. I wasn't desperate for love, but I certainly welcomed the possibility of a satisfying and mutually fulfilling sexual encounter (eagerly).

Leaving the shop, the allure of a sexual connection with Xavier remained undeniable. His attractiveness lingered in my mind, stirring a desire to explore the potential for a different kind of relationship—if, of course, Xavier was open to it. The idea of venturing into uncharted territory with him held a certain intrigue, igniting a spark of curiosity within me.

Christmas Is in the Air

"Hey! Christmas is just around the corner! Let's do something!" I texted Xavier, brimming with excitement. It had been two months since we last saw each other, and I was eager to reconnect during this festive season.

"This Saturday, 6:00 p.m. See you then!" came his prompt reply.

Filled with anticipation, I had even carefully selected the clothes I wanted to wear the night before. I straightened my hair and applied light makeup, paying attention to every detail. The excitement coursed through me as I ventured out of my home on the designated day, even though the temperature had dropped to one degree that night, braving the freezing temperatures that had descended upon Barcelona.

Upon arriving at Plaça de Catalunya, I positioned myself on the Zurich Cafe side of the road, ready to make my way across to Las Ramblas. And there, standing right at the beginning of Ramblas, I spotted Xavier. His eyes lit up with a radiant smile behind the mask, a clear display of his eagerness as he patiently awaited my arrival. Crossing the street became a delightful journey toward his welcoming presence.

Pausing in the midst of the bustling crowd, Xavier and I embraced tightly, sharing a warm hug and exchanging two kisses on the cheek. Despite the lingering effects of the pandemic, the streets of Las Ramblas were transformed into a festive wonderland, adorned with an array of vibrant decorations that illuminated the night. The city lights danced with a dazzling radiance, reflecting off the glistening surfaces and creating a magical atmosphere.

"Where should we go?" I asked, not having planned anything ahead of time.

"I will take you to this new exhibition by Jaume Plensa, a famous local artist known for his sculpture works," Xavier replied with his Spanish accent, which I found quite sexy, as he guided me toward the gallery. He continued, "I think you will enjoy it."

There's a positive sensation that comes with knowing someone is thinking of you, even in the simplest gestures, like making plans for a night together. It filled me with immense gratitude to have Xavier by my side, if only for a single evening. The fleeting nature of our time together amplified its significance, making every moment feel precious and magical.

While walking along the Ramblas, shoulder to shoulder, he shared with me the intriguing history of this renowned street. He explained how the face of the city has evolved since the 1992 Olympics, transforming from a once-troubled drug-infested area into one of the most popular destinations on the planet. Additionally, he shared insights about what it felt like to be a local living with overtourism. It was difficult for me to fully comprehend the concept of overtourism, as COVID-19 struck just five months after I arrived in Barcelona as a new resident. Amid the challenges of settling down and navigating a broken marriage, my first experience of strolling around the city was during the pandemic, when everything appeared quiet and serene.

Suddenly, he pointed toward a money exchange store on the side of the Ramblas, saying, "I bought my first guitar there."

In the exhibition, Xavier graciously shared his experiences as an artist, enlightening me on the collaborative efforts between the community and government in Barcelona to foster artistic growth. He also provided insightful commentary on the techniques showcased in the artwork. Together, we exchanged our thoughts on the pieces we admired, even secretly comparing the prices to see if they resonated with our values. It was truly enriching!

Leaving the gallery behind, Xavier led me to a charming terrace bar nestled near the Palau de la Música Catalana, revealing his thoughtful planning for our next destination. As we strolled along the street that led to the opera house, my gaze was immediately caught by the awe-inspiring installation by Jaume Plensa called *Awilda*, prominently displayed in front of the Palau de la Música Catalana. The sculpture was a mesmerizing sight, featuring the figure of a woman seated with her eyes closed, intricately crafted from metal mesh structures. Plensa's distinct style of intertwining forms showcased a harmonious blend of grace and contemplation. The experience of witnessing this artwork only intensified my admiration for Xavier's attention to detail and thoughtfulness in creating meaningful moments.

As we entered the bar Xavier had enthusiastically recommended, he excitedly informed me about the charming terrace embellished with lush plants. With a friend working there, he assured me that he would make every effort to secure a spot for us. To my delight, we spent the remainder of the evening beneath the only tree at the center of the terrace, thoughtfully arranged by his friend and adorned with enchanting light decorations. Entranced by each other, we relished the moment, sipping on our San Miguel beers and indulging in the delectable nachos his friend treated us to.

It was approaching 11:00 p.m., past my usual bedtime. Normally, I adhered to a disciplined routine of mindful living, prioritizing sufficient sleep and maintaining a healthy diet. Keeping a strict 10:00 p.m. bedtime in my room had been a steadfast practice since my separation. However, on that particular night, I was unwilling to let the enchantment end so abruptly. As we walked together, side by side, toward the Plaça de Catalunya metro station, the bustling crowd engulfed us, their hurried movements surrounding us from all directions. Standing in the middle of the whirlwind of activity, Xavier's voice cut through the chaos, softly whispering, "I want to kiss you." At that moment, we came to a standstill amid the vibrant backdrop of one of Barcelona's busiest streets. We instinctively removed each other's masks, his fingertips gently encircling my neck, and he pulled me closer to his lips.

The people rushing past us, the twinkling Christmas lights, and the ambient music surrounding us seemed to fade into the background. In that moment, time stood still. Nothing else mattered.

Sometimes, it's not the words exchanged but the moments created that leave a lasting impression.

I don't vividly remember the details of our conversation that night. Yet, looking back now, I realize that our time together became an indelible memory, etching itself as one of the most unforgettable dates I've shared with Xavier. In that moment, I allowed myself to fully relish the experience, embracing the present without any anticipation or concern for judgment. It was a night of pure presence and connection, where worries melted away, leaving only the profound joy of being in each other's company.

Traditionally, on a first date, I would often find myself caught in misery, changing my outfit repeatedly, meticulously prepared in advance, consumed by the worry of what my date would think of me. Every aspect of my behavior and appearance would come under scrutiny as I sought to make a perfect impression. The fear of being judged or falling short created an overwhelming sense of nervousness within me, amplified even more by the fact that it had been fifteen years since my last date.

The rawness of the experience added an extra layer of vulnerability and uncertainty.

However, Xavier was different. His down-to-earth nature allowed me to gradually let go and be myself more and more each time I saw him. By the night of our memorable date, I had departed from my usual routine of self-doubt. Effortlessly, I showed up for our date, embracing the moment authentically and without pretense. Gone were the elaborate preparations and excessive concerns about appearances. It was a refreshing change to simply be myself and savor the joy of our time together.

There was a liberating feeling in letting go of those self-imposed pressures and fully embracing the genuine connection we shared. The traditional patterns of fancy restaurants, movie theaters, or upscale bars did not bind our date. Instead, it was a night of spontaneity and pure fun, without anticipation or expectations, which allowed me to break away from the expected norms. It was a shift from the traditional dating paradigm to a more carefree and enjoyable experience, where the focus was on simply having a great time together.

Traditionally, I would never be the one to take the initiative in making contact. I was always the shy and somewhat snoopy lady who hesitated to reach out for a date. It was a pattern that I had become accustomed to, and it limited my opportunities for connection and exploration. However, everything changed when I started practicing mindfulness and understanding the language of the Universe.

Through my mindfulness journey, I learned to tune in to my desires and intentions, to communicate them with clarity and openness. I discovered that making things happen required a proactive approach and a willingness to step out of my comfort zone. The magic truly happens when you align your thoughts and actions with the energy of the Universe, and when you actively participate in shaping your reality.

It felt as though the Universe had intentionally brought Xavier into my life, someone who was completely outside the realm of anyone I had encountered before. His unique personality and individualistic nature challenged me to explore and discover a different way of approaching people. As I embraced this new mindset and opened myself to new possibilities, I started to witness the magic taking place in my life. It was a realization that if I had never taken the initiative to contact Xavier, with his intriguing hot-and-cold personality, I would have missed out on the romantic Christmas night that remains one of the most cherished memories in Barcelona to this day.

It was a testament to the power of stepping outside my comfort zone and embracing the unknown. So as I continue on my journey, feeling like I have unlocked the first door, the door that takes me from perfectionist to adventurer, I embrace the spirit of the journey. Feel the journey!

"Hey! How are you?" came the text from Xavier, sparking excitement within me.

"I'm doing well! I'm admiring the stunning interior of the Palau de la Música Catalana," I replied promptly. I took a seat in the center of the concert hall alone, sharing my whereabouts with him.

As I stood in awe within the resplendent Palau de la Música Catalana, I was immediately entranced by the grandeur of the main concert hall. The space emanated a timeless charm, a testament to its rich history and architectural mastery. Every corner of the hall was a visual feast, adorned with opulent Modernistic-style embellishments that delighted the senses.

The walls of the hall were adorned with intricate carvings, depicting scenes of musical motifs, mythical creatures, and delicate floral patterns. Each stroke of the craftsmanship showcased remarkable attention to detail, inviting the eye to explore and appreciate the artistry that adorned the space.

But it was the celestial masterpiece above that truly stole the show. The stained-glass ceiling, a work of art in its own right, cast a mesmerizing array of colors and patterns throughout the hall. As daylight filtered through the intricate glass panels, a kaleidoscope of hues bathed the space in a soft, ethereal glow. The ceiling seemed to come alive, transporting me to a realm where music and light merged harmoniously.

"I must play a piece of music for you then," Xavier responded sweetly, causing butterflies to flutter in my stomach once again. His words sparked my imagination, and my mind began to paint vivid scenes like a rainy day in Raval. This time, I envisioned my artist serenading me with his music while I stood inside the awe-inspiring Musica de la Catalana, a UNESCO World Heritage concert hall. "Would you like to come to my place this Saturday?" he openly invited me, leaving me excited for the upcoming weekend.

In the days leading up to Saturday, my thoughts swirled with anticipation and contemplation. "Okay," I pondered, "the moment of intimacy is approaching. Let's be honest with myself. I have desires, both physical and emotional, and it's important to acknowledge them." Yet amidst these musings, questions lingered: "Who are we to each other? Should we have a conversation about our intentions and expectations? Or Do I even want this conversation? Should I let this ensue naturally, without imposing any preconceived notions?"

Traditionally, dating guidelines often suggested waiting for a certain number of dates or a specific timeframe, like ten dates or three months, before engaging in physical intimacy. However, with Xavier's invitation, I questioned myself whether those guidelines still apply (especially after divorce). Despite having known each other for over six months, it felt like our romantic journey had only recently begun. I couldn't help but feel doubtful myself, wondering if this was the right time to take that next step.

But guided by my mindfulness practice, I wanted to trust my inner voice without judgment. If a sexual connection was important to me and I felt a genuine connection with Xavier, with mutual consent, I saw no reason to adhere to arbitrary rules or timelines. The labels such as "boyfriend" or "girlfriend" held less significance for me. Instead, I preferred to test the waters and explore the chemistry physically. It felt more authentic to me. This approach was the best equation for a fulfilling experience.

On that Saturday night, we surrendered ourselves to each other's embrace. Our passion ignited as we found ourselves entwined in bed, his kisses tracing a tantalizing path from the top of my chest, lingering on my neck, until our lips met in a fervent dance. With every gentle caress behind my ears, my body responded, awakening sensations and unlocking desires. He began to explore further, moving down and kissing every inch of my body, lavishing attention on every sensitive spot with his playful tongue. It was as if an LP song echoed in my mind, its lyrics resonating with the intensity of our connection: "I'd swallow the moon and the stars to follow the beat of your heart."

The Music of Authenticity

Xavier's apartment gradually transformed into our cherished haven as we continued to spend more time together. It became the place where we felt most at ease and could truly be ourselves. Whether it was taking a leisurely stroll to Montjuïc mountain, where Xavier would often practice his percussion, or simply visiting the cozy café nearby, we often found ourselves gravitating back to his welcoming abode.

Within the walls of his apartment, we forged countless memories and shared intimate moments. Xavier has a special passion for comics. As I entered his apartment and made my way through the hallway, I noticed the bookshelves with an impressive collection of books. Most of them were dedicated to the world of art, particularly comics. There were also some family photos scattered around the bookshelves.

"You were blonde?" I exclaimed, staring at the photo in surprise. The man standing in front of me had hair that had no resemblance to blonde.

"Yes! Many people are like that. Blonde hair tends to fade as they grow older," he explained.

Sometimes, he would proudly share his collection of Japanese comics with me, knowing that I could resonate with them due to my upbringing in Taiwan. Like him, Japanese culture deeply influenced me, particularly through its captivating world of comics. I would recount to him the nostalgic tale of my younger days, when my brother and I would venture to comic bookstores that occupied entire buildings. These establishments offered a serene environment where enthusiasts could lose themselves in their favorite comics undisturbed. The shops charged by the hour, providing not only a space for reading but also a place to savor delicious food. My brother and I spent countless hours within those walls, engrossed in the pages of fascinating stories together.

Once, he went to his bookshelves and pulled out two things. The first was a book titled *Le Voyeur, Barcelona,* with a cover featuring a sketch of a bus filled with people. At the bottom center of the booklet was his signature. He explained that this book was published for an exhibition he did long ago when he was still honing his sketching skills. It was a project where he randomly sketched the people of Barcelona, capturing their moments in everyday life. Some were depicted sitting on a bench at the metro platform, engrossed in their phones, while others leaned against the bus window, deep in thought. The book's content consisted of black-and-white sketches composed of different styles of strokes. The sketches ranged from delicate, thin lines of full-body drawings to intricate, bold strokes of portrait headshots.

Another item he pulled from the shelves was a piece of paper that caught my attention. It turned out to be a detailed map of the Raval neighborhood in Barcelona. One side of the paper featured a map with various locations marked, while the other side provided comprehensive listings and tourist information.

The Raval neighborhood is situated in the heart of Barcelona and is renowned for its lively and diverse atmosphere, attracting both locals and tourists alike. Its narrow streets, historic buildings, and cultural mix contribute to its unique charm. Over the years, Raval has undergone a remarkable transformation from a once rough area to a thriving cultural hub. It is now home to an array of art galleries, museums, theaters, and music venues that draw in artists and creatives. The neighborhood's bohemian and alternative vibe appeals to a diverse range of people.

Notably, the MACBA (Museum of Contemporary Art of Barcelona) stands as a prominent landmark in Raval, showcasing alluring contemporary artwork and hosting engaging exhibitions and events. It was through Xavier's commission to produce this remarkable work that he had the opportunity to introduce the neighborhood to others.

We spent a considerable amount of time exploring the map together, retracing our steps where he showed me the artistic side of Barcelona during a rainy outing a few months ago. He pointed out the locations we had visited, including the *El Gato* statue, where we engaged in a three-hour conversation, attentively listening to each other's stories. We also reminisced about the formal art academy we walked through, with its enchanting hall of orange trees. The map featured various intriguing characters scattered throughout, and we shared our favorite ones with each other.

In the end, he generously gifted me both the map and the book. He mentioned that he didn't even have a copy of them, but he wanted me to have them as cherished mementos. I accepted the gifts with profound appreciation, feeling a familiar flutter of excitement in my stomach once again.

What struck me the most about these conversations was how refreshing they felt. Prior to my time in Barcelona, my monotype social circle consisted of individuals with almost the same types of hobbies and career paths, so the conversation with Xavier opened up a whole new world for me. We would engage in deep discussions that spanned a range of topics, from music and art to life's most profound questions. It was a space where we could laugh, explore, and simply enjoy each other's company without any pretenses or constraints. Xavier's apartment became more than just a physical space; it became a reflection of our growing on-and-off connection.

"I have a live performance this weekend," switching topics, Xavier shared this with enthusiasm as we sat together in his living room, nestled comfortably on his couch. Another two months had passed without us seeing each other. His voice reverberated with passion for percussion. Aside from his main responsibility as a painter, he enjoyed playing live performances as a hobby from time to time.

"I would like to go if it's not too far, and if I can work out my co-parenting schedule with the kids' father," I asked carefully, trying to balance my desire to be there with the need to respect his boundaries. I didn't want to come across as too eager or presumptuous. And at the same time, I wanted to protect my fragile heart, aware that a rejection could potentially cause discomfort or hurt.

"Yes. Please come." He immediately showed me the location, and I could see the sparkle of welcoming emotions in Xavier's eyes.

I arrived at the performance venue thirty minutes before it was scheduled to begin, taking in the surroundings with a keen eye. The setting was a charming and unassuming old factory with high concrete walls that shielded the venue from the outside world. Peering over the walls, I could see wild grasses growing tall, adding a touch of untamed beauty to the scene.

As I stepped inside, I was greeted by the vibrant graffiti art that adorned the walls. The eclectic mix of colors and designs added a sense of urban grittiness to the otherwise industrial space. The stage was positioned at the center of the open, outdoor old factory, where the first group of the performance was already onstage.

The venue eschewed the opulent embellishments commonly found in larger concert halls, opting instead for a boutique atmosphere that exuded intimacy and warmth. I noticed the absence of extravagant decorations or elaborate stage setups. Instead, the space was simple yet with charming accents.

Colorful flags, delicately suspended, added a touch of vibrancy to the surroundings. They fluttered gently in the air, creating a lively and whimsical atmosphere. Additionally, small light bulbs were strung above the stage, stretching out toward the audience in an eye-catching spider-like formation. Their soft glow illuminated the space, casting a warm and inviting ambiance. These subtle adornments, while modest in nature, added a unique and authentic charm to the venue.

As I continued entering the venue, my eyes immediately met Xavier's. Xavier gave me that familiar smile and walked toward me, and we embraced each other with a sense of familiarity. Taking my seat, I chose a spot in the middle of the audience, ready to fully appreciate the experience. Settling down, I let my observant nature take over. Coming from a background in marketing agencies where I was accustomed to event planning, my eyes scanned the surroundings, taking note of every detail. From the setup and sound crew to the food and beverages being served, I silently assessed the number of staff involved and instinctively calculated the budget in my head. It was an instinct that had become ingrained within me.

Xavier swiftly joined me shortly after I took my seat, settling in the chair beside mine. With a gentle touch, he placed his hand on top of my knee, a comforting gesture that made me feel his presence and our connection. In his hand, he held a cup of gin and tonic, extending it toward me as an offering. I smiled appreciatively, feeling the warmth of his gesture. Although I declined the sip for now, his thoughtfulness and the shared moment added an intimate touch to the experience. We sat there fully enthralled by the music emanating from the stage. Every now and then, he would turn his head toward me, sharing anecdotes about the band and the intriguing history behind the location of his factory.

Xavier excused himself, explaining that he needed to prepare for the performance. I watched as he joined his band members on stage, taking his place as the percussionist on the far right side. The band consisted of a guitarist, a bass player, a lead singer, a clarinet player, and a qanun instrumentalist, creating a fascinating fusion of Turkish music.

Despite the presence of five other talented musicians on stage, my gaze was drawn to Xavier. His earnestness, creativity, and courage to always try new things made him charming. There was an undeniable magnetism about him as he played, with his passion for percussion shining through every beat. Sometimes, I caught him glancing at the audience, his eyes searching until they met mine. In those fleeting moments, a shared understanding passed between us, and he would offer me a gentle, subtle smile that felt like our little secret.

As the music filled the air, a spirited energy swept through the audience, inspiring them to take to the stage and dance freely. The atmosphere was infused with joy and excitement, amplified by the gentle May breeze that caressed our skin. The early evening sun cast a warm glow, casting vibrant hues through the dancing, colorful flags that adorned the venue. It was a mesmerizing sight, as if the very essence of the music had come alive, swaying in harmony with the rhythm and the laughter that filled the air. Some audience members joined the band members, dancing on the center stage. Some even Turkish belly danced, and the combination of music, dance, and the enchanting play of light created a vintage ambiance that transported us to a time of carefree and pure enjoyment.

From my personal experience, I had never attended a live musical performance that exuded such positive vibes. It was a truly extraordinary moment. In that split second, as I witnessed the band playing with passion and the audience dancing joyfully, with a minimum of decorations, a brief thought crossed my mind. It felt as though the Universe had heard my words in Palau de la Música Catalana, my imagination of my artist playing music in front of me, and had manifested it into reality. It was a beautiful affirmation of the law of attraction and how high vibrations can develop when we let life flow the way it is without any expectations.

Two hours later, as the performance neared its end, Xavier took center stage for his final solo. The spotlight illuminated his passionate presence, commanding the attention of everyone in the venue. Accompanied by each beat of his percussion, a lady from the audience with curly hair joined him. With her simple style and deep passion for music, she danced alone on the center stage. Waving both her arms in the air and moving her feet to the rhythm, she seemed unstoppable, as if two spotlights were shining just on her and the percussionist for a glorious thirty seconds. Their energy radiated through the air, captivating the hearts of the audience. As the performance came to a close, the rest of the band members gathered, joining in the applause and expressing their gratitude to the crowd.

I rose from my seat and went to the back of the venue. From there, I watched as Xavier, filled with gratitude, personally interacted with the audience, expressing his heartfelt appreciation for their presence and support. I feel a deep sense of joy and pride for him. Even in that busy moment, his eyes scanned the crowd, searching for my presence. And when our gazes finally met, a smile spread across his face as he approached me as soon as he could. Without hesitation, Xavier leaned in and planted a gentle kiss on my lips, followed by a long hug. In that fleeting moment, time seemed to stand still. It was a beautiful expression of affection and affirmation, leaving an indelible mark on my heart.

With the entire story unfolding before me that night, I was immensely grateful for being a part of such a remarkable experience. Every minute that passed held its unique magic, seamlessly weaving together to create a tapestry of perfection. There was an undeniable beauty in how things occurred, in the moments shared, and the emotions felt.

As I reflected on the evening, I realized that perfection wasn't about everything going according to plan or the presence of extravagant gestures. It wasn't about fancy restaurants or expensive gifts. Instead, it was about embracing imperfections and cherishing the authenticity of each moment. It was about finding joy in the simplicity and the genuine connection we shared.

I headed home from the concert that night, knowing I had just added another memory to my personal story. It made me truly believe that the Universe was actively listening to us! The manifestation of my desires was starting to become a tangible reality.

Fading Brushstrokes

As our time together grew, I started to notice that Xavier was a sensitive person. It became apparent to me that he could become quite detached when we were physically apart. His moods seemed to be influenced by the changing seasons, weather, or sometimes without any apparent reason. There were moments when we had the opportunity to meet frequently, cherishing each other's company. However, there were also times when we would go without seeing each other for extended periods, as long as two months. This inconsistency often left me feeling confused about his true desires and, in turn, my own.

Apart from our dates and the satisfying sexual aspect of our relationship, I was still grappling with my insecurities stemming from my recent divorce. These conflicting thoughts and uncertainties created internal conflicts within me. I still didn't know how to communicate my feelings openly, and I had never tried to talk about my confusion.

Although our connection was deepening, we had not broached the subject of the nature of our relationship. We seemed comfortable with the status quo without the need for explicit clarification. While our dates and the fulfilling physical intimacy brought us joy, I couldn't shake off the lingering insecurities stemming from my recent divorce. Being someone who struggled to communicate emotions openly, I was avoiding discussions about my confusion. These internal conflicts left me grappling with uncertainty.

While I hesitated to disrupt the status quo by discussing our relationship status, I also maintained a boundary around my personal life. Up until this point, Xavier hadn't visited my place yet. The undefined nature of our connection created a gray zone that strangely felt like a comfortable zone too. However, amidst this uncertainty, I wondered if our intermittent meetings were normal. I did want to understand more about his feelings for me. Yet, he had never verbally expressed his emotions. The unspoken boundaries and lack of communication in our relationship left me pondering if such a dynamic existed, where two individuals navigate a complex connection without fully unraveling its mysteries.

In addition, as I embraced the present moment with an open mind, I couldn't ignore the echoes of past pain lingering within me. The wounds from my previous marriage still had a hold on my heart, instilling a cautionary fear of being hurt once again. While I was willing to explore the unknown, I knew deep within that I still guarded my heart, and I did so with a measured sense of self-protection.

With a guarded heart, I was reluctant to invest more in the relationship. I desired to maintain control, convinced that it would shield me from potential heartbreak. Yet it came as no surprise that the more time we spent together—or rather, apart—the more my confusion grew. Our communication was lacking, and we both hesitated to express our emotions, fearing the vulnerability that could lead to pain. Consequently, we allowed the uncertainty to linger, leaving me feeling troubled. The moments when he was in a low state proved particularly challenging, as his energy deeply affected me and created a sense of distance between us. While our times together were blissful, the periods of separation were marred by a cloud of confusion. I gradually realized that the romantic artist I had once idealized was becoming increasingly difficult to navigate.

For months, these internal dialogues persisted without being addressed between us. It felt as if I had regressed to that initial stage of our relationship, sitting across from Xavier on our first date, sipping sparkling water and pretending that everything was just fine while keeping my true thoughts and feelings hidden. It seemed that he, too, struggled with navigating his emotions, as he was an artist accustomed to solitude.

Months later, I attended another of Xavier's performances at a nightclub for the second time within a year. It was a cool November evening, and though I knew he wouldn't anticipate my presence, I recognized the significance of the night for him. Wanting to show my support, I grappled with the decision of whether or not to go. Hours were consumed by questioning the extent of my commitment and weighing the effort required. The performance was slated for 11:00 p.m., well beyond my typical bedtime. I calculated the distance, the effort required, and the potential consequences of my choice. My mind raced, considering if I was investing too much, given that we weren't in a defined romantic relationship, and whether the potential exhaustion would outweigh the benefits.

I fell ill for several days following that night's performance. As expected, Xavier and I didn't exchange texts, and in my frustration, I blamed him and convinced myself that he didn't care. The ironic part was that he had no knowledge of my illness in the first place. I immaturely ignored his first text, trying to avoid conversation, and he responded by ignoring my subsequent texts, which led to a breakdown in communication. During that period of frustration and heated emotions with Xavier, we seemed to struggle to find our harmony again. At that moment, I recognized the signs from the Universe, urging me to shift my focus inward.

I tried to comprehend what kept drawing me back to Xavier, and it dawned on me that our passionate moments in bed were probably the main culprit. It had become a peculiar pattern where we would disconnect from each other only to come together for a few hours of intense intimacy. We weren't fully committed to each other or even to addressing our doubts, but there was an undeniable physical attraction that we simply couldn't resist. It's funny how I now adore the tobacco scent, which used to annoy me when I was with my ex-husband. I suppose I appreciate the feeling of being "reunited with fresh hope" after those moments of disconnection.

Three weeks later, during the heart of the Christmas holiday season, I received a positive COVID-19 test result for the Omicron variant. Despite the challenging circumstances, I was glad my children were in good health and safely spending time with my ex-husband and his family, traveling from Brazil and England. To be honest, as happy as I was for my children to have the opportunity to hang out with them, it wasn't easy to digest that they got to hang out first while I remained stuck in Barcelona, dealing with COVID and not having seen my own family in years. It was a lonely Christmas.

"I caught COVID, feeling terrible," I texted Xavier, hoping to grab his attention after weeks of not talking.

"Oh no, I'm sorry to hear that. I hope you feel better soon," he replied coldly one day later, and we did not speak again for another year. It became clear that it was time to let go of my favorite artist. Days after my COVID recovery, I traveled to Berlin, feeling that the physical distance would provide me peace from Caetano's family reunion and Xavier.

Chapter 2:
Focus on the Positive

"Where focus goes, energy flows. And where energy flows, whatever you're focusing on grows. In other words, your life is controlled by what you focus on."

- Tony Ribbons

In the middle of the winter season and enduring the winter blues, I lacked the motivation to venture outdoors. It seemed as though the entire country was caught in a slow-paced rhythm. Perhaps it was the persistent cold weather or the fatigue from the Christmas festivities.

On one of the coldest days in January, I returned to my hot yoga practice following a one-month Christmas break. Stepping back into the 40°C room, my legs shook, my breath deepened, and sweat dripped down my face as I focused every ounce of my effort on another pose.

I stood there, preparing myself for the first of the twenty-six poses, the pranayama breathing exercise known as standing deep breathing. As I entered Mountain Pose (Tadasana), I clasped my hands at the base of my chin, ready to begin the rhythmic journey. Inhaling slowly through my nose for a count of six, I lifted my elbows toward the sky. Then, exhaling for another count of six, I released the breath through my mouth, visualizing the release of unwanted energy as my elbows came together and my head tilted back.

This particular part of the practice always challenged my mental focus, and it often went something like this:

Me (breathing in): Let's focus.

My mind (breathing out): Ugh, I can't believe how annoying the gas company is!

Me (breathing in): Come on, stay present!

My mind (breathing out): And don't get me started on the terrible apartment management. They completely ignored my email.

Me (breathing in): Root, find strength. No more distractions.

My mind (breathing out): Maybe I should just go straight to the gas company's office. Oh great, now I'm stressing about my Spanish skills too. One problem on top of another!

We transitioned to the second pose of Bikram yoga, known as the Adhra Chansarana or Half-Moon Pose, which involves a three-part movement to warm up the side body and transition into a forward fold. With both hands brought together overhead and forefingers pointing upward, I prepared to start the sequence.

On an inhale, I elongated my spine, reaching upward, and then slowly started arching left and right a couple of times. Just as my yoga instructor often encouraged, I used this opportunity to wipe out any mental noise, letting it dissipate like a windshield wiper clearing the view. Coming to a complete stop, I took a deep inhale, lengthened my body, and arched to the right, forming a graceful half-moon shape. Finally, I returned to the center and gracefully formed a *C* shape with my body, arching to the other side. The flow of the movement, combined with the metaphorical cleansing of the mind, brought a sense of fluidity and tranquility to the practice.

Next in the sequence was a gentle backbend, engaging the glutes and abs to provide support to the muscles in the lower back. Up until this point, I was starting to manage to align my body and mind. As I focused on taking deeper breaths with each inhale and exhale, I could feel the brain fog slowly dissipating. With my gaze fixed upon my extended forefingers pointing behind me, I aimed to deepen the backbend with each breath.

As I reached the final stage of the Adhra Chansarana, I gracefully transitioned into a forward fold, allowing my spine to release and my hamstrings to stretch. Surprisingly, the noise that had cluttered my mind seemed to vanish naturally, without any force or control. The stillness and serenity within me allowed me to fully embrace the present moment and the soothing flow of the practice.

The initial seventeen poses of Bikram yoga primarily focus on standing postures, which aim to enhance balance and strengthen the lower body. During these poses, I often lose balance or struggle to maintain my posture. However, this mirrors life itself, where we may stumble or fall at times. And that's perfectly alright! The key is picking ourselves up, practicing, and giving ourselves the time and patience to progress. By embracing this approach, little by little, we will ultimately reach our goals.

The final pose of Bikram yoga concludes with the Savasana, also known as the Corpse Pose. It is often considered the most significant pose in yoga, although some individuals may choose to skip it or shorten its duration. In Savasana, practitioners lie on their backs in a state of stillness and silence, with their eyes closed. This pose serves as a crucial opportunity to rest our awareness, connect with the subtle essence of our being, and calm the central nervous system after the stress of physical movement.

During Savasana, the practitioner is encouraged to observe their thoughts without attachment or judgment, allowing them to come and go without getting caught up in them. By practicing present-moment awareness and focusing on the breath, Savasana becomes a meditative experience that promotes mental clarity, emotional balance, and a heightened sense of self-awareness. Savasana holds significance beyond the confines of the yoga mat; it can be integrated into our daily lives as a tool for restoration. After experiencing moments of stress or burnout, Savasana allows us to relax and enter a state of being that lies between wakefulness and sleep. It offers a valuable respite, promoting deep relaxation and rejuvenation.

Practicing yoga has provided me with a profound awareness of the consistent response of our bodies to the same exercises. It has taught me the significance of listening to my body, honoring its needs, and being present in the moment. This approach extends beyond the yoga mat and influences how I navigate life's challenges. In a world filled with daily obstacles, never-ending tasks, and constant demands, cultivating a clear and calm mind allows me to approach these challenges with clarity and resilience. By bringing the principles of yoga into my daily life, I am better equipped to face and overcome whatever comes my way.

Most importantly, those were the golden ninety minutes that I could give myself without any interruption from external factors. In a world with so many things going on, I grant myself the gift of solitude, silence, and peace.

Footprints in the Wilderness: Lessons from the Trail

Toward the end of winter, I started to feel a longing to venture outdoors, seeking solace and serenity amidst nature's embrace, prompting me to join a hiking group through a social community Meetup app. This platform served as a hub for various activities, ranging from language exchanges to painting and dancing. It provided a fantastic opportunity for like-minded individuals to connect and forge new connections.

I undertook moderate hikes to discover hidden waterfalls at La Foradada with a group of fifteen hikers representing eight nationalities from all over the world, each with their unique reasons for landing in Barcelona. However, on that day, our diverse paths converged with a shared goal—to immerse ourselves in the beauty of nature. During the car ride to the hiking site,

I engaged in a thought-provoking conversation with Maria, a Russian lady in her twenties. With fiery red hair cascading to her shoulders, she intensively discussed her perspective on the recent Russia-Ukraine conflict. Emotions of anger, disappointment, and sadness flowed through her words as she expressed her deep concern for the ongoing events.

"I've been actively participating in the protests at Plaça de Catalunya since day one. We want the Ukrainian people to understand that the decisions from the government do not reflect our sentiments or choices," she explained.

With sensitivity, I asked, "What do the opinion polls say about the war?" Drawing on my background and training in public relations, I've learned to approach political subjects like this with a neutral mindset. I listen attentively to each person's story, asking questions to gain a deeper understanding of their perspective. This approach extends to discussions surrounding the Catalonia-Spain independence issue as well. Coming from Taiwan, a place with its own political divisions, I've learned the importance of keeping our personal opinions to ourselves, and I understand the importance of respecting different opinions. However, I find it fascinating to explore the various angles and viewpoints that shape these complex narratives.

In response, "It's terrifying to know that Russian propaganda is incredibly effective in manipulating information. You hear stories of people living in Russia with relatives in Ukraine, yet they refuse to believe the accounts of their Ukrainian family members who describe the risks they face."

"Do you believe this war is primarily driven and instigated by power struggles and business interests involving all parties, including America, NATO, Ukraine, and Russia?" I asked carefully.

"I may not be well-versed in politics and power dynamics, but I've come across many Russians who firmly believe that the country is in a defensive position, with the government taking necessary measures to protect national interests. From their perspective, they see Ukraine being viewed as a lucrative opportunity for the USA and NATO, leading to provocation. However, from my point of view, the human cost of this conflict, with people dying and living in poor conditions, is unacceptable on any level. I will join the street demonstrations tomorrow morning to protest against these terrible massacres," Maria said.

Two hours later, we finally arrived. It was a pleasant day in late February. Despite the lingering remnants of winter, a subtle shift was in the air. The trees, still adorned with their barren branches, stood tall and sturdy, awaiting the arrival of spring. The flowers had yet to bloom, and the landscape retained its wintry charm. However, the gentle kiss of the sun's rays illuminated the surroundings, signaling the gradual awakening of nature from its slumber. It was a day filled with the promise of the new season to come.

Nataly, one of the fifteen hikers, swiftly became my hiking companion. Standing tall at over 170 cm, she possessed flowing golden hair that cascaded down to her waist. Her purple sweater beautifully complemented her choice of white hiking shoes. Nataly, like me, after enduring a long winter of staying at home, felt the need to embark on this journey, desperate to stretch and awaken her body. As we walked side by side, we exchanged stories, forging a connection through our shared experiences.

"I moved here to co-parent my children," I explained.

"Oh, I'm separated too! I don't have children; it was a tough period," she responded. In that instant, an unspoken understanding passed between us, acknowledging the detrimental impact that toxic relationships can have on one's energy and well-being.

"Latvia! You're the first Latvian person I've met. I know so little about your country that I can't even begin to imagine what it looks like," I exclaimed as we carefully navigated the walking trails, our steps synchronized. The soothing sounds of rustling leaves and cheerful birds chirping filled the air, creating a harmonious backdrop to our conversation.

"Latvia is magnificent, with its expansive forests, picturesque landscapes, and rich cultural heritage. Growing up in Latvia, we developed a profound connection to nature. But I have found a new love for Barcelona. Nowadays, my family and I make annual summer visits to Greece, where my sister resides."

Living in Barcelona offers a unique and remarkable experience due to the city's incredible diversity and abundant opportunities. Among the people I've encountered here, many are nomads who constantly explore new destinations, expats like me who have chosen to settle here from different parts of the world, and numerous expats who possess extensive international living experience. It's common to find individuals fluent in more than three languages, and it's fascinating to learn that many have family members residing in various corners of the globe.

"Where do you usually spend your Christmas?" This question is always on my lips, as it provides a glimpse into a person's familial ties or cultural background.

"Latvia," Nataly responded proudly.

While the hiking spirit was still strong, I took the kids to Andorra for a magical trail called the Forest of the Menairons the following week. Located in La Massana near the village of Pal, it marked our first hiking adventure together since moving to Catalonia. It was also their first time venturing outside of Barcelona's city center since COVID. The weather was mild, devoid of the winter's chill and absent of snow. With a touch of trepidation mingled with excitement, I hoped to guide them through the charming realm of mythical creatures that resided in the forests of Andorra, praying that my limited natural survival skills wouldn't lead us astray. As we started our journey, we eagerly anticipated what awaited us along the four-kilometer trail, which would take us approximately two hours to complete.

With the guidebook I had prepared in advance, we stood at the wooden entrance portal, ready to enter the enchanting world of the Menairons. A wooden plaque greeted us, adorned with two handprints and a heartfelt message: "Before I enter, I promise to respect this place, to help the Menairons, and to leave no trace. If I encounter one, I'll keep my distance and only mention 'smelly farts' in that instance. Dragon's tail and snail poo, if I break my promise, a stinky shoe I'll turn into!" The message was written in Catalan.

"We have to be respectful, calm, and well-behaved." With excitement, I guided my children to place their hands on the wooden plaque. Together, we made a solemn vow to protect the forest and its magical inhabitants. We pledged to keep the wonders we were about to witness a secret, sharing the joy of our experience only within the confines of our family.

As their little hands pressed against the wood, a sense of responsibility and wonder filled the air. We understood the importance of preserving this magical realm, respecting its delicate balance, and leaving no trace of our presence behind.

During the hike, we discovered approximately ten magical "hidden" surprises along the route, all conceived and produced by local artists and craftsmen using quality, sustainable materials that respect the natural environment and seamlessly integrate into the landscape. We had also finished the sandwiches we had prepared in advance, and as we walked, we reached out to touch the surfaces of several trees, listening to nature's sounds. Additionally, we eagerly searched for mini-beasts on the forest floor, behind trees, and underneath rocks. We also had silly chats like, "Can you live inside this wooden house by yourself?" or, "Can you sit on the tree branch like the statue on the top up there?" adding an extra sense of adventure to our journey.

Nataly and I stayed in touch. She invited two other new hikers and me to take a walk along the peach blossom trails in Aitona Lleida. The air carried the delicate scent of blooming peach trees, and the landscape transformed into a picturesque scene with vibrant pink petals adorning the branches, creating a breathtaking tapestry of colors. Despite occasional gloomy weather and looming clouds, the sun intermittently pierced through the gray blanket, casting a radiant glow upon the blossoms. As we hiked, we witnessed the enchanting sight of people biking alongside the river on one side while the other side showcased an endless field of peach blossoms. It felt like a scene from a movie or a painting come to life. During lunchtime, we found an empty space on a small hill, where we sat to enjoy our meal while overlooking the vast expanse of the peach blossom field. The view was simply breathtaking. The overall experience was nothing short of a Michelin three-star dining experience.

To wrap up our spring hiking adventure, it was safe to say that we hadn't had enough. Nataly and I decided to hike the cliffs from Collioure to Banyuls-sur-Mer in Southern France, where we were treated to breathtaking views of the Mediterranean Sea. This hike proved to be the most challenging of our hikes in the past few weeks. If you have a fear of heights or suffer from vertigo, this hike will undoubtedly put you to the test. It wasn't just the uphill climbing that made it difficult but also the height itself that proved to be a challenge to manage. We could barely engage in conversation, as our attention needed to focus solely on each step we took. The trail was narrow and scattered with small rocks, and the thought of slipping on one of them was something we didn't even want to imagine.

Throughout the five-hour hike, we passed by vineyards that overlooked the Mediterranean Sea. The curves of the cliffs resembled shapes we could find on a map. The wind continued to blow, causing the sea to dance in harmony with its gusts. It wasn't a sunny day; the waves moved abruptly, one after another, disappearing into the foggy horizon. The lack of a clear line added an air of mystery to the scenery.

As I walked, I encouraged myself to be brave and focus on each step. I reassured myself that I could handle it. I parallel this hike with my life at that time. It felt rough and foggy, with no clear end in sight. But with each mindful step, I knew I would eventually reach my destination.

A glass of French wine and a classic croissant were the sweet rewards awaiting us at the end of that challenging hike, and let me tell you, they tasted like a buttery victory.

The Dutch Way: Standing Tall and Calm

A few weeks before my trip to Berlin, which occurred about one month before Christmas, my husband (we still had not finalized the divorce yet) decided to move closer to the kids' school for the purpose of co-parenting. It appeared that he had started to rebuild his life, finding a new job with a steady income. This newfound stability allowed him to afford a new car, a new apartment, ski trips, and frequent gifts for the children. While I preferred not to shower the kids with presents too often, only for more special and meaningful occasions, I recognized that co-parenting involves finding a delicate balance. The key, for me, was to respect each other's boundaries as long as we were all doing our best and avoiding anything significantly detrimental.

One week before Christmas, his family traveled from Brazil and the United Kingdom to Barcelona for an almost three-week Christmas reunion. (That's the other reason why I felt the need to be in Berlin, using distance to find peace—apart from the situation with Xavier.) Renting a hotel room for such a duration was certainly not something you would do if you had financial limitations, at least not to my knowledge. Seeing all the money my husband and his family were spending, I had insisted that he begin shouldering 50 percent of the kids' expenses, after taking care of most things for years. Despite the mixed feelings I had experienced during our separation, I genuinely felt happy that he was starting to get his life back on track. After all, he was the father of my children, and I wanted him to be well.

I truly felt that the Universe had finally let the sun shine through my gloomy cloud. My husband and I had finally found harmony in co-parenting and dealing with each other. We could actually have conversations without them turning into a heated dispute. This progress in our newfound "friendship" after the separation was significant.

"I met Jos's father at the playground earlier today. He invited us to Jos's birthday party tomorrow. Can you take the girls?" a WhatsApp message from Caetano popped up on my phone screen; There's something about Spanish culture where most kids hang out at the playground at least once a day, making it one of the easiest ways to arrange playdates or meet other parents.

On Saturday morning, we arrived punctually at the birthday party venue. It was held at a sprawling indoor playground, bustling with excitement. As we stepped inside, a towering figure man standing at an impressive height of 200 cm greeted us warmly, ushering my girls and me to the upper level where all the festivities and games were taking place. Strangely enough, his face seemed oddly familiar. After a brief exchange, he excused himself to welcome other families who were just arriving, leaving us to settle in.

The birthday party took place in a vibrant space that spanned two floors. The first floor catered to the parents, offering a cozy setting to enjoy refreshments, food, and conversations. As we ascended to the second floor, we entered a beautifully decorated area adorned with long tables featuring an array of themed paper plates, balloons, lively music, delicious snacks, and an enticing birthday cake. At the far end of the floor, the entrance to the kids' party zone beckoned with a delightful assortment of toys, balls, and slides. The energetic ambiance was amplified by the joyful commotion of at least twenty kids gleefully jumping and running around.

To be honest, I've never quite felt at ease when it comes to navigating social circles centered around parenting. In moments like these, I tend to retreat into my world, preferring to observe quietly rather than actively engage. I naturally sought out a cozy corner where I could keep an eye on both of my girls without the need for much interaction.

Just as I was beginning to settle into my solitude, I suddenly found myself in the company of Jos's father, who stood right next to me. "Hi, do you want anything to drink?" he asked politely, extending a friendly gesture.

"Would you like to join the other parents?" he inquired, perhaps sensing my shyness and wanting to help me feel more at ease.

"No, thank you! I'm fine here," I replied, reaffirming my preference for solitude. I smiled back and couldn't help but think, "Wow, those blue eyes!" I wanted to ask, "What does it feel like to have a pair of blue eyes?" As an Asian who grew up with black eyes, it fascinated me to see them up close. They were so beautiful, I thought to myself once again.

A few moments of silence and slight awkwardness followed. In those micro-awkward seconds, our gazes wandered toward the direction of the children's playground. However, I could sense from his body language that he was attempting to strike up another conversation.

"So, yeah, I saw your husband at the park and took the opportunity to invite the girls to Jos's party," he shared.

"We are separated. Nonetheless, thank you for inviting us," I responded, acknowledging his kindness.

"Oh! Me too," he revealed, and for a brief moment, our eyes met, conveying an unspoken understanding. Just then, his ex-wife approached and engaged in conversation with another mother nearby. The atmosphere grew quiet and awkward once again as we stood silently next to their conversation, unsure of what to say next.

In an attempt to alleviate the awkwardness, we excused ourselves and went our separate ways.

"Thank you for inviting us! The girls had a fantastic time," I messaged the birthday WhatsApp group after the party.

"Hey! I'm glad the girls enjoyed the party! We could arrange a playdate at some point if you're interested, considering we live so close," a notification message popped up on my phone screen. It was him!

Oh my, it just dawned on me that I never asked for his name!

"Yeah, let's find some time for a playdate. That would be fun for the kids! We could meet up for a coffee too," I suggested, attempting to bridge the gap and salvage the conversation, attempting to recover from my earlier bluntness.

"By the way, my name is Hsin," I quickly added, hoping to rectify my oversight. As I texted those words, a whirlwind of thoughts flooded my mind. "Is this another opportunity? That's interesting. I used to dream about dating a tall guy, not like 200 cm, but tall! And he has a pair of blue eyes. Boy, he's Dutch, and I love Amsterdam! I love it so much that I used to be a KLM frequent flyer member, making sure to pass through Amsterdam every time I traveled back to Taiwan during my years in Sao Paulo, Brazil. The tulips! Oh, how I adored visiting Keukenhof Gardens and marveling at the beautiful array of tulips. I even discovered Giethoorn before it became overwhelmed with tourists. The cheese, the canals, the fresh cool air! Who doesn't love Holland? It's been ages since I met another Dutch person, apart from that one girl I encountered fifteen years ago during my Central America backpacking trip. And he's a single father, too, which resonates with me.

"But most importantly, he seems so proactive and decisive in pursuing what he wants, and that's charming!" My mind started creating a mental checklist of all the positive attributes I could think of in someone I had only spoken to for five minutes. Yet I still didn't know his name. I went as far as, "He is 200 cm tall. Is every part of his body also proportional?" if you know what I mean. Well, at least it nourished my mind for a delightful two minutes. That was fun.

"I'm Max," he replied, finally sharing his name.

The memory of encountering Max somewhere still lingered in the recesses of my mind. Suddenly, a flash of recollection struck me. We had crossed paths approximately six months before at another birthday party for a mutual friend's child. Although we didn't engage in conversation on that occasion, I distinctly remember catching a glimpse of this tall gentleman with striking blue eyes, subtly ducking his head to avoid hitting the ceiling as he entered the kitchen, where I happened to be standing.

"Hey, Hsin, hope your week is off to a great start! What does your schedule look like for tomorrow? Maybe we could grab a morning coffee at any place of your choice," he texted me a few days after our last conversation after the party.

"Tomorrow morning works for me!" I replied quickly.

In the remaining day leading up to our morning coffee, my mind occasionally drifted to thoughts of Max. I contemplated the possibilities and wondered about the kind of person he was beyond our initial interactions. As the hours ticked closer to our rendezvous, a mix of nerves and excitement danced within me, creating a delightful flutter in my chest.

I was just so excited to have an opportunity to meet somebody new after six months. Although I still wasn't sure how I felt about being ready to fall in love, there was no denying the awakening of my libido, sending signals in my head.

I carefully chose my outfit, aiming to strike a balance between comfort and reflecting my unique personality. I decided on a black sleeveless top paired with denim shorts, my trusty

Birkenstocks, and a pair of sunglasses. This ensemble had become my signature morning look.

Preparing to leave home and meet Max, I took a deep breath, grounding myself in the present moment and letting go of any expectations. The intention was to approach the day with an open mind, setting the tone for what lay ahead.

Stepping inside Serrajòrdia Taller de pa cafe, the delightful aroma of freshly baked bread enveloped me, filling the air with a comforting warmth. The interior design seamlessly combined rustic charm and modern elegance, resulting in an inviting atmosphere that beckoned me further.

The wooden panel walls reflected the craftsmanship and tradition of the bakery, giving the space a sense of life and history. My gaze was drawn to the wicker baskets lining the shelves, displaying an array of freshly baked bread loaves. Each loaf was thoughtfully arranged, showcasing the artisanal quality of the bakery's offerings. The scent of warm dough and crisp crusts lingered in the air, growing more enticing as I approached the counter. Every detail in the shop reflected a deep appreciation for the art of baking. From the thoughtfully curated selection of bread to the precise placement of artisanal bread knives and cutting boards, no element was overlooked.

Amongst the bustling crowd and the tables filled with patrons, I scanned the room in search of Max. Being the first to arrive, I claimed a small, cozy table tucked away near the heart of the shop. Its placement provided an intimate setting amidst the energetic hum, allowing us to enjoy each other's company while immersed in the vibrant ambiance. Soft lighting fixtures hung gracefully from above, casting a gentle radiance that enhanced the organic beauty of the wooden surroundings, creating a warm and inviting atmosphere.

And just like that, within forty-eight hours, I was sitting next to Max, free from the presence of our kids or any other parents. It was just the two of us, starting our get-to-know-you morning. I ordered a café con leche, while Max opted for a cup of American coffee. With Max sitting across from me, I was mesmerized by his blue eyes, once again, as he shared his story.

Among the many topics that typically arise on a first date, we didn't get into our marital statuses. Curious about the atmosphere, I cautiously asked, "How is your relationship with your ex-wife?" I wanted to gain a better understanding without intruding into someone else's personal life.

"It could be better," he replied, sharing just a few words to summarize his situation. Sensing his desire for privacy, I quickly concluded the topic with a simple statement, "Yes, finding balance is what matters." I spoke as if I had finally achieved my own sense of balance with my husband, feeling content with my current circumstances.

Max, a Dutchman with a similar international background to mine, had lived in various places, including London, Chile, and Spain, where he had resided for nearly ten years. Like me, he was passionate about maintaining a healthy lifestyle and followed a strict, almost vegan diet. He proudly mentioned the trophies he had acquired at a young age and was always on his bike. As a computer scientist, he has worked remotely from home since the onset of the COVID-19 pandemic, which explained his availability for a Tuesday-morning coffee meeting. I was impressed by his high energy and calm vibes.

As I leisurely strolled along the narrow streets, making my way back home after our first date, Max's presence lingered in my thoughts. He had undeniably made a positive impression on me, drawing my attention with his charm. Thoughts started to surface in my mind as I reflected on our time together.

"Oh, he's also a single father. That's a matchy quality to have."

"He's almost vegan, like me. I find that very appealing."

"He rides a bike. I've always been attracted to active men."

"He also follows a healthy lifestyle and sleeping routine, just like me."

"And, he has lived in different parts of the world; a multicultural mindset is a plus."

Despite these thoughts swirling around in my head, I was still uncertain about the true extent of my feelings toward him. It was as if I unconsciously fell into my familiar pattern of overthinking and excessive analysis, which tends to cloud my judgment.

In the days that followed our coffee meeting, we didn't have much communication except for me sending him a random YouTube clip. It was an episode of *Last Week Tonight* with John Oliver, where he discussed the topic of Taiwan. I thought it would be a nice way to share a glimpse of my country with him, mainly since we talked about Taiwan at the cafe. I was surprised to learn that he had never tried the signature Taiwanese drink "bubble tea" or even heard of it before. This amazed me, and I felt a sense of duty to change that. With my diplomatic and patriotic heart as a Taiwanese, I knew I had to do something about it.

Two Worlds Collide: A Casual Connection

"Hey! How have you been? How about meeting up this Saturday at 7:00 p.m.? Let's take some time for ourselves without the kids! I'm looking forward to hearing more about Taiwan. Let's grab a drink." He used the video clip as an excuse to set up a date.

Honestly, at this point, I still had many uncertainties about whether it was a good idea to date a parent who was connected to my parenting social circle. I had reservations about potential complications arising from previous relationships and the merging of parenting responsibilities. In my view, it was important to maintain two separate families. However, on the upside, it would be nice to expand my support system and the possibility of arranging playdates. Despite my concerns, I believed that the Universe had brought Max into my life for a reason, and I wanted to embrace a mindset of going with the flow. Whether our connection evolved or not, he seemed like a lovely man whom I could trust. With gratitude and respect, I approached this budding relationship with an openness to explore its depths as long as he was comfortable keeping our relationship private, low profile, and casual.

Additionally, I must admit that my libido was quite alarming!

"Okay! Let's meet at 365 this Saturday," a bakery store just around the corner from my apartment, I replied, ready to enjoy the journey.

"Hey! Are you already there? I just need a few more minutes." It was Saturday, and Max's text came in as I stood at the front door of 365, awaiting his arrival.

A few minutes later came another text, "I'm here," he said. "But I don't see you." I could picture him rushing to the front door of the other 365, scanning the entire place in search of me.

"Oh, my bad! Of course, it's that 365. I went to the wrong place. Give me another five minutes please," he quickly responded without waiting for my reply.

As he arrived at 365, we embraced each other. He quickly apologized for his lateness and promised to explain what happened once we settled into a restaurant for a drink. We started walking down the narrow streets of the old town, searching for a decent and quiet place to enjoy our drinks. He promptly suggested a medieval town plaza nearby and guided me there.

As Max walked beside me for the first time, I noticed his towering height. I wondered, "So this is what it feels like to be next to someone who is 200 cm tall." When I hugged Max, I had to tiptoe slightly, and during our conversations, I had to lift my chin to meet his gaze.

We settled in one of the few restaurants open at 7:00 p.m. Fortunately, it had available terrace seats with open air, and we ordered a glass of white wine to start the evening. The evening was pleasant, taking place in late May 2022. Barcelona had already experienced the first heatwave, with temperatures surpassing the 40°C mark, indicating a hot summer ahead.

Mealtime in Spain is something I have never fully adapted to, and it's often a topic among foreigners. In the typical Spanish culture, they eat after 9:00 p.m., and sometimes even later. You can't help but think how they go to bed with a full stomach of food. How do they digest? Well, the Spanish can, and they appeared to have the longest life expectancy in the world, second only to Japan!

I remember when I first arrived in Barcelona in 2019, I had an intense craving for a delicious pizza. I called a restaurant at 6:00 p.m. to order a pizza for pickup at 7:00 p.m. To my surprise, the restaurant informed me that the oven didn't even light up until at least 8:00 p.m. That was probably my first experience of culture shock. In my hometown, most restaurants are already preparing to close by 9:00–10:00 p.m. The difference in dining customs was quite striking to me.

Three hours later, we had indulged in several tapas, a few glasses of wine, and a jar of sangria. That was certainly a departure from my usual "healthy diet." My tolerance for alcohol is usually limited to two glasses of wine, but that night we exceeded our limits. As we prepared to end the beautiful evening in this medieval town, he kindly offered to walk me back to my place. During our fifteen-minute journey, he pointed out some of the restaurants he had visited that served healthy food. He also shared with me some areas in the neighborhood that I could explore with my kids. Additionally, he promised to introduce me to more friends in the community who could help me expand my local support system in this small town.

We came to a complete stop at the beginning of the street where my apartment was located. I pointed in the direction I had arrived from and thanked him for accompanying me on this beautiful night. Everything seemed to pause momentarily as we faced each other, our eyes locking. Before I knew it, he leaned his body forward and kissed me. Without any resistance, I embraced that beautiful moment, allowing myself to experience it fully.

As we kissed, I could sense that we were growing closer. Although our connection was deepening, I wasn't sure how much I liked him other than my libido was alarming me to take action. When we pulled back and looked into each other's eyes, it was as if we were both waiting for an unspoken invitation to take the night further, perhaps to someone's place. Well, I am typically hesitant to invite anyone to my home, so I knew very well that I would not extend the invitation. However, a part of me secretly hoped he would suggest continuing the night at his place, taking the lead.

A minute later, it felt like the Universe had heard my unspoken desire and delivered it directly to Max's mind. Without hesitation, I accepted his invitation to have a drink at his apartment. However, deep down, I knew I couldn't handle another sip of alcohol.

Stepping into his living space, I was immediately enthralled by the meticulous details. Everything seemed to be in its rightful place, a testament to Max's organized and tidy nature. Coats and jackets hung neatly on racks, and shoes were arranged on shelves neatly. Underneath the doorbell monitor, there was a box hanging with a bunch of colorful ribbons of Lord of Bonfim in Salvador.

"I have the exact same colorful ribbons hanging next to my door too!" I exclaimed with a hint of excitement as if it were a romantic, meant-to-be coincidence. "You've been to Salvador in Brazil?" I asked.

I moved further into the space when he was explaining his Salvador World Cup story. My gaze was drawn to the family photos adorning the wall, capturing precious moments frozen in time.

"That's my mother, and that's my sister." He pointed his fingers at the photos, his voice filled with delight as he spoke about his family. "And that's my father with Jos." I observed his happy energy and silently thought to myself, "He is a true family man." With each step I took forward, the wooden floor emitted a faint creak, adding to the cozy atmosphere of the welcoming living room.

The living room and kitchen emanated the same sense of tidiness and organization as the rest of the apartment. However, my gaze was stopped by the four Chinese characters, 心堅穿石 (*xīn jiān shí chuān*), hanging upside down on the wall. The sight of it elicited a spontaneous burst of laughter, breaking the silence and the tension inside me. Seizing the opportunity, I playfully explained the meaning of the four words and humorously pointed out their incorrect orientation, adding a lighthearted touch to the moment.

We spent the rest of the night embracing each other but found it difficult to sleep well. The truth is, it takes time to readjust and get used to sleeping in someone else's bed after without sharing for a period of time. Despite the satisfying sexual experience we had, the combination of alcohol and its impact on our sleep quality made it challenging to have a restful night. It made me wonder how I managed to sleep soundly on someone's shoulder in my twenties without compromising the quality of my sleep. During my time with Xavier, I often thought about why we never tried to spend the night together. We would always wrap up our dates by heading home in separate ways. He never attempted to keep me with him, and I never considered inviting him to my place. But with that one-night experience with Max, I realized I had outgrown the cuddling-all-night-long theme. I evidently sleep better alone. Max and I often laughed about that night when our desperation to fulfill our sexual desires came at the expense of our sleep quality and regular routine.

(Heart-shaped emoji) I left his apartment the following morning at 9:00 a.m.

After returning home from a bustling morning, I finally found a moment to reflect on the eventful twelve hours that had just passed. Staying the night at Max's place wasn't part of my original plan, yet I didn't actively prevent it from happening. Again, I must admit that the entire night was driven by my desire to fulfill my sexual cravings.

From the first time we met on the playground to the night we spent together, it all happened within a span of two weeks and less than two dates.

My approach to sexuality has always been a struggle. I had experiences with one-night stands before marriage. It stopped not because I agreed that women should not advance sexually too soon, but because I concluded that one-night stands never led to fulfilling intimacy. Mind-blowing sex needs a connection!

I reflect on the lessons I was taught while growing up, emphasizing the importance of self-love and being cautious about accepting advances from men, especially in terms of intimacy. As a result, whenever I engage in sexual encounters that may be considered too soon by societal standards, I often find myself harshly judging and questioning whether I fall into the derogatory category of being labeled promiscuous. Additionally, I ponder how I would like to educate my daughters about making decisions regarding sex and intimacy.

One of the beautiful things about being an almost forty-year-old single mom who has been through shit in recent years is that you naturally rise above the standard judgments and learn not to give too much importance to what other people think. It has become clear to me that everyone has the right to decide about their bodies and experiences without fear of condemnation. It's more important to focus on cultivating a healthy and respectful relationship with my desires and boundaries and trust myself to make choices that align with my values and personal comfort.

In my single parenting journey, I have learned that sexuality is a deeply personal aspect of human existence, and there is no one-size-fits-all approach or timeline that applies to everyone. By rejecting judgment and embracing self-acceptance, I can develop a healthier and more empowering perspective on my own sexuality and relationships. With this intention in mind, Max and I are on our way to creating a strong sexual bond regularly.

I continued to reflect, deeply grateful for the unexpected encounter with Max at a children's birthday party. It was a gathering that my husband had confirmed randomly at the park, but due to unforeseen circumstances, he couldn't be there to accompany our girls. I was amazed by the beautiful coincidences. The Universe seemed to have woven together a series of seemingly unrelated occurrences, serving as a gentle reminder of the enchanting and unpredictable nature of life.

It had been nearly two years since I began practicing mindfulness. Alongside being present and embracing uncertainty, this practice taught me the importance of emotional self-management. I noticed that when stress arose, whether it was related to work, friendships, or co-parenting, my body reacted instantly, often leading to impaired functioning and disrupted sleep in the days that followed.

In my journey with Max, regardless of its duration or destination, my intention was to approach our casual relationship by being present in the moment and accepting things as they happened without judgment. However, how about Max?

As I reflected on the recent events and processed the details, various questions arose in my mind. How could I navigate the delicate balance between organizing playdates for our children and engaging in casual dating? In the past, I had believed that keeping my dating life separate from my role as a parent was the simplest approach. Yet fate had intertwined our children's lives even before ours.

Defining the boundaries between organizing playdates for the kids and merging our personal lives became a crucial consideration. I contemplated how to navigate this casual dating situation without causing any undue alarm to the children, our parenting circle, and our ex-partners. Most importantly, I questioned whether pursuing this path was a good idea in the first place.

The feeling of uncertainty about Max's thoughts and the idea of merging our two worlds evoked a range of mixed emotions within me, primarily worry. While I was intrigued by the potential for deeper connections and shared experiences, I also had concerns. At that point in my life, I still valued the freedom of keeping things separate and maintaining a casual approach. I was cautious about blending these aspects too quickly and potentially disrupting the delicate balance I had established. Amidst my concerns about preserving my personal space, I also acknowledged the significance of embracing the opportunity to explore this relationship. I was ready to invest the necessary effort to foster a meaningful connection with Max. Proceeding with caution was important to me, ensuring that each element retained its individuality while exploring the possibilities ahead. Additionally, I recognized that I wasn't ready for love. In fact, I didn't want to go close to the word *love* at all.

In this uncertain space, I realized the importance of communication with Max. It was an area where I had struggled in the past, often being less open-minded and always going along with the flow of others. Reflecting on this, I was fully aware that I could have alleviated much of the suffering I had experienced over the years by being more willing to express my thoughts and emotions honestly. Practicing mindfulness helped me hear my voice, but I needed to openly discuss my expectations, desires, and concerns so that my life could be driven in the right direction.

It was clear to me that a change was necessary to shape the experience! And it was my choice.

"Hey, I need to talk about us! About kids and us. I mean the expectations, you know what I'm saying? Have you given it any thought?" I tried to squeeze out the right words to form a decent sentence, lying beside him.

"Of course, yes! We can do it casually. Occasionally set up playdates. But let's take things slowly and not rush into anything, keeping each other company." I felt relieved upon hearing his response, unsure whether I fully understood or if we were on the same page. Nevertheless, I interpreted it as an agreement to maintain a casual relationship without "invading" each other's privacy and personal lives.

"Wow, that's quite a gift from the Universe," I thought, realizing that at this stage of my life, I was surrounded by people who shared my hobbies and interests. Unfortunately, when it came to sex, I felt the need for external assistance. What I mean to say is that I was happy to be with this incredible Dutchman to whom I was attracted, and one thing we prioritized for each other was spending quality time together and enjoying a fulfilling sexual connection without the need for commitment.

"That's a good idea," I replied, keeping my words minimal, as I sensed our mutual understanding. As single parents, there was an unspoken connection between us. We were both in the process of turning the page, leaving the past behind, and moving forward. It was like imagining the fingers of the thumb and index finger still gripping that single page and turning it midway through. It felt as if the Universe had orchestrated this moment for us to cross paths. We understood the importance of prioritizing our healing and the well-being of our children, which allowed us to approach this connection with a shared understanding. Adding any additional weight or roles to our relationship felt unnecessary. Moreover, there was an unspoken acknowledgment of fulfilling each other's sexual needs during this time.

The feelings I continually got from Max were uncomplicated, good vibes, lightweight, and free. The synchronicity felt like the missing piece of the puzzle to my life balance!

"Hey! How about we plan a day to visit the Picasso Museum? I remember you mentioning that you enjoy museums," a text message popped up on my phone.

"Picasso Museum?" I was aware that Max had been undergoing therapy to ease the chronic foot pain resulting from his past athletic pursuits and his height, which added extra pressure on his feet. Considering that walking would cause him discomfort, especially given the distance from the nearest metro station to the museum and the effort required to navigate the exhibition, I was pleasantly surprised and deeply touched by his thoughtfulness. It meant a lot to me that he wanted to explore and spend time together, engaging in an activity that brought me joy.

"Awww, he is such a sweet guy," I thought.

As we walked from Plaça de Catalunya to the charming neighborhood of El Born, which is where the Picasso Museum is located, we were mesmerized by the vibrant energy of Barcelona. The bustling streets were filled with a diverse mix of locals and tourists, creating a lively atmosphere. It struck me that nearly two years had passed since the lockdown was lifted. It felt as if COVID had never happened, as there were barely any masks to be seen on the streets. The city was buzzing with an influx of tourism, and Barcelona was gearing up for the upcoming summer season.

As we made our way through the crowd, the sounds of people chatting, laughter, and snippets of different languages filled the air. With each step, we gradually left behind the more commercial areas and ventured into the enchanting labyrinth of narrow medieval streets that define El Born. The transition was almost magical. The noise of the crowd faded, and we found ourselves enveloped in a sense of history and authenticity.

The narrow streets, adorned with centuries-old buildings, were lined with small boutique shops, art galleries, and hidden gems waiting to be discovered. The sunlight filtered through the cracks between the buildings, casting a warm glow on the cobblestones beneath our feet.

As we wandered through these charming streets, the narrow passageways created an intimate setting, allowing us to connect with the rich past of the neighborhood. We admired the architectural details, the vibrant street art, and the occasional glimpse of hidden courtyards.

We entered the Picasso Museum in Barcelona, immediately greeted by a sense of artistic immersion. The museum itself is housed in a beautiful historic building, adding to the overall ambiance and setting the stage for our encounter with Picasso's masterpieces.

The museum's interior was thoughtfully designed to showcase Picasso's diverse body of work, taking us on a journey through the different stages and styles of his artistic evolution. The galleries were arranged chronologically, allowing us to trace Picasso's artistic development from his early years to his later periods.

The museum showcased Picasso's work from his early period, when he was still crafting his skill before Paris, including his Blue Period, Rose Period, and Surrealist-inspired works. Each gallery offered a unique glimpse into the artist's inner world and the influences that shaped his artistic expression.

I stood in front of *A Blue Vase* by Pablo Picasso, mesmerized by the intricate details and the vibrant hues. With bold brushstrokes and vivid blue tones, the painting depicts a simple vase transformed into a striking and emotive work of art. Standing behind me, Max reached for his phone without me knowing and captured the moment, which he only showed me later on after we left the museum. What intrigued me even more were the perspectives captured in the photos he took from behind me, with the camera positioned above my head. I was seeing myself through a different lens of a 200 cm tall man, exploring a whole new vantage point. "Wow, that's his perspective!" The images held a sense of novelty and excitement, infusing my personal dating experience with a delightful twist. The unconventional angles and unexpected glimpses added an element of surprise, making each photograph a treasure trove of memories.

As we explored the museum, I noticed that Max's discomfort in his feet began to bother him, hindering his ability to appreciate the artwork fully. He reiterated that he wasn't particularly fond of museums. Despite this, I was touched by his willingness to accompany me and engage in an activity that he didn't necessarily enjoy, purely to bring me happiness.

We continued to spend time with each other for weeks to come. He shared his experiences navigating the complexities of divorce, adapting to life as an expat in Barcelona, and embracing the challenges of single parenting. I also uncovered the depth and richness of his character beyond his impressive stature. In the face of adversity, Max radiated a contagious motivation and unwavering optimism. He opened up to me about his daily meditation practice and the importance of a vigorous morning routine, waking up promptly at 7:00 a.m. I was inspired by his commitment to personal growth and well-being, and his positive outlook on life became a magnet for my aspirations.

Max's dating style emanated a refreshing simplicity, practicality, and directness typical of Dutchmen (Yes! My stereotype of thinking). Being Dutch, he embodied the cultural values of open and honest communication in relationships. Coming from a traditional Taiwanese family, I observed the striking contrast between the gender dynamics prevalent in my society and Max's belief in equality and mutual respect. He saw his partner as an equal, sharing responsibilities in the relationship. In contrast, Taiwanese men are still often seen as holding dominant roles in relationships. Witnessing his unwavering commitment to fairness in our connection was enlightening.

Max epitomized a casual and easygoing demeanor, often donning a T-shirt layered with an unbuttoned shirt and complemented by comfortable khaki shorts adorned with numerous pockets. His trusty bicycle served as his preferred mode of transportation, reflecting his active and adventurous spirit. He derived happiness from life's simple pleasures, opting for activities like leisurely bike rides, picnics in the park, or casual meetups for drinks at a nearby local spot. Max gravitated toward informal settings that fostered a sense of relaxation and authenticity, prioritizing the company and conversation over formalities such as fine dining.

When it came to matters of the heart, Max may not be the grand romantic who orchestrated candlelit dinners adorned with roses. Instead, he expressed his affection through genuine actions and heartfelt sincerity. He placed great value on authenticity and treasured meaningful connections built on compatibility and shared values. Rather than relying on flowery words, Max let his actions speak volumes, demonstrating his commitment and devotion in tangible ways.

And Max prepared the most delicious and flavorful salads, earning him the title of Best Salad Maker on the Planet. And because he is Dutch, there was always cheese. Cheese is a lifestyle in Max's world.

"Do you have the kids this weekend? If so, how about we plan a picnic day?" I got his text with two weeks left before the end of the school term.

"Yes, let's do it. But can we go around 9:00 a.m., before the sun gets too hot," I suggested due to the summer heat. While part of me preferred to stay in the shade, I appreciated his encouragement to engage in activities. Otherwise, I could easily see myself at home in the shade with my two girls, seeking refuge from the sun and trying to avoid getting burned.

Upon our arrival at the park, my eyes darted around searching for a comfortable spot, preferably one that offered ample shade. The priority was to shield ourselves from the sun rather than seek out the most comfortable spot. We settled on a location adjacent to a sprawling playground, where I unfurled my picnic blanket and unveiled the homemade cake and madeleines I had prepared the previous night. Max produced a thermos of coffee Americano for the both of us, along with a delightful treat of sugar-free Greek yogurt ice cream that he had made for the kids to relish.

I quietly observed how Max interacted with the children, intrigued by the contrast between his dominant personality and his gentle approach to parenting. I witnessed his tender and nurturing side shining through in his interactions as he effortlessly connected with the kids and created a playful and engaging atmosphere.

Max had the potential to be a valuable support system for me in the parenting world, and I could already see the positive influence he had on me. His presence brought a sense of calm and reassurance, reminding me that I didn't have to navigate parenthood alone. Together, we could create a harmonious balance between our personal lives and our shared connection. I started to believe our casual relationship could work if we could maintain boundaries, privacy, and space.

Finding Calmness in the Storm

"Hey, I need to talk to you," I received a text message from my husband, and a wave of anticipation immediately washed over me. I've become familiar with that opening line over the years, and it usually signifies something *huge* is about to happen.

"Yes!" I replied almost immediately, my curiosity piqued. "Just tell me now. I'm reading your text," I urged, eager to discover the news he had to share.

Without disclosing too much information, it was a situation that left me to solve an urgent financial issue that involved thousands of euros within a short period, to be more precise, within two weeks. I was furious when I read the text message. In the midst of all the expenses—new apartment, new car, his family's visit during Christmas, trips, restaurants, and more—how could he leave me a problem like that? Inside my head, I was screaming at the top of my lungs. I was seething with anger and overwhelmed with emotions, unable to find a proper word to describe how I felt. "This can't be possibly true. Why can't you handle the situation?"

It was incredibly challenging for me to put into words the monsoon of emotions I experienced—fury, disappointment, and a sense of hopelessness. I felt an overwhelming wave of anger, as if all the mindfulness I had practiced to control my emotions went completely out the window.

"Hey, you wanna come over for lunch today?" appeared on my phone screen, Max's message breaking through the turmoil of my thoughts.

Arriving at Max's place, I struggled to fully grasp the magnitude of what had just transpired. Despite my anger and frustration, being in his presence had a remarkable effect on me. It was as if my rage dissipated instantly, and I was able to adopt a more composed and solution-oriented mindset. I was able to explain my situation and seek a resolution, thanks to the calming influence Max had on me. The most extraordinary part was that he didn't have to do anything other than sit there and listen, his peaceful demeanor serving as a catalyst for my inner transformation.

To add a twist to my divorce journey, just two weeks after managing to pay off all the debts with the invaluable support of my family, I expressed my desire to take the kids back to Taiwan. With the easing of lockdown restrictions and not seeing my family for three years, combined with the high cost of living in Europe during the summer, it seemed like a sensible choice. However, my soon-to-be ex-husband vehemently disagreed. He insisted that we wait until the children were older, teenagers, so that they could make the decision for themselves, with the fear that I wouldn't bring the kids back to Spain again! To compound matters, he insisted that I didn't deserve sole ownership of my blog, where the contents were 100 percent produced by me, because he put in his effort to host my blog on his hosting server! I mean, come on! He went as far as suggesting I share my affiliate income with him. It was a clear sign that our relationship had reached its breaking point.

At that point, I realized that the peaceful moments I had experienced in the past few months were a gift from the Universe, an opportunity to practice mindfulness in a perfect condition, and Max had been sent to me as close mental support just shortly before the storm arrived, preparing me for the challenges that lay ahead. The Universe was now putting me to the test!

Unfortunately, divorcing is a process that can take from two months to over two years. During this challenging period, Max played an immense role in supporting me. He didn't dictate what I should do, but his mere presence kept me grounded and focused. Max always gave me a sense of, "I understand; I've been there, and I know how you feel."

There was a particular instance when I opened up to Max about what had happened, and true to his nature, he remained calm and composed. It was in that conversation I realized how unfair it was to project my negative energy onto him. During my emotional turmoil, I had lost sight of the importance of keeping personal matters private. It was never my intention to involve Max or burden him with my problems. I simply needed an outlet to release my frustrations, but I felt a sense of remorse afterward. I came to understand that I needed to cultivate the same level of composure and calmness as Max in order to resolve my issues.

I appreciated having Max by my side during this tumultuous divorce process. His presence allowed me to reflect upon myself when I became emotional. The standards he set for mindfulness and inner peace consistently guided me back to a zen place, enabling me to view the situation objectively rather than allowing my emotions to consume me. Meditation became a part of my life at this point, and while it may not have helped me relax, it certainly helped me stay focused. Through practicing mindfulness, I learned to see my divorce as a separate entity, detached from my identity. It was merely a circumstance and not a reflection of who I was. When stress arrived, mindfulness allowed me to recover quickly. Moreover, Max possessed remarkable emotional intelligence, offering me the support and attention I needed without getting entangled in the narrative of my failing marriage.

With a sense of peace, I collected my thoughts and reminded myself to embrace the summer ahead with my children and live in the present moment. I consciously decided not to let the recent events with my soon-to-be ex-husband consume me. Come September, as the new school term began, we would initiate the legal process of divorce, and I was fully committed to reclaiming my and my kids' freedom, no matter what it took.

"Hey! I'm at the park enjoying a beer and live music with friends. You should join us," read the message on my phone on a Saturday evening. I was at home working on my paper when the message caught my attention.

As I read the message, a wave of hesitation washed over me. Deep down, I needed a day of solitude and self-care. While I understood his intention to help me connect with new friends and build a support system, I simply didn't feel like going out. Today was meant to be a "me day."

"Thank you for the invitation, but I've decided to stay home today. I hope you have a fantastic evening," I replied, finally making a decision after hours of contemplation. I chose to honor my own needs.

As midnight approached, I received another text from Max: "Hey, can I come over to your place?" while watching a YouTube video clip of a comedy bit, a small guilty pleasure I allowed myself before bedtime. Remember those COVID days? I would watch endless stand-up comedy shows, finding comfort and laughter in the performances of comedians like Ellen DeGeneres, Chris Rock, Dave Chappelle, Jimmy Fallon, Jimmy Kimmel, Ricky Gervais, and Conan. I even binge-watched Jordan Schlansky from Conan's late-night show. The algorithm went as far as recommending international comedians, from Graham Norton to Uncle Roger. The computer robot understood what I wanted and gave me everything it could to lighten me up! There's an American who says, "Fake it until you make it," which I embody as I work on my facial expression, from smiling to laughing, training myself to find internal amusement.

The suddenness of Max's request caught me off guard, leaving me uncertain about how to respond. Since I moved to this new apartment, separate from my husband, I never invited anyone to stay overnight. I always guarded my personal space so fiercely that opening the door to someone felt like an intrusion. However, despite my initial reservations, just fifteen minutes later, I was unlocking the door and welcoming Max inside to my very private space.

As Max entered my place with his bicycle parked at the entrance, I greeted him wearing my silky pajama dress. The scent of alcohol mingled with his body odor, adding a hint of intoxicating allure to the air. We leaned in to greet each other with a kiss on the lips, feeling the electricity between us intensify. With confidence and familiarity, he took the lead and guided me to my room. His touch sent shivers down my spine as his hand moved from the bottom of my hip, sensually gliding upward. In an exquisite display of desire, his hand found its way to the front, heightening the anticipation of what was to come. Our bodies were entwined in a passionate dance, exploring each other's depths with an insatiable hunger. The room became a vessel for our shared ecstasy as the electric energy between us propelled us into a realm of unbridled pleasure, leaving us both craving more.

As Max lay beside me, his body spent from our passionate encounter, he quickly succumbed to sleep. I, on the other hand, remained awake in the quiet darkness, my mind filled with a subtle unease. While the sex was undeniably satisfying, the unfamiliarity of another body in my bed disrupted my sleep, causing me to toss and turn throughout the night. It wasn't a restful night by any means. The first time we spent the night together at his place, neither of us could sleep well, and I thought I'd gotten over the cuddling-all-night-long theme. However, the same unease lingered the second time we spent the night together, this time at my place. I wondered if we weren't as deeply connected as it seemed. It didn't hold the romantic allure; it felt foreign to me.

In retrospect, it turned out to be the final occasion throughout our casual relationship. For reasons related to personal space and the sleeping issues we both experienced, we silently agreed to spend quality time together, primarily at his place. It was understood that I would always make my way home before bedtime. As we established this habit, it gradually became a routine for us.

As we grew closer, we discovered a cherished Sunday afternoon slot that allowed us to spend time together. Max would often reserve his Sunday mornings for beach volleyball, and I would attend yoga practice. Then we would set aside the afternoon or evening to enjoy a few hours together, whether it be sharing a meal or watching a movie. Despite our plans, sex would always find its way into our time together.

With each Sunday afternoon we spent in his apartment, our understanding of one another deepened. We engaged in open and non-judgmental conversations, delving into various topics. We shared our experiences, discussed the people we met, and revealed personal stories. It was within this space that we found a sense of comfort, where we could be ourselves without encroaching upon each other's boundaries, all while maintaining a regular and fulfilling sexual relationship.

We often engaged in candid and open conversations about our sexual desires and fantasies. These discussions created an atmosphere of trust, allowing us to explore and share our desires without fear of rejection. We expressed our fantasies, discussing the elements that excited and aroused us, sharing our wildest dreams and secret yearnings. Through these conversations, we built a greater understanding of each other's desires and preferences. We found joy in discovering new aspects of our sexuality and exploring different avenues of pleasure together. Together, we pushed boundaries, respected each other's boundaries, and navigated our shared exploration with trust, respect, and mutual consent.

He was the kind of man who understood the importance of creating a sensual environment to enhance our intimate experiences. He went the extra mile to set the mood by lighting candles, carefully selecting the perfect music playlist, and creating an ambiance that ignited our senses. These thoughtful gestures showed his commitment to making our moments together extraordinary.

In his presence, I felt seen, cherished, and celebrated as a sexual being. His enthusiasm for exploration, attention to detail, and commitment to our mutual pleasure created an experience where our physical connection could thrive. With him, I felt free to explore, grow, and fully embrace the joys of our shared sexual journey.

Rooted in my traditional Taiwanese upbringing and hindered by a lack of body confidence, I always felt hesitant to explore the realm of sexual activities. However, my mindfulness journey has brought about a profound transformation in my perspective. It has granted me the ability to approach these experiences with openness and freedom. By releasing the weight of judgment and self-criticism, I have wholeheartedly embraced the introduction of new elements into my sexual journey, letting go of feelings of intimidation and shyness along the way.

Nurturing a non-judgmental attitude toward my own body has unlocked a path of self-discovery and self-acceptance. I have learned to attune to the sensations and needs of my body, deepening my understanding and appreciation for its intricate workings. I have become adept at listening to my desires, honoring my boundaries, and communicating my needs with confidence and clarity. These practices have become second nature to me, empowering me to fully embrace my sexual experiences and foster a healthy and fulfilling connection with myself and my sex partner.

Parenting Across Cultures

Max and I made it a point to occasionally arrange playdates without revealing the true nature of our "underground casual relationship." Our intention was simply to provide an opportunity for our kids to enjoy each other's company.

In the process of separating from my marriage, learning how to be a single parent became an integral part of this journey. Before meeting Max, I frequently hesitated to take my children on outings outside my comfort zone. I often dreamed about taking them hiking or visiting the nearby waterfall, but I lacked the confidence to navigate the city alone with my children. However, my horizons expanded by observing Max as a single father and learning from his experiences. His guidance not only helped me deepen my bond as a parent with my children but also showed me how to navigate similar circumstances. He often said, "When in doubt, just ask!"

Additionally, witnessing Max teach his child how to ride a bike was inspiring and amusing. I thought to myself, "The Dutch are renowned for their cycling prowess, so the Dutch must have the best methodology for teaching kids how to bike. I have to steal their secrets." Fueled by this humorous thought, I enthusiastically invested in new bicycles for my two kids and took on the role of their cycling instructor. Mama was on fire in the middle of the summer—heat wave!

As I let go of the training wheels and anxiously ran behind my girl, grabbing onto wherever I could to help her balance, sweat dripping down my forehead, I tried my best not to let go.

"Mama, let go of the bike!" My daughter shouted confidently. The bike wobbled left and right as I watched my child give her best to stay upright and control her direction. In her first attempt, I saw her riding the bike all by herself, cruising away from me. It was an unforgettable and monumental moment, especially for me as a mother!

"Good job, ladies! You both did it!" Max approached me from the other end of the playground, his face beaming with happiness and pride.

I vividly recall the first playdate at Max's place, as it marked my initial encounter with the combination of Dutch culture and his distinct personality. As a gesture of gratitude for welcoming us into their home and sharing their toys, I instructed my children to bring a small toy as a token of appreciation. However, upon our arrival, it was evident that Max wasn't particularly thrilled by the gesture. "We have enough toys here," Max said, and I quickly understood his message. When we were invited back to his house weeks later, Max proactively reminded me they had toys at his place. Though I felt it was unnecessary, I respected his instructions. It was a small but significant moment that highlighted our cultural and parenting differences.

We had planned a zoo day with a few other families. Max was the kind of person who wanted to make the most of every minute and see all the animals, probably feeling he had paid for the tickets. On the other hand, I was more relaxed and went with the flow. Even if we only ended up seeing one gorilla and spent the whole day at the playground, I would be perfectly fine with it. As long as the kids were happy, I accomplished my goal of a zoo day.

I remember I once asked if Jos had finished his homework that was assigned from school every other Friday. "We tried, but Jos seemed to lose interest after one page, so we stopped and moved on to something else," Max responded. However, coming from a traditional Taiwanese family, where being a student meant taking responsibility for homework assignments, I was taught that I should finish it, whether I liked it or not!

Max would greatly emphasize disciplining Jos's eating and sleeping habits. "Jos ate everything," he would say, and "I put him to sleep by 7:30 p.m. with no screen time or candy!" On the other hand, my approach was more flexible. If my kids expressed that they were full, I respected that. They don't need to finish all the food. Sometimes, I used snacks to manage sibling crises when I felt almost suffocated. Of course, I found acceptable amounts of screentime, such as when I needed a moment of peace while cooking or cleaning the house, to be totally fine. However, on our commute to the city, I would strictly ask my child to stay seated in their chair without disturbing anyone else on board. Meanwhile, Max had no problem with Jos running up and down in the metro cabin! Neither of us was right or wrong; we were just so different in many ways.

These small instances of differences became valuable opportunities for me to see things from various perspectives. One thing that happened in my marriage was the tendency to react swiftly and strongly to situations that didn't align with my desires or expectations, resulting in anger or frustration. However,

I have found space through mindfulness practice to explore, reflect, and accept myself. I have learned to understand situations from a different perspective and recognize that it's okay for things to be different from what I want. With each new difference that arises, I gain a deeper understanding of myself. I am relieved to have moved away from relying on anger and heated arguments to seek balance in my life and relationships. Instead, I have learned to approach disagreements with a calmer and more measured perspective.

Bordeaux, France

It had been nearly six months since we integrated each other into our routines. As an avid traveler, I was planning a trip to Bordeaux, France, to explore the city's charm during its harvesting season. Contemplating the idea, I carefully considered the potential implications of inviting Max to accompany me. Throughout our time together, I had come to know him as someone who thrived on routine—always on his bicycle, surrounded by the same group of friends, dedicated to meditation, reading, maintaining a healthy lifestyle, and indulging in beach volleyball. However, I thought that breaking away from his regular routine for a while could be refreshing for him while also providing me with a pleasant companion during my travels. It seemed like the perfect opportunity for us to experiment with this new approach without jeopardizing the casual nature of our relationship.

"Hey, I'm planning a trip to Bordeaux. I wanted to extend an invitation for you to join me. It would be wonderful to explore the city together, but please feel no pressure to decide. I'll have a great time regardless, and I want you to make the choice that feels right for you." I sent the invitation to Max, making sure to emphasize that I would enjoy the trip with or without him.

Our relationship had been casual and focused on the present moment, without any discussions about the future. The furthest we had ventured into the realm of future planning was our anticipation for this very trip to Bordeaux, which was now taking place before our eyes.

A few weeks later, our journey brought us to Bordeaux. As we stepped off the plane and boarded a bus to the city center, it was nearing 9:00 p.m., and the bus was only a third full. A sudden scene unfolded before us with just ten minutes remaining until our stop. Eight policemen boarded the bus, and a wave of nervousness washed over me. Memories from a backpacking experience in Salvador, Brazil, flooded my mind. It was a time when several police cars stopped the bus I was on with Madoka, my adventurous photographer friend from Japan who is now living in Berlin. (Apart from my artist Xavier and my husband's family visit, she was the first, primary, and most important reason I visited Berlin.) The officers carried imposing weapons and commanded silence among the passengers. They moved slowly and methodically down the narrow aisle, their eyes scanning the faces of the passengers. A sense of uncertainty hung in the air as everyone on the bus remained unaware of what was happening. Time seemed to stand still as the atmosphere grew increasingly tense. Without uttering a word, the police singled out two men seated in front of Madoka and me, escorting them off the bus. The men showed no visible resentment, but the tension in the air was palpable. It was later revealed that the men were wanted suspects. I refrained from asking whether they were carrying weapons or not; some things are better left unknown. The experience was incredibly intense.

In that Bordeaux moment, the sight of eight policemen entering the bus evoked a chilling memory. The contrast between the tranquil beauty of Bordeaux and the sudden intrusion of authority created a stark reminder of the unpredictability of life.

As I nervously anticipated the approach of the police, Max, my travel companion, calmly reminded me that we hadn't paid for our bus tickets. The driver had waived the fee at the airport due to a malfunctioning machine. He wanted to reassure me that the police presence was likely just a routine ticket check. However, seeing eight officers verifying tickets on a single bus felt unusual, fueling my lingering suspicions.

In a low voice, barely taking my eyes off the police, I quietly expressed my concerns to Max. I urged him to be prepared with passports, sensing that this situation might require more than just ticket verification. The officers were moving slowly closer to our seats while the bus continued its way forward.

As I reached into my purse to retrieve my passport, mentally preparing for the encounter with the police, Max took the initiative and confidently approached the officers. Speaking a mix of Spanish and French, he explained our situation. Despite Max being right next to the police, calmly engaging in conversation with everyone, my mind remained locked in a state of uncertainty, convinced that something major was transpiring on the bus. The memory of encountering armed police on a bus in Salvador had left a lasting impression, making it challenging to shake off my sense of apprehension.

While Max engaged in conversation with the officers, the minutes ticked by slowly as I anxiously awaited Max's return. Finally, after what felt like an eternity, he came back to his seat with a relaxed smile on his face. My brain decided to believe that it indeed was just about the tickets. The police, having understood our predicament, displayed understanding and kindness. They accepted Max's explanation and allowed us to continue our journey without further issues. At that moment, I felt a mixture of emotions for Max's assertiveness and relief that my fears had been unfounded.

As we settled back into our seats, the tension inside my head began to dissipate. I shifted my focus back to enjoying the journey through Bordeaux. With a sense of relief and gratitude, our stop finally arrived.

Taking the train from Bordeaux city center to Saint Emilion was the plan for our first day. Upon arriving and leaving the Saint Emilion train station, we made our way toward the UNESCO center of the city. As we turned, an enchanting sight filled our eyes—a vast expanse of vineyards stretching as far as the eye could see. In the far right corner, nestled atop a hill, a Chateau stood proudly, adding a touch of dreamy allure to the picturesque landscape.

As we ventured through the beautiful city of Saint-Émilion, we wholeheartedly embraced the opportunity to be fully present in every precious moment. Continuing along the main street of Saint-Émilion, Rue Simard, we found ourselves drawn toward the heart of the town. The picturesque street guided us through lush vineyards, where row after row of vines stretched as far as the eye could see. The early morning arrival ensured a tranquil atmosphere, with the absence of cars enhancing the sense of serenity. Overhead, the sun-drenched sky expanded gradually, casting a soft, radiant glow upon us. Its warm rays delicately kissed our skin, while in the shaded areas, a cool and gentle breeze whispered through the air, offering a refreshing embrace. The breeze carried with it the invigorating scent of the surrounding vineyards. Continuing our journey along Rue La Gaffelière-Ouest, we couldn't help but be awed by the magnificent architecture of Chateau La Gaffelière. The exterior of the vineyard building proudly displayed its name, logo, and distinction of being a First Grand Cru Classé.

We finally arrived at the entrance of the UNESCO site, and the town was still quiet, as the shops were just preparing to open. We ventured toward the center on the cobbled pathway through those narrow alleys, casting dappled patterns on the ancient stone walls, blending ourselves into the rich tapestry of history and architectural beauty. The Romanesque churches stood as testaments to the town's past, their intricate details telling stories of centuries gone by. Among them, the monolithic bell tower stood tall and proud, commanding attention with its imposing presence.

The medieval town exuded a rustic charm that transported us back in time, evoking a sense of nostalgia and wonder. In the heart of the old town, we discovered a spot near the church and bell tower. We settled at a cozy table on the terrace area, basking in the gentle morning breeze as it carried the fragrant aroma of freshly brewed coffee.

Knowing that it's a universally recognized coffee choice, I ordered a cup of cappuccino, allowing me to navigate without worrying about pronouncing *café au lait* correctly in French. From our vantage point, we observed the quiet morning life of the town. As we savored our coffee, I also explained our plan to visit Château Coutet for an organic wine tasting in an hour. Every now and then, we snapped a couple of photos, capturing moments to share with our children later on.

Making a checkpoint to how I felt about Max at that moment, I wasn't exactly experiencing a romantic French moment. However, his energy was so present and realistic that I felt more like I had a dependable travel companion with whom I shared a mutual sense of looking out for each other. With Max by my side, I could focus on gathering the information I needed to complete my upcoming assignment on sustainable travel in Saint-Émilion. He even reminded me to declare this trip's expense during the tax season. He was that practical and grounded.

After enjoying our coffee, we set off toward Château Coutet, renowned for its exceptional organic wines. With a blend of work and leisure in mind, prioritizing sustainable travel, I promptly booked a wine tour immediately after purchasing my airline ticket, even before inviting Max to join me on this trip.

As a conscious traveler, I was determined to explore the vineyards without relying on a car. I presented Max with the choice of either cycling from the Saint-Émilion city center to the Château or taking a thirty-minute leisurely walk. He opted for the latter.

We followed a narrow street as we walked from the Saint-Émilion city center to Château Coutet. With Max leading the way and the UNESCO Center behind us, I was so entranced by the surroundings, constantly scanning left and right with my phone camera in hand, capturing the moments. We passed by Château Beau-Séjour Bécot, and I quickly commented, "Hey! I visited this chateau the last time I came."

As we continued to stroll from the Saint-Émilion city center to Château Coutet, we meandered along a narrow street lined flanked by two-meter-high walls, which I learned were built to protect against wolves in the past. I eagerly captured the moments with my phone camera.

However, we got a little lost between Rue Ramonet and La Carte, as we were enveloped by vineyards. They all seemed the same, without a clear street sign to guide us. Unfazed, Max, with his characteristic problem-solving skills, spotted two individuals about three hundred meters away and approached them, using his mix of Spanish, English, and French to ask for directions. Meanwhile, I continued to wander and enjoy the idea of getting lost amidst the vineyards. I knew that if I were alone, I would fully trust my inner orientation and continue to pave my way through the middle of nowhere.

Our classy wine tour experience commenced shortly after our check-in, led by our knowledgeable guide, who educated us through the process of making biological wine in Château Coutet. We stepped inside, and a refreshing coolness enveloped us, heightening our senses. As we made our way through the family cellars, the air became saturated with an enchanting medley of aromas, growing more intense with each step. The neatly arranged aged oak barrels stood as a testament to the craftsmanship, while our guide shared insights on their cost, the values, and the importance of recycling. As we reached the final leg of the tour, our guide revealed that the harvesters had just completed their work the day prior, instantly infusing the air with the earthy fragrance of freshly crushed grapes in my head.

The tour concluded with tasting vintage wines, which I found to be a self-indulgent experience. My judgment of a wine's quality was based solely on whether I liked it or not. That being said, my wine knowledge is quite limited. As our guide presented each glass with its vibrant hue, they proceeded to explain the distinguishing features of young and aged wines. They demonstrated the proper technique of placing one's nose at the center of the glass, cupping it to fully appreciate the aroma, observing the colors, and concluding with a gentle rinse in the mouth.

With anticipation, like the other international travelers in our group, we raised the glasses to our lips, letting the flavors dance upon our palates. As I observed the various expressions around me, some revealing a symphony of tasting notes and others savoring the graceful balance of fruitiness, I quietly thought to myself, "Mmmm, I like it." Though I found it challenging to put into romantic and descriptive words, our visit to the winery left our palates satisfied and our hearts brimming with gratitude as we bid farewells.

Over the next three days, we remained inseparable, and it became evident that this was the most extended, uninterrupted period we had ever shared, with no intention of parting ways. In our individual personal journeys, it represented a significant milestone, as it was the first time we had ventured so intimately with someone since the separation from our previous marriage. This experimental trip allowed us to explore our connection further, yet we approached it with caution, hoping to preserve the comfortable dynamic we had as a casual relationship.

In terms of the definition of a casual relationship, it was so clear that we were literally engaging in an open and serious conversation as we concluded our trip at the bustling Bordeaux airport, waiting to board our flight. We aligned that this journey had been nothing more than a delightful companionship experience with no further expectations or attachments.

As we prepared to bid farewell to Bordeaux, a bittersweet feeling washed over me. During my previous visit to Bordeaux, I was headed toward the beginning of my marriage. However, this time in Bordeaux, I was on the beginning path to its conclusion.

Whispers of the Universe

We seamlessly transitioned back into our routine after Bordeaux. Our Sunday hangouts resumed, offering a comforting sense of familiarity and stability. Throughout my moments with Max, we did not encounter a conflict, as he possessed a magical ability to diffuse disagreements with his peaceful demeanor. Also, as a not-so-outspoken me who doesn't usually talk about my thoughts or feelings, he often referred to me as an "unconfrontational person."

In general, we have contrasting natures. Max was mighty and domineering, being an outspoken individual who preferred face-to-face communication and freely shared his ideas. On the contrary, I tend to be more reserved, keeping my preferences to myself and often opting for WhatsApp as a means of communication to avoid immediate reactions. If we were in a classroom, Max would always confidently raise his hand to discuss his opinions and share his knowledge openly. At the same time, I would be the quiet observer, diligently taking notes and seamlessly blending in with the surroundings.

In terms of dietary preferences, we both had a strong inclination toward healthy eating, which initially made me think we could be a good match. I consider myself a flexitarian, prioritizing vegetables and fish in my meals. However, I'm not strict about being vegan and still occasionally enjoy meat. Just to address any concerns regarding the children's nutrition, their father is Brazilian, and meat is a significant part of his lifestyle, much like soccer is in Brazil. He ensures they have meat with him, and supporting Brazil during the World Cup is a "religion." On the other hand, Max took his dietary control to a higher level. He would study the different nutrient categories and has even had his blood tested to identify superfoods.

"Tomato is not good for me" was the catchphrase I heard from him during approximately 80 percent of the meals we shared together.

I recall a time when we had planned to take a stroll around Barcelona, immersed in the vibrant Christmas atmosphere. My intention was to visit a Christmas market, preferably one near the Gothic Quarter, or perhaps even venture down to Port Vell. However, we ended up deviating from those plans as Max suggested a different course of action the moment we arrived at the city center—heading directly to a restaurant. Despite my preference for a longer walk, I acquiesced and agreed to his proposal.

On that night, we were fortunate to secure a table at Vinitus, one of Barcelona's renowned tapas restaurants, without the usual wait of at least forty minutes. As we perused the menu and decided to share some tapas, I realized that our options were somewhat limited. Max's preference would aim for lighter, vegetable-based dishes, avoiding tomatoes (of course) and sugar-free. It was quite an interesting experience because I'm the type of person who tends to be enticed by whatever delectable dishes I spot at nearby tables.

Sometimes, when Max invited me to his place for coffee, even after months of explicitly stating my preference for coffee with milk, he would still serve me a coffee with Coffee-mate. In those moments, my usually non-confrontational self would raise my voice (in my head, of course), saying, "I want real milk, fresh milk, not Coffee-mate!"

Whenever we decided to do something together, he would have already sorted out the plan, the route, and the estimated time it would be. This is another classic example of the difference between us. I, on the other hand, tend to understand the "overview" of my plan while happily wandering around. I enjoy getting lost and not knowing what will happen next, finding joy in the unexplainable beauty of the world around me.

As our relationship settled into a comfortable rhythm, our weekly sexual activities followed a predictable routine. Slowly, I noticed a change within myself. The ease and stability we had established started to feel somewhat stagnant, creating a subtle sense of uneasiness. While I wasn't involved with anyone else romantically, my intuition nudged me to acknowledge that despite the many positive qualities I admired in Max, there was a certain lack of connection. My struggle to fully open up and express my emotions persisted. Although these thoughts occasionally resurfaced in my mind, I hesitated to take any action that might alter the course of our relationship. Time continued to pass, and the contrast between our personalities became increasingly evident with each passing day.

During our last few weeks together, I noticed myself unintentionally fixating on aspects that didn't align with my preferences rather than appreciating the harmony that had enveloped us months ago. The desire to have my own space and spend Sunday nights alone at home or with friends started to outweigh the comfort of being at his place.

Some of our conversations went like this:

"Lunch today? You can choose your preference," he kindly offered.

"How about this one?" I chose an option.

"No, I don't feel like having that. How about this instead?" he politely declined and offered another suggestion, which we ended up going with.

This pattern extended to our movie selections as well. Despite expressing my love for documentaries, we never ended up watching a single one on our Sunday movie nights. To be fair, I enjoyed all the films we watched, and he always asked for my agreement before starting. However, it never landed on my first choice.

Along with many other minor details that don't warrant mention, I felt hesitant to take any action to address the situation. Instead, I attempted to rationalize my concerns, convincing myself that the issue solely resided within me. After all, Max was genuinely kind and one of the best things that had come into my life since my divorce. He fulfilled and protected that specific piece of the puzzle, meeting my sexual desires without encroaching on other aspects of my life. Through his mature character, I believed I could grow into a better version of myself than before we started seeing each other a few months ago. Our casual relationship seemed to be perfectly aligned, so why was I feeling the need to complain? I questioned my own emotions and hesitated to acknowledge the mounting dissatisfaction brewing inside me.

On a random Monday morning, in a small town, mutual parenting community, coincidentally, I found myself walking next to Max's ex-wife, who remained unaware of my relationship with Max. We had always maintained a low-profile approach to our connection. However, as we engaged in conversation, there was an unmistakable tension in the air.

"Hey, how was your weekend?" I asked politely, trying to keep the conversation light.

"Jos told me about the playdate. I know everything! Everything!" she replied abruptly, rolling her eyes with tension-filled words.

Feeling caught off guard, I quickly responded, "Yeah, we had a playdate with a few friends over the weekend." I hoped my explanation would alleviate any concerns.

"I'm surprised your small apartment could accommodate so many people," she retorted, her tone implying more than just a passing remark.

I struggled to sleep well for the next two days, unable to fully comprehend what was bothering me to such an extent that I couldn't brush off the conversation lightly. Perhaps it was the accumulation of all the internal dialogues I had created in my mind. In the early stages of my spiritual learning experiment, I didn't always have complete faith in this inner voice of wisdom.

I vividly recalled Oprah Winfrey's words, "The Universe will whisper to you, first in a gentle breeze. If you ignore it, it will get louder and louder, like a thunderstorm." Those words resonated within me as I struggled to suppress the mounting signs and whispers that urged me to pay attention. The growing dissonance between my true desires and my current circumstances couldn't be ignored. The Universe was sending me messages, nudging me toward self-discovery and fulfillment. It was my responsibility to listen to those whispers and summon the courage to embrace change.

Another question that bore significant weight on my mind was the profound contradiction between pursuing a casual relationship and craving for a deeper connection. Intrigued by this quandary, I delved into the depths of online resources, seeking to understand the nuanced distinction between sex and intimacy. Were they not, in essence, two sides of the same coin?

Sex is the physical act, the intimate connection between two people. It's the shared experience, the vulnerability of being physically close. On the other hand, *intimacy* goes beyond the physical; it's the emotional and psychological connection that deepens over time. While sex can be a part of intimacy, intimacy encompasses a broader spectrum of feelings, trust, and understanding. I contemplated their relationship, drawing parallels to the dichotomy of private versus secret. While these concepts shared similarities, they were not precisely identical. *Private* denoted information belonging exclusively to oneself, shielded from disclosure, while *secret* encompassed a sense of unease or embarrassment associated with withholding such information.

One thing I knew for sure was that in our casual relationship, clear boundaries were drawn. It was always in my head that I was dating Max, keeping everything under control and rationalizing my actions. However, to foster the growth of intimacy in a relationship, one must be willing to open their heart.

I pondered whether these two desires could truly coexist or if they were inherently incompatible. I tried to decode my mind and feelings. It was a conundrum that forced me to reflect on my needs and aspirations and the type of relationship I truly desired. During this introspective process, I began to reevaluate the definition of my "casual relationship." Did it encompass an open sexual relationship? And if I wanted more connection, how much could I give in return? Was the frequency of our encounters too frequent, blurring the boundaries I initially sought? Or was it simply that I wasn't that into him?

In Buddhism, there is a saying, "Learn to offer no resistance to what *is*; learn to allow the present moment to *be* and accept the impermanent nature of all things and conditions." Everything happens for a reason. It became clear that I needed space and time to explore these complexities, and understand the nuances of my heart. How did I want to appear and exist in the realm of love? Where was the key to my heart? With gratitude, I ventured forth.

Chapter 3:
When the Past Becomes Present

"The past has no power over the present moment."

– Eckhart Tolle

Caetano and I initiated the legal process immediately after the kids returned to school following the long summer vacation. Months of negotiations ensued, starting with a 50/50 custody arrangement and gradually transforming into a situation where I pleaded for every inch, desperately seeking permission to take the children to Taiwan and explore the world, just as I had always done. Negotiations reached a point where I began accepting every term he requested. My mind had wandered so far that I even considered reaching out to government authorities for assistance, convinced that Caetano was hindering my children's freedom by refusing to issue passports and permitting me to travel outside of Spain until they reached their teenage years.

In a futile attempt, my lawyer presented a few obscure laws to Caetano, showing that I had no historical record of ever violating or leaving my residential location without any preparation or closure. On the contrary, I had put enormous effort into establishing a new life in Spain. There was absolutely no way the judge would believe I was intentionally planning to "steal" the kids and never return to Spain. It was preposterous. Both the lawyer and I repeatedly tried to explain to Caetano that the main purpose of arriving in Barcelona from the beginning was what we had agreed upon—co-parenting the kids. If I had intended to steal the kids, I would have done it long ago, before COVID struck, with their Taiwanese passports. Requesting Spanish passports for my children was to ensure our return to Spain from travel without any hiccups from immigration.

My lawyer, with unshakable conviction, made it clear to my husband that if this matter were to proceed to court, his chances of winning were slim to none. Yet the relentless question that tormented me was whether I should subject myself to a trial. The exorbitant financial and emotional costs loomed heavily, casting a dark cloud over my already burdened spirit. The thought of engaging in a protracted legal battle, baring my deepest vulnerabilities for all to see, was a source of immense pain and frustration. However, above all else, I had to prioritize the well-being of my children. It is well-documented that involving children in court proceedings can severely damage their overall welfare. With this knowledge, I was acutely aware that finding a resolution without resorting to a court order was undeniably the best course of action, even though it felt like a heart-wrenching concession.

Three months after the legal process started, on a November day, Caetano requested a face-to-face conversation without mediators or lawyers—just the two of us. He said, "I'm giving you a chance to explain to me." So with a humble heart, setting aside my ego and reminding myself that this was a process to resolve a situation, not a reflection of my identity, I decided to go for one last and final attempt. I vowed to stay calm, avoid conflict, and detach myself emotionally.

Clutching my small notebook from The City Lights Bookstore in San Francisco and a blue pen made in Taiwan, I entered Cafe 365 as agreed. I scanned the room and spotted a small corner table that would afford us some privacy. Without exchanging polite greetings or making eye contact, I took a seat, ready to begin our conversation.

"I cannot bear how you left our apartment, abandoning the kids and me." Caetano's words pierced through me, one painful accusation after another. "I cannot accept that you reached out to my parents for help," he continued, his voice filled with hurt. "I cannot forgive you for that trip to Cologne," he added, each word carrying the weight of resentment. "You were a terrible wife, confessing in your diary about feeling for someone else during your backpacking trip fifteen years ago." And then came the final blow: "Look into my eyes! You created a story of being the victim of this marriage, which was a lie! Look into my eyes."

"I'm sorry, Caetano. I apologize for the way you're feeling. Whatever happened is history; the past has no power over our present. That's not important anymore. Let's move on! We are talking about something that happened from 15 years ago to nearly two and a half years ago," I said firmly, my voice filled with frustration.

Since the summer began, I had been avoiding direct communication with him. I believed every moment spent engaging with him was a waste of my precious time, draining my energy and impacting my well-being. All communication revolved around lawyers.

As Caetano emotionally laid out his grievances, I grappled with the weight of our impending decision. "Caetano, in just thirty minutes, we will determine whether or not we go to court. Do you truly believe it's worth taking that path?" I expressed my deep sorrow over the fact that after fifteen years of being together, we were in this situation. I didn't expect a fairy-tale ending, but I also didn't want our story to end in bitterness.

"I want to apologize for what happened in Cologne and during my backpacking trip in Central America. It was unfortunate that you dug into my diary and read through it without my permission," I acknowledged, admitting to my emotional infidelity. "I have repeatedly assured you that nothing physical happened between me and Stefan. I deleted him from my contacts and removed him from Facebook." To be more specific, I deleted all my German friends' contacts after Caetano and I had a massive argument due to Brazil's loss to Germany, 7 to 1, in the FIFA World Cup in 2014. I stood in front of a bar in San Francisco during my business trip, watching this humiliating game playing out before me. Within a minute after the game, I received a text message from Caetano demanding that I delete all my German friends immediately. Meanwhile, Stefan sent me a text message with a GIF image of a monster gorilla with a German flag on top, humorously "destroying" Brazil.

Our eyes locked with each other for the first time in months. "I was fighting for years to save our marriage, Caetano. We have children, and I wasn't willing to give up on a 'perfect family' for other people. If I had wanted to do something reckless, I had all the opportunities in Central America and during the night I spent in Cologne. Two years after the separation, I'm still here trying to work on everything we have left to work on. I didn't dive into Stefan's arms. In fact, we were not in contact at all."

"Move on, Caetano. It doesn't matter anymore! Live your life and be the father you want to be. Over the course of fifteen years, I have made mistakes and said things I'm not proud of, and for that, I am truly sorry. I was young and immature, and I mishandled situations that were important to you. Believe me, I exhausted every possible avenue to salvage our marriage. Whatever you feel about me being a bad wife, I am again sorry for how you feel. It wasn't my intention to ruin the marriage! Let's move on. It is a learning lesson for both of us!" I emphasized. "Caetano, what happened in our past is no longer significant. Let's close this chapter and turn the page," I pleaded, hoping to convince him of the need for closure.

"It's already November, and I've essentially agreed to everything you requested in our divorce agreement. Let's proceed with signing the necessary documents soon. Please permit me to travel with the kids, allowing them to see the world and spend time with both sides of our families in the coming years. If we can do this, we can wrap up this process and embrace the approaching year of 2023 together. Isn't that a positive sign, a fresh start?" I begged one last time.

"Okay, I will give you a chance," Caetano responded emotionally. We concluded the meeting with the understanding that he would sign the agreement. However, another month passed without the agreement being signed, as he claimed to be too busy to review his version of the last two drafts that I had accepted without changing a single word.

I often repeated the phrase, "What can you do? We'll just have to wait until he becomes less busy, right?" Deep down, I believed that the Universe had presented this test to me for a reason. During this negotiation period, I experienced an emotional roller coaster, but I managed to not respond to everything he said. It was a newfound sense of maturity and inner peace. I felt like I was detaching myself from the situation, focusing on the resolution, and allowing myself to approach the issues in a manner that would not impact my well-being and, therefore, not negatively impact my children. The sequence of events in life can be incredibly intriguing, and it's hard not to see the connections and patterns that emerge.

Paris, France

Just two days after the transformative conversation in the cafe, I was on my way to Paris. It was a momentous occasion as I reunited with my dear friends Ray and Rina from Taipei, Taiwan. They were the first two people I had seen from my pre-COVID life in a long time.

Although the COVID period played a significant role in dividing my pre-marriage and post-marriage life, it was an unfortunate event that many people suffered around the world.

However, looking at the bright side, I am thankful for this experience, as it cut me off from all my previous support systems that could have created noise and distractions as I ventured forward into a new life. It was an event through which the Universe placed me into solitude and asked me to handle it bravely. The time alone in a new country taught me to navigate the situation without relying on the various sources of comfort I used to take for granted. It was a time that the Universe forced me to grow and become more self-reliant.

Just one week before seeing them in Paris, I was typing them a short text message about the pickpocketing issue in a big city like Paris, a gentle reminder for them as first-time travelers to Europe. We definitely needed to be extra careful since the atmosphere was completely different from Taipei.

Living in Taipei, you feel safe, with the city being known for its cleanliness and organization. Most people would have felt comfortable leaving their phone on an empty table in a cafe as a sign of "occupying the table." Walking around with your phone in your hand is not a problem, and you generally don't have to worry about pickpocketing.

On the other hand, Paris has a different reputation when it comes to security and pickpocketing. The city is bustling with tourists and locals alike, making it an attractive location for pickpockets. It's essential to be cautious and vigilant, especially in crowded places and tourist hotspots like museums, famous landmarks, and public transportation.

Unlike in Taipei, leaving your phone or valuables unattended on a table in Paris is not advisable. It's best to keep your belongings close to you and use anti-theft measures, such as securing your bag with a zipper or a lock. Many experienced travelers recommend carrying a crossbody bag and being mindful of your surroundings to avoid falling victim to pickpocketing.

Both cities have their unique charms and security considerations. While Taipei provides a sense of safety and comfort, it's essential to stay aware and take necessary precautions while exploring the beautiful streets of Paris.

Reminder!

Sending a quick reminder in our group chat:

1. Please be mindful and avoid leaving any valuables unattended on the table while enjoying your coffee or meal, whether you're inside or outside the restaurant. Keep an eye on your mobile phones, wallets, and bags at all times.
2. Remember to hold onto your luggage with one hand and avoid getting distracted by your phone when you're on the move. Never let go of your belongings, and always keep one hand on your luggage.
3. To ensure better safety, carry your bag in front of your body rather than hanging it on the chair or placing it on the table when you sit down.
4. And if you're using the metro system, be cautious when the train is about to stop. Refrain from using your mobile phone during that time, as items can be easily grabbed and stolen. Purchase a phone leash if possible.

Looking forward to seeing you all soon!

As I hit send on this message, in metro line 2 from Sagrada Família, I raised my head and witnessed a pickpocket incident right before my eyes. It served as a stark reminder that we should always be extra vigilant, especially when living in a big and complex city like Barcelona or Paris.

Seeing Ray and Rina standing next to the carousel of the majestic Eiffel Tower, it hit me with a sense of nostalgia and a clear distinction between the pre-COVID and post-COVID eras. I held back my emotions, approached them, and embraced them with a long-awaited tight hug. It was a comforting feeling to be in the presence of old friends in a foreign city, where the sound of Mandarin filled the air and conversations revolved around memories of Taiwan. For a brief moment, I was able to escape the weight of my burdens and thoroughly enjoy myself in the warmth of their company.

Rina and I were once co-workers in a bustling marketing and communications agency, where our lives were consumed by the fast-paced demands of the industry. Days and nights blurred into one another as we tirelessly worked on client projects, often staying in the office close to midnight. The office became our second home, and we spent countless nights brainstorming, meticulously working on proposals, and ironing out every single detail of events. Despite the challenges and the pressure, we found solace in each other's company, bonding over our shared passion for our work.

Our connection went beyond that of mere co-workers; we became genuine friends. Our conversations shifted from work-related matters to personal ones, and we started to hang out even after office hours. Our lives became intertwined, and I often saw Rina more frequently than my husband or anyone else in my life.

Working in an advertising agency was undoubtedly challenging, but it was also an exhilarating experience. The industry demanded creativity, innovation, and the ability to think on our feet. Deadlines were tight, and stress was a constant companion. However, we thrived in a fast-paced environment, finding fulfillment in the projects we delivered and the satisfaction of meeting our clients' expectations.

The late nights at the office, the adrenaline-filled pitches, the moments of celebration for successful campaigns—all of these experiences brought Rina and me closer together. We weathered the challenges side by side, supporting each other through the highs and lows of our careers.

Looking back on those days, I cherish the memories of our shared struggles and triumphs. Our time in the advertising agency may have been demanding, but it also forged a bond between us that would endure beyond our professional lives.

Ray, Rina's husband, was someone I got to know during our time in the advertising agency. Back then, he was still a budding illustrator, eager to get his work recognized. Now, he has become a renowned illustrator in Taiwan known as A RAY, working closely with the president's marketing team.

Ray is a bit introverted and tends to keep to himself around unfamiliar people. However, once you become close to him, he unleashes his sharp wit and sarcasm, often incorporating playful banter with his close friends into his creative works. For instance, he loves to playfully highlight funny and slightly twisted Chinese phrases in his illustrations.

Initially, Ray gained fame for his Fat Otaku and A RAY characters, but over time, his artwork evolved to reflect current events and political issues that deeply resonated with young people. Politics had never interested him until the Sunflower Student Movement in 2014, a significant social and political movement in Taiwan opposing the Cross-Strait Service Trade Agreement with China. Through this movement, he realized the inseparable connection between politics and life.

Since then, Ray has fearlessly expressed his political stance through his artwork, even though his family advised him to stay out of politics. However, he insists that as long as it benefits Taiwan, he will continue to draw and make his voice heard. His humorous and satirical approach to his art allows him to speak out against injustice and advocate for positive change.

Wandering around the Eiffel Tower, we took in its breathtaking beauty, illuminated by a dazzling display of lights. The sparkle of the Eiffel Tower at night is a magical sight to behold, as thousands of glittering lights dance and twinkle, turning the iconic landmark into a mesmerizing spectacle, and filling the air with a sense of wonder. We couldn't have asked for a more perfect setting to capture our joyous reunion, and we eagerly took our very first photo together with the magnificent Eiffel Tower as our backdrop.

As we continued strolling around the Eiffel Tower, I shared some of my experiences traveling in Europe over the last few years. "European commutes are quite frequent, and airports are often packed with people, leading to daily flight delays," I said. "But what caught me by surprise was the way some pilots fly the airplanes. It almost feels like they're handling them like New York taxi drivers, making sharp turns and quick maneuvers."

"In Taiwan, whenever we're on an airplane, the pilot usually takes a moment to pause before making a move, be it a turn or an announcement before takeoff. But my first time taking a budget flight in Europe after COVID, the pilot practically took off immediately after turning. It was quite an exhilarating experience!" We laughed together. "There's no time to stop!"

We stumbled upon a charming, classic restaurant bar nearby, reminiscent of the cozy spots found in the heart of the city.

"Bonjour," I greeted politely, "*trois personnes*."

The server responded by asking if we would be dining in the restaurant, and none of us understood a single word, so he politely switched to English and led us inside. The space felt intimate, with tables placed closely together, and the round table he chose was small and cozy. The chairs were petite, and the overall ambiance exuded a classic charm, harkening back to the traditional Paris restaurants.

Before the waiter returned again, I had secretly practiced in my head *vin blanc* and *bière* in French. I insisted that I should at least "localize" myself with a couple of words on my first day.

With a playful wink and a confident smile, I attempted my best French accent, uttering, "*Deux vin blanc*," while pointing to myself and Rina, followed by a casual gesture toward Ray as I announced, "*un bière*." To my dismay, the server seemed utterly perplexed by my attempt at acting like a local. Feeling a tad defeated, I chuckled to myself and decided to switch to Spanish, hoping it might alleviate the awkwardness. After all, it's a well-known myth that Parisians find it rude when tourists assume they speak English, so I thought I'd play it safe and add a dash of humor to the mix.

"How did COVID look like in Spain?" Rina inquired with genuine curiosity.

"It was really bad. Everything was shut down. Spain had a strict lockdown where you couldn't go out anywhere. Asian countries like Taiwan, Japan, and South Korea did a great job mainly because their cultures are more collective, and people are open to wearing masks when they are sick, not just for COVID. However, it took weeks for Europeans to accept the idea of wearing masks. My guess is that they couldn't stand the government controlling what they should do. You know, the whole human rights thing plays a strong role in Europe. On the other hand, Asian countries work collectively, so when faced with a situation like COVID, everyone works together, leading to better success. We've seen that in the last two years. While the rest of the world was suffering, Taiwan seemed to be partying, having events and concerts, and everything else appeared normal. The only downside was the restriction on travel and entry into the country."

"Some of the policies were quite funny. I remember when a group of my friends wanted to have lunch together. At that time, the policy allowed a maximum of four people per table for dining out on the terrace. Unfortunately, there were five of us. The restaurant server suggested that we sit at two separate tables due to the law. It was so ridiculous that we decided to take the food to go and go to the park for a picnic instead. In the end, all five of us were still standing together, waiting for the food and eating in the park. When it comes to masks, it looked more like a chin guard!" We laughed at the absurdity of the situation, appreciating the humor amidst challenging times.

"Have you been vaccinated?" Ray asked. "How was the experience?"

"Yeah, the government notified us through various media platforms based on our age group. We had to go to the official website to register for a vaccination date." I continued to explain, "When we showed up at the CAP, which is the government health center, we presented our IDs to the front desk. A nurse then guided us to the station where we should be vaccinated. The nurse confirmed our names and asked if we had tested positive before. After that, they administered the injections, and we were asked to wait in the waiting room for fifteen minutes before leaving in case of any discomfort due to the vaccination."

"You didn't get to choose the brand?" Rina asked

"No! I didn't know what brand I was injected with until I saw my vaccination record." I laughed like choosing wasn't even an option.

"Are most people open to vaccinations?" Ray continued to ask.

"No, in fact, most people I know didn't like the idea of needing to be vaccinated. Some of them even got furious. Their faces and necks would turn red just from expressing their frustration about the situation. On the other hand, there was another group of people who reluctantly decided to get vaccinated because of work and travel requirements, even though they didn't really want to."

"In Taiwan, many people were furious that the government didn't have enough vaccinations ready from the beginning. People were desperate to get vaccinated as soon as possible. You could even see charts published everywhere showing the side effects of each vaccination brand. The experience I had was once I arrived at the vaccination station, I was seated, and the nurse came to me with the brand I chose. After the injection, they handed me another bag of painkillers and fever medicine just in case. Basically, I didn't have to move; the nurse came to me," Rina explained the differences, feeling so proud to be Taiwanese, as it's a service-oriented country.

"The government didn't even need to impose any law enforcement to ask people to stay at home or to allow employees to work from home. It all happened automatically. Taiwanese were just so afraid of the virus that they would do anything to collaborate with the government," Ray added. "We had SARS once in 2003, and we knew we couldn't handle another one."

"So what brought you to Paris?" I asked.

"I'm on a business trip, and the German company I'm working with sent us to Strasbourg for private employee training. We were testing our new kitchen appliance, making pizza! The flight had to come to Paris, so we decided to take extra days off after the training," Rina explained.

"You mean your German company sent you to France to make Italian food!" I chimed in with a grin, playfully teasing Rina's culinary adventure.

Our night continued with catching up on what had happened in our lives over the last few years, sipping our French wine, fully present with each other in the charming ambiance of the restaurant. It was a reunion filled with laughter, shared memories, and the joy of reconnecting with dear friends.

Over the next few days, we decided to explore Paris by strolling along the picturesque Seine River. Despite being November, the winter days felt surprisingly pleasant, with the sun shining warmly upon us. The brilliant blue sky adorned with fluffy white clouds created a serene and inviting atmosphere. As we walked beside the river, the gentle breeze carried the essence of the city, and we marveled at the iconic landmarks that lined the Seine's banks toward the Notre Dame de Paris and the independent bookstore Shakespeare and Company.

Rina and I found a random chair by the riverbank and took a moment to relax and admire the surroundings. The soothing sound of the flowing water and the vibrant energy of the city provided the perfect backdrop for our heartfelt conversations. Meanwhile, Ray, with his digital sketchbook and pen in hand, was passionately capturing the essence of Paris in his artwork.

The highlight of our trip was visiting Bourse de Commerce, a magnificent building that beautifully merges history with the present. Designed by the renowned architect Tadao Ando, this iconic structure was once a historic stock exchange in Paris. It was later acquired by François Pinault, a prominent French businessman and art collector, who transformed it into an extraordinary art museum.

As we stepped inside, we were immediately impressed by the seamless blend of the old and the new. The original architectural features, such as the grand dome and the stunning frescoes, have been meticulously preserved, while modern elements have been integrated to create an awe-inspiring space for contemporary art.

The art collection housed within the Bourse de Commerce is nothing short of spectacular. François Pinault's private collection includes an impressive array of masterpieces by renowned artists from various periods and artistic movements. From contemporary artworks to classical pieces, every corner of the museum seems to hold a treasure waiting to be discovered.

The history of the building and the incredible art collection within its walls served as a powerful reminder of the richness of French culture and its enduring commitment to the arts. Walking through the galleries, we couldn't help but feel a profound sense of appreciation for the preservation of history and the celebration of creativity.

Our visit to Bourse de Commerce was a true feast for the senses, where the past gracefully merged with the present to create an unforgettable experience. It was a testament to the power of art to transcend time and connect us to the essence of human expression and emotion.

As I wandered through the Bourse de Commerce, it was a true feast for the senses, where the past gracefully merged with the present, the seamless blend of the old and the new resonated deeply with the last few years in Spain and the reunion with Ray and Rina in Paris. Our meeting symbolized the merging of cherished memories and new experiences, creating a truly unforgettable journey in the heart of Paris.

Marseille & Avignon, France

As fate would have it, I was also headed to Avignon to meet Madoka and Maggie for a wedding immediately after my Paris trip, a celebration of love for a friend we had met during our time in Brazil over a decade ago. These individuals held a unique place in my past life. The Universe seemed to be orchestrating these encounters, weaving a tapestry of reconnections and reminding me of the intricate web of relationships that spanned across time. As I caught up with Madoka and Maggie, it felt like flipping through the pages of a history book. We first met in a Portuguese language school in Sao Paulo in 2009 when I had just moved to Brazil. We were all foreigners, navigating a new country and culture together, which quickly forged a deep bond between us. Madoka was a Japanese friend now residing in Berlin, as I had mentioned earlier, and Maggie was an American living in Washington, DC. We had all left Brazil before the 2014 FIFA World Cup excitement engulfed the nation.

Having known Madoka for over a decade, our bond has grown to resemble that of sisters who share a similar background. We have always felt detached from our conservative Asian culture, preferring the freedom and thrill of living around the world. When we are together, the conversations flow effortlessly, and we can talk for days on end. However, when we are apart, we rarely engage in constant communication, fully absorbed in our respective lives. It's as if we have a secret code, an unspoken understanding that despite the distance, we always think of each other and make it a point to connect at least once to twice a year.

Together, we have embarked on countless journeys, starting from Sao Paulo to Rio de Janeiro, then to Salvador, and even a few trips to Taiwan. Most recently, I had the opportunity to visit Berlin, and now, thanks to Madoka's invitation as her "plus one" for the wedding, the charming city of Avignon. Whenever we are with each other, our topics of discussion span a wide range, from art and architecture to life, travel, and the unique experiences of living as expats in Barcelona and Berlin. Every story that emanates from Madoka's mouth leaves me spellbound, much like reading a riveting tale from the pages of Harry Potter.

Throughout our fifteen years of traveling together, we have shared a common approach: modest budgets and a passion for walking. Prior to our arrival in Avignon, we had already trekked thirty thousand steps in a single day while exploring Marseille. Our preference has always been to truly immerse ourselves in the local life of each city, bypassing the well-known tourist spots in favor of the lesser-known neighborhoods.

We would burst out laughing about the *Titanic* joke, commuting on the bus:

"The *Titanic* is about to sink, the captain shouted to let people of different nationalities jump in," Madoka said.

American → If you jump into the sea, you are a hero!

English → If you jump into the sea, you are a gentleman!

French → Don't jump into the sea!

Italian → A beautiful woman is swimming in the sea!

German → It's a rule to jump in!

Japanese → Everyone is jumping in!

South Korean → The Japanese have already jumped in!

"What would the Taiwanese person say?" Madoka asked.

"There's money in the sea." We come from a culture where most people live to work, and income is an important variable for happiness.

Rather than visiting the Basilique Notre Dame de la Garde or admiring the Cathédrale de la Major, we decided to explore Le Corbusier, also known as Unité d'Habitation or Radiant City. This iconic architectural masterpiece, designed by the renowned architect Le Corbusier, fascinated us. As we ascended to the rooftop, the panoramic view of Marseille served as a backdrop for our discussion on the architectural history and significance of Le Corbusier's work. From the rooftop, we gazed upon the cityscape, engaging in conversations that seamlessly transitioned to exploring Le Corbusier's other notable creations. By the time we reached the ground floor, our dialogue had extended to Tadao Ando's impressive reputation as an architect in Japan and Taiwan. We marveled at the play of concrete, lights, and structures, appreciating the intricate details that brought this building to life.

We would forgo extravagant breakfast meals and instead set out on a quest to find the most exquisite croissants in the local bakery. After Madoka's diligent research, we decided to give Pain Pan Boulangerie a try. To my delight, their croissants proved to be unrivaled, surpassing any I had ever tasted before, not just in Marseille, but anywhere else. The best part was that they were priced at a mere one euro each, a true culinary delight that didn't break the bank.

Armed with our takeout coffees and croissants, we found a cozy spot in a nearby park to savor the serene simplicity of the morning. With the first bite, the delicate layers and golden crust of the croissant made a delightful sound, giving way to the luscious sensation of butter melting in my mouth. It was a genuine culinary pleasure, and I relished every mouthful as the warmth of the November sun enveloped us.

I playfully shared a humorous anecdote with Madoka, saying, "You know, in Spain, they use pork fat instead of butter in croissants just to spite the French. It's their way of showing their rivalry!" We both chuckled at the playful banter.

Madoka expressed her admiration, sighing wistfully, "Ohhh, I wish we had bakeries like this in Berlin. It's so rare to find such high-quality pastries at such reasonable prices."

I couldn't help but respond with a playful smile, saying, "Well, you have the best potato recipes, and let's not forget about the German sausages! They're my absolute favorite!" We burst out laughing, playfully teasing each other.

On the other end, I hadn't spoken to Maggie since she left Sao Paulo in 2012, and our connection had mostly remained limited to being social media friends. However, despite the time that had passed, I could still sense the familiarity in her presence. Maggie exuded kindness and positivity, always being the nurturing figure who cared for everyone around her.

As Madoka and I arrived at the Airbnb from Avignon train station, where Maggie and her twelve-year-old daughter Lora had already checked in, I couldn't contain the rush of emotions that overcame me when I embraced her. My eyes grew watery, and I tried my best to hold back tears, not wanting them to see the depth of my emotions. It was a powerful moment, reuniting with someone who had played a significant role in my past.

"Lora, the last time I laid eyes on you, you were still in your mother's tummy," I reminisced, overcome with a profound sense of how swiftly time had passed. "Now, here you stand before me as a beautiful teenager."

As we settled into the apartment, Lora swiftly retreated to the room she had chosen, leaving Maggie, Madoka, and me to gather comfortably in the kitchen dining area with our cups of tea.

Without delving into the intricacies of my divorce, I briefly mentioned to Maggie that our relationship had reached a point where it no longer worked, and we had both changed during our time in Brazil. It was a difficult decision, but we were now in the process of getting a divorce after years of struggling. I didn't want to burden everyone with more negative information about my marriage and self-identity crisis during our special reunion in the romantic city of Avignon, focusing instead on the positive moments.

However, Maggie, in her turn, began sharing her journey over the past ten years, particularly the last two, during which she bravely fought against breast cancer, enduring chemotherapy and surgery. Despite the pain and challenges she'd faced, she stood before Madoka and me with kindness and the warmest smile, saying, "Look! Everything is fine."

A profound realization washed over me as I listened to Maggie's story. In the grand scheme of things, the difficulties I faced in my marriage and divorce seemed insignificant compared to the immense challenges Maggie had endured. Not that my path was an easy one, but she had to navigate a challenge that threatened her life while also shouldering the responsibilities of motherhood and working full-time. It felt as though the Universe had wanted me to witness firsthand Maggie's strength and resilience.

Her story served as a poignant reminder that each person carries their burdens and confronts their trials. It is not the weight of these challenges that defines us, but rather our approach toward them. Maggie's positivity and determination to overcome adversity left an indelible mark on me. It inspired me to reframe my perspective and approach my struggles with renewed courage and resilience.

Before the wedding welcome reception in the evening, we decided to spend a day sightseeing. In late November, Avignon greeted us with its chilling winds and cold temperatures, setting the stage for our exploration of the enchanting old town. Bundled up in our coats and scarves, we ventured through the narrow cobblestone streets adorned with charming medieval buildings and ancient walls. Some Christmas decorations were already up, and the atmosphere was filled with a sense of history as if the whispers of the past were carried on the wind.

Our first stop was Pont de Avignon, a magnificent bridge that gracefully spanned the Rhone River. We stood on its ancient stones, transfixed by the breathtaking scenery before us. The wind was blowing so strongly that my hair was just flying all over the place. With Maggie's nurturing demeanor, she had already queued and obtained all the tickets while Madoka and I were still meandering about, walking upon the heap of autumn leaves strewn across the ground to touch the ancient stone beneath our feet.

As we walked along the bridge, we marveled at the intricate details and the stories etched into its weathered stones. Each step seemed to whisper tales of travelers who had crossed this path centuries ago. We imagined the bustling trade that once took place on this very spot, with merchants and artisans from distant lands converging to exchange goods and ideas.

"Maybe it's better to find a cozy cafe?" Maggie suggested. We all agreed that the relentless wind made it difficult to fully enjoy exploring the city. Seeking refuge from the elements, we settled into a warm, inviting cafe, ready to indulge in a much-needed break.

As we sipped our steaming cups of coffee, Maggie empathetically remarked, "Hsin, it must be incredibly tough for you to be a single mother." Her words carried a deep understanding, born from her unique journey.

With genuine candor, I acknowledged that my own experiences as a single mother were just a fraction of the challenges Maggie had faced. I recognized that it was not an easy path to navigate, with a multitude of responsibilities to balance. However, I shared with Maggie how becoming a single mother had allowed me to truly embrace and enjoy the journey of motherhood itself. It has allowed me to prioritize self-care, understand myself better, and gain the confidence to flourish in my role as a mother.

"Can you imagine that we thought life was so difficult when we got stuck in the rainforest fifteen years ago in Brazil?" I reminisced, bringing back our shared adventure memories on Ilha Grande (Big Island) in Sao Paulo. "Remember that knee-deep mud, the swarms of mosquitoes buzzing around us, constantly keeping an eye out for snakes and other wild animals lurking nearby, and watching the sky grow darker? We truly believed it was the end of the world." As we chuckled and reflected on our past experiences, we realized how our perspective on challenges and difficulties had evolved over time. What seemed insurmountable then now became cherished memories of resilience and camaraderie.

"I love living in Spain (or at least the town I've chosen) because of the open-mindedness of most people here. I've never felt judged, and in fact, even strangers seem to understand and accept me when I'm alone. In my kids' class, there are parents from diverse backgrounds—some are single parents and others are same-sex couples, and there's even a special case of a mother-by-choice whose child grew up without a father from the beginning. The school ensures that the kids' mental well-being is handled by normalizing these situations and creating a supportive environment for their growth. I feel incredibly grateful for the direct and indirect support from everyone around me." Expressing my gratitude, I emphasized the importance of prioritizing the happiness and well-being of both parents rather than trying to preserve an unhappy union for the sake of the children. I firmly believe that two content and fulfilled individuals, even if separate, could provide a more nurturing and positive environment for their children than a stagnant and unhappy relationship ever could.

As our heartfelt conversation continued in that cozy cafe, it became clear that we were not alone in our struggles. Each of us carried our burdens and faced unique challenges, but it was our attitude and resilience, as well as the support we offered one another, that allowed us to find strength and march ahead. In the warmth and comfort of that moment, we knew we could overcome the hurdles that life presented.

Leaving Avignon two nights later, an immense wave of gratitude enveloped me as I contemplated the abundance of blessings that life had graciously bestowed upon me. I expressed my appreciation to the Universe for bringing my old friends to the present, where we shared stories and supported each other as strong women.

Catalan Christmas Traditions

Arriving back in Barcelona, Spain, I noticed the Christmas lights were already up, preparing for the festive season. It was my fourth Christmas since moving here, and it had taken us about four years to truly settle down after an international relocation. During our first Christmas, we were still caught up in the overwhelming relocation process, so our celebrations were modest, mainly focused on setting up a Christmas tree and preparing a few simple presents. The following Christmas, in the middle of COVID, most shops were closed and all events were canceled.

In the third year, the kids and I caught COVID for three consecutive weeks and missed out on the entire festive scene due to quarantine. Additionally, the kids' grandparents from Brazil were visiting Barcelona for the first time since our move, and I wanted them to spend as much time as possible with them.

Now, in our fourth year of celebrating Christmas in Barcelona, I have gained a deeper sense of familiarity and understanding of the Spanish way of celebrating. The Christmas spirit in

Catalonia is truly remarkable, filled with vibrancy and enriched by unique traditions. The atmosphere becomes infused with Christmas-is-in-the-air vibes as the city lights up during the first week of December. It's a special time for us as we cherish the final gatherings with our friends before they head back to their respective homes for Christmas. Many others I know will be leaving the city between December 18 and 23.

The Christmas celebration in Catalonia spans from December 24 to 26, and one fascinating tradition involves the beloved character known as El Tió de Nadal or El Caga Tió, a wooden log with a smiling face and a traditional Catalan red hat. Children "feed" the wooden log with treats and gifts throughout December, and on Christmas Eve or Christmas Day, they gather around to sing songs and hit the wooden log with sticks, prompting it to "defecate" the hidden surprises. This joyful tradition brings excitement to families, particularly the little ones who eagerly anticipate the log's "releases."

Another intriguing character in Catalonia's Christmas traditions is the Caganer, a peasant with a traditional Catalan red hat like the Caga Tió, depicted in the act of defecating. Often found hidden in the nativity scene, the Caganer symbolizes good luck, fertility, and prosperity for the upcoming year. This humorous and irreverent addition adds a unique touch to the traditional nativity display.

Victoria and I always joked about how there seems to be a fascination with poop in Catalan culture, which prompted me to do some research on the matter. It turns out that poop was indeed considered a symbol of "fertilization" in ancient Catalan beliefs, and it was believed to bring luck, happiness, and abundance to the household.

On Christmas Eve Day itself, Catalans gather with their loved ones to enjoy a festive meal. The typical Catalan Christmas dish is *escudella i carn d'olla*, a meat and vegetable stew. Christmas is often symbolic as the time for families to come together, share stories, and create cherished memories. In addition to the main meal, various sweet treats are enjoyed during the Christmas season, such as *turrón* (a nougat-like dessert, with *Xixona* being a personal favorite), and *neules* (thin, crispy wafers). These delicacies add a touch of sweetness to the holiday celebrations that will last until December 26.

On New Year's Eve, one of the unique traditions in Catalonia, as well as in many parts of Spain, is the custom of eating twelve grapes as the clock strikes midnight. This tradition, known as *las doce uvas de la suerte* or "the twelve lucky grapes," is believed to bring good luck and prosperity for the upcoming year.

The ritual involves eating one grape with each strike of the clock at midnight, representing the twelve chimes that mark the arrival of the new year. It is important to eat each grape in sync with the chimes, ensuring that all twelve grapes are consumed before the last stroke of midnight. This tradition is taken quite seriously, and many people gather around the TV or the town square to watch the clock and eat the grapes together.

The origins of this tradition can be traced back to the early twentieth century in Spain. It is said that grape growers in the region of Alicante had a surplus of grapes one year and came up with the idea of promoting them as a symbol of good luck. The custom quickly gained popularity and spread throughout the country, including Catalonia.

I have also developed the habit of buying grapes before New Year's Eve. However, as I began to prioritize a good night's sleep, staying awake until midnight became a bit challenging. I often find my eyelids drooping by 11:30 p.m., and I struggle to keep myself awake. Those twelve grapes that were neatly arranged for the occasion would end up being enjoyed as part of breakfast the next morning. "Well, I'll try harder next year. I'm sure the Universe will understand and still give me good luck in the coming year!"

Almost a week after the New Year countdown, on January 6, Catalonia celebrates the Dia dels Tres Reis (Three Kings' Day) or Epiphany. This day is highly anticipated, especially by children, as it is when the Three Wise Men arrive to deliver gifts. Families often attend parades known as the *La Cavalcada de Reis*, where the Three Kings throw sweets and small presents to the crowds. On this day, a special cake called *Rosca de Reyes* is enjoyed. It is a round cake with a hole in the center, often filled with whipped cream or other sweet fillings. Inside the cake, a small figurine and a dry bean are hidden. The one who finds the figurine is considered lucky, while the person who finds the bean is expected to pay for the cake the following year.

That's how the Catalans celebrate their Christmas holiday in true Catalan style!

Our Kind of Christmas

Christmas in my home was more about embracing the cultural celebration rather than focusing on the religious aspects. As a Taiwanese individual, where Christmas isn't typically celebrated as a family day, and having spent the majority of my life in foreign countries, my previous Christmases were often spent alone. However, apart from my time in Brazil with my former in-laws, without feeling any pain associated with a broken marriage or the intrusion of COVID, I was genuinely in a holiday mood, free from depression and loneliness, and fully in the vibes of spending this wonderful time with my kids.

The Christmas season has always held a special place in my heart. It radiates joy and love, and there's an undeniable energy in the air as people eagerly anticipate gathering with their loved ones. It has been my dream to establish Christmas as a cherished family tradition, creating a dedicated day and space where, no matter where life takes us, my kids and I will always prioritize and make time to be together during the holiday season.

The weather forecast for Christmas in Catalonia made headlines with the prediction of "abnormally warm" weather and rain. The year 2022 proved to be an interesting year for weather in the region, as heatwaves arrived as early as May, and the country experienced one of its hottest years on record, coupled with drought conditions. By December, the weather felt unusually pleasant, almost like fall, which was not typical for winter. These signs of global warming were hard to ignore, serving as a reminder of the ongoing climate changes affecting our planet.

Setting up the Christmas tree was different this year, and my daughters joined in to help me. As the kids grew older, I felt less like a one-woman show, and the whole family, meaning the three of us, began to embrace the Christmas spirit. I made an Advent calendar filled with hairpins, small chocolates, candies, and a bunch of other goodies to impress my kids, allowing us to countdown together each day.

The kids and I would visit the Christmas market in front of the eighteenth-century Monastery of Sant Cugat. In this charming Catalan town, we could experience the most traditional holiday scene right before our eyes. Families would gather in the Plaza de Octavià, enjoying each other's company while the kids kicked a ball and the bells of the monastery rang in the background. We indulged in roasted chestnuts (*castanyes*), and a cup of hot chocolate, and the town's small Christmas train delighted families with free rides. The Christmas decorations were elegantly simple, adorning the trees.

We passed by several wooden kiosks that displayed Catalan nativity scenes, poinsettia, and Caga Tió figures in all sizes. We didn't personally incorporate the Caga Tió into our celebrations due to its more *active* nature and my non-Catalan background. However, I believe it's important for our children to be aware of their Catalan heritage, as a quarter of their bloodline is Catalan from Caetano, and so any family member from his side of the family wished to involve them in Caga Tió activities, it would be more appropriate to do so, as the Catalan roots are stronger.

In our family tradition, we write letters to Santa, bake cookies for him, and eagerly await his arrival. Instead of receiving gifts from the Three Kings, Santa Claus delivers our Christmas presents. Although some Spanish children receive gifts from both, the Three Kings are cooler than Santa. On one of the Christmas nights, my older daughter even requested that we place a recorder near the Christmas tree to capture the sounds of Santa and his reindeer enjoying the cookies and delivering the presents. It's fascinating how kids never fail to remind me that I come from a different generation, as they were born into the era of tablets and technology. Times have certainly changed, but the magic of Christmas remains timeless.

To make Christmas even more special, we received an invitation from the Ukrainian-American parents of my older daughter's best friend, who had moved here last year just before the war started. Initially, I thought it was just going to be a playdate, so we embarrassingly arrived with nothing! I was pleasantly surprised to see their house beautifully decorated with Christmas ornaments, lights, a Christmas tree, and even presents for the kids. The fireplace was lit, candles were spread throughout the house, and a Christmas wreath hung on the door.

It had been two and a half years since I sent out that WhatsApp text to the parenting group asking for playdates and friends. Besides my own colorful social life, my kids' social lives were also expanding. They were forming their best friendships and enjoying playdates. Actually, my children had more social events than I did. Thanks to their best friends, we were able to experience "international playdates" with families from Sweden, Russia, Brazil, Israel, Venezuela-American, and Ukrainian-American.

The kids were incredibly well-behaved, immediately gathering and entertaining themselves upon arriving at the playdate location, relieving us parents from giving them constant attention.

I must confess that I occasionally attended these playdates with my main interest being the food and drinks. Whenever we attended playdates with Brazilian families, we were treated to a feast of Brazilian BBQ and traditional dishes such as *farofa* and Brazilian vinaigrette. Even the pizzas had homemade toppings with a Brazilian twist. Russian family gatherings offered an abundance of sausages and chicken wings. If you are wondering, vodka was not on the menu. The Ukrainian-American family always generously served us delicious American-style roast beef. These playdates were like my mini international fair, filled with interesting stories shared by all these parents.

I categorized this group of parents as "the parents of my kids' best friends," which meant that certain topics were frequently discussed, while others, such as my preference for casual relationships, didn't quite fit socially. Our conversations often revolved around the reasons behind our moves, the relocation process, settling into the new environment, plans for weekends and holidays, travel destinations in Southern France, work, and visa-related matters. We all moved to this town and enrolled our children in the same school for various reasons, including job opportunities, co-parenting arrangements, escaping from war, or simply being fed up with the corrupt government in the home country.

Whatever reason brought us together, at the Christmas table, we joined hands and expressed our gratitude. "We are grateful for this delicious meal before us, grateful for the wonderful people gathered here to share this meal, and grateful to be in the city of Barcelona for a better life. Merry Christmas, everyone," Jake, the American father, said. There was a shared spirit of, "We are all here, striving to build the life we want."

The Three Kings Parade

I was standing at Plaça Octavia in Sant Cugat waiting for the arrival of Three Kings with my kids and the Israeli family, Ofek, his wife Zohar, and their two adorable kids, who also happen to be my younger daughter's classmates. This family recently relocated to our town in August, bringing the excitement and freshness of a new beginning, moving to a new city with a sense of adventure and discovery as newcomers.

Ofek is the kind of father who openly shares his dreams of establishing a new life here. He is dedicated to working hard, and I mean truly admirably hard, to provide a comfortable life for his family. Not only is he a devoted family man, but he is also very present in his children's lives. In his pursuit of starting afresh, he makes genuine efforts to reach out to various available resources and channels. Whether learning the local language or finding ways to communicate effectively, he puts in his best effort to connect with others in the community and make this new place feel like home.

Zohar is a young mom, and by young, I mean anyone born after 1990 just sounds really young to me. But age is just a number, and she has shown remarkable grace in handling the entire moving process. When emergencies arose, she was surprisingly calm and composed, always knowing how to handle the situation. She pushes herself to go the extra mile. I remember her telling me once that she was determined to practice her Spanish so that she could fully "settle down," refusing to rely on her neighbor's assistance to communicate with the gas company and resolve a gas leak issue. Her determination struck a chord with me, prompting some self-reflection. It made me realize that I also needed to pull my Spanish together! Oh, by the way, she is also fantastic at pole dancing. It never fails to amaze me, as I can hardly even climb a pole, but I've witnessed her effortlessly performing daring moves upside down on the pole.

I must mention Chasy, too, the family dog, whose name I mistook as Tracy for many months until I got it figured out!

Thanks to Ofek's proactive efforts, our families started to build a strong connection, becoming a support system for each other. Ofek and Zohar openly shared with me their experiences and reasons for choosing to be in Barcelona. They warmly invited us to their family pancake breakfasts on weekends and organized fun playdates. Together, we've shared many memorable experiences, such as a delightful day trip to the science museum and celebrating the Chinese New Year festival. The level of trust between us grew so much that even after knowing each other for just a few months, I felt comfortable giving them a spare key to my home. That gesture speaks volumes about the bond we've formed and the genuine friendship we cherish.

As a single mother trying to organize a birthday party for my daughter all by myself, they went above and beyond to help me with every single detail, making my daughter's dream come true! I was appreciative and could not find the right words to express my thanks. Having this wonderful family in my life feels like the Universe's way of sending support and love, and they have become like siblings to me, offering care and assistance that goes beyond the usual school-parent relationship. Their presence has enriched my life in so many ways, and I'm filled with gratitude for having them by my side.

The atmosphere was filled with excitement and anticipation during the Three Kings Day celebration at Plaça Octavia. The square was bustling with a lively crowd, and it felt like every single member of this small town was gathered at this very spot, eager to witness the arrival of the Three Kings. As the Kings made their grand entrance, there was a collective applause from the spectators, cheering and applauding their arrival. The air was filled with a sense of wonder and joy.

To add to the festive ambiance, fireworks lit up the sky above the Monastery of Sant Cugat. The spectacle of the fireworks added a touch of magic to the event for both children and adults alike. Following the arrival of the Three Kings and the fireworks display, the Three Kings parade commenced, where all of us started to gather at the sideroad of the designated route, patiently waiting for the Three Kings to pass by, accompanied by music, dazzling costumes, and tons of candy!

As the cars carrying the Three Kings approached, you could feel the heightened anticipation in the air, particularly among the children, as if they were preparing to compete in a one–hundred–meter race at the Olympics. As the Kings' cars passed by, the enthusiastic shouts of, "*Aqui, aqui*!" (meaning, "Here, here!") could be heard from every corner as children eagerly tried to catch the attention of the Kings and receive more candies. Once a handful of candies was thrown down, there was a flurry of excitement as all the kids scrambled to the ground, eagerly picking up as many candies as they could.

"Chicas, be careful, please!" I shouted anxiously as I watched my child enthusiastically dive onto the ground, determined to collect as many candies as possible. Being my first year fully participating in this parade, and to ensure their safety, I held onto both kids' jackets like a protective leash, ready to pull them back in case of any unexpected emergency. It was a comical sight within a festive madness.

Boston, Massachusetts, USA

One week after Three Kings Day, the kids were back to school. I was gearing up for a trip to Boston to attend the wedding of one of my closest friends from college, Brennan. Our friendship has spanned over fifteen years, witnessing both the highs and lows, including the rise and fall of my relationship with my ex-husband. He is this big tall guy with the sweetest heart that has always been there for me. During those crazy COVID days, he was there reading my dramatic texts every day without leaving me alone.

I vividly remember sitting in the lobby bar of the W Hotel with Brennan and his now-wife Nellie in 2009, pouring my heart out about how deeply in love I was with Caetano, even though the distance posed a challenge. We were determined to overcome it because our love was "unbreakable." We still laugh about that conversation to this day. Over these fifteen years, I've experienced the roller coaster of dating, marriage, pregnancy, motherhood, and ultimately divorce. Meanwhile, Brennan and Nellie casually decided to "get serious" and finally organize a wedding six years after he proposed.

Boston has always held a special place in my life. I spent a remarkable seven years in Beantown, from my college days to my first job and completing my master's degrees. The city witnessed my wild and crazy antics, from making lifelong friends to engaging in some memorable escapades. I worked relentlessly and partied with equal fervor. Boston has given me invaluable lessons and experiences that make me forever indebted to this city. It's also where I first crossed paths with Caetano, whether it was a mere coincidence or a plan by the Universe. Just two days before heading to Boston, I received an email from my lawyer informing me that he had finally signed the agreement, signaling the last step before submitting the documents to the court. The overwhelming feeling of relief and closure washed over me, allowing me to start my trip with a sense of liberation.

Brennan had steadfastly supported me throughout my journey, being there for me virtually every day as I navigated the process of ending my marriage. He patiently listened and read through all my negative and angry messages, offering a comforting presence without becoming directly involved. As I was on my way to attend Brennan's wedding, it felt as if the stars had aligned perfectly, the combination of timing, location, and circumstances. It was as if the Universe had orchestrated this moment, allowing me to take a physical journey back to where everything began, express my deep gratitude to Brennan and the city of Boston, and reconnect with key friends who may have drifted away during my identity and marriage crisis over the years.

Boston marked my first significant journey since relocating to Barcelona, significantly defined by the distance away from my children. One of the amazing aspects of living in Europe as an expatriate is the proximity of countries, as if they are all just a two-hour flight away. It's fascinating how a statement like, "I'm heading to Germany," would have sounded like a daunting fourteen-hour international voyage with exorbitant prices for most of my life, but now it's a mere two-hour journey costing less than one hundred euros. The accessibility and affordability of travel within Europe are remarkable.

As a frequent traveler and lover of exploring new places, I have never quite managed to overcome my fear of flying. So you can imagine the rush of panic that surged through me when the pilot calmly announced that one of the engines had failed. Although the pilot reassured us not to worry, explaining that we would be making an immediate U-turn back to Heathrow Airport and assuring us that the other engines were functioning fine, it was difficult to simply sit tight and relax.

"How could one find comfort and enjoy the rest of the journey knowing that an engine had failed?" I thought to myself, panic gripping my insides. Despite the rising fear, I mustered all my strength to maintain a facade of calmness, pretending to read the book *Life's Golden Ticket* by Brendon Burchard as if nothing out of the ordinary was happening.

There were no explosions or fires, and I really thought that it would have been much easier to handle if the pilot had simply announced that we had forgotten to load the meals onto the airplane and needed to make a U-turn to retrieve them for our in-flight dining.

After what felt like an agonizing twenty hours, the flight finally landed safely twenty minutes later. Without wasting a moment, I grabbed my phone and sent a text to Caetano: "Please tell the kids that I love them and will always love them no matter what happens," overwhelmed with emotions as I sent the text.

"You will be fine. Actually, you ARE fine!" he replied.

The passengers were asked to remain on the airplane for an additional three hours while the technical engineers investigated the issues. As time passed, frustration grew, and it felt like an eternity. Finally, after four long hours, the decision was made to change airplanes. A collective sigh of relief swept through the cabin. Thank goodness for the resolution.

During those three hours, numerous thoughts raced through my mind, with one prevailing question: "If I had perished that night, would I have any regrets or unfinished business?" It was a moment of introspection, contemplating the significance of my life and the things left undone.

In response to that question, I reflected on my fortunate upbringing and the multitude of experiences I've had. I realized that many people in the world would eagerly exchange their lives with mine, despite the pain I've endured over the past eight years. Those challenges were necessary for my personal growth and ultimately led me to have two beautiful daughters, who now reside with me in the breathtaking city of Barcelona. I reassured myself that I would have been content if I had died that day because I was immensely thankful for everything I had experienced, especially the last two years of living an authentic life after my separation.

However, my only lingering concern was for my parents and children. Yet I also recognized that they would be in good hands, as abundant resources are available to ensure their well-being in the future. My parents would have a support system to care for them in their old age, and my children would continue to receive love from the many people around the world who care for them deeply.

The process of entering the USA border tends to be notably more tense and rigorous compared to my experiences with other countries. For example, it stands in stark contrast to entering Japan, where visitors are greeted with polite smiles and a warm welcome. The moment you approach the immigration checkpoint, a sense of seriousness fills the air, and anticipation builds as you wait for your turn to speak with the immigration police officer. They sit behind their desks, maintaining a stern expression that conveys the importance of their role in safeguarding the country's borders.

As you step forward, the officer's gaze scrutinizes your documents—passport, visa, and any supporting paperwork—with a keen eye for detail. Every question asked is precise and deliberate, as if they are searching for any inconsistency or discrepancy in your answers. The officer's tone is professional and commanding, leaving no room for ambiguity or misunderstanding.

I often found the way they questioned pretty intimidating, as if they were already making the visitor feel "guilty" without any accusation of a crime. The tension only escalates as you provide your responses, navigating the fine line between staying calm and composed while effectively communicating the purpose of your travel and your intentions. The immigration officer's stern demeanor can be quite imposing, as if they continuously evaluate your credibility and assess potential security risks.

My anxiety about crossing immigration was likely established during my teenage years when I traveled from Vancouver back to my high school in Hawaii after a winter vacation. Due to some visa issues that I still couldn't fully understand, I was confined to a "private waiting room" for hours (and, yes, I missed my flight). I remember being surrounded by a few handcuffed men who were also waiting for some kind of resolution. The experience left a lasting impact on me, and since then, crossing immigration has always been a nerve-wracking process for me.

"Where did you fly in from?" the officer asked.

"Barcelona," I replied firmly.

"Listen again, where did you fly in from?" the officer emphasized the question and asked again.

"Oh, London Heathrow Airport," I corrected my answer.

"What are you doing in Spain?" the office continued questioning.

"Co-parenting my kids with my ex-husband," I answered.

"What do you do in Spain?" the officer repeated the question as if my answer wasn't perfect.

"Freelance writer," I corrected again.

"Why are you in the States?" the officer continued questioning.

"For a friend's wedding."

"For how many days?"

"One week."

"Have a good day." The officer handed me my passport with a light smile after stamping it. I quickly felt a sense of relief, as if I had passed an obstacle in a labyrinth of bureaucracy.

Finally leaving Logan Airport close to midnight, it was three degrees Celsius outside. I was supposed to have arrived a few hours earlier to enjoy a dinner with Brennan amidst his hectic wedding preparations, finalizing details, and welcoming friends and family from all corners of the globe. Unfortunately, we had to cancel our plans.

It was nearly ten years since my last visit to Boston. My first time in the city was during the summer of 2002 when I went for a college visit, and it was during that summer that I met Caetano. The following year, in September, I moved to Boston as a full-time undergraduate student at Northeastern University, and it became my home until 2009. There are countless memories buried deep within my mind that I haven't had the chance to revisit. During my trip to Boston, I didn't feel the urge to organize grand reunion parties with all the Bostonian friends I knew. Instead, apart from attending the wedding, my focus was on creating meaningful, intimate moments with only a few key friends—Sarah and Katherine.

Sarah is an intelligent and authentic woman who attended a prestigious college and launched her career in a Fortune 500 company at a young age. She is an uplifting, positive person, never gossiping, never judging, and never complaining; she always puts on a smile to support the people around her by saying: "Everything is going to be okay. I'm so happy for you." She has this magical power to make you feel relaxed and comfortable. Whenever I reach out to her, she gives me her undivided attention. Now, she has found the love of her life and is blessed with two happy children, residing in Princeton. Sarah and I were once known as the dynamic duo, famous for our wild nights at Boston bars and clubs. Embarrassingly, we had countless drunken black-out nights together (but who doesn't have a past?).

I still vividly recall the moments when she would enthusiastically describe her husband, Nicholas, and open up about her feelings during our short breaks while working at JP Morgan Chase in downtown Boston. She was one of the very first college friends to settle down in a long-term relationship and seamlessly transitioned into the role of a dedicated wife and mom. They live a simple yet joy-filled life in the peaceful countryside of Princeton, which I visited once. She drove me to the organic farm and the small town, showing me her life. She just seemed to have all the puzzle pieces put together!

"I'm planning a trip to Boston to see you, and I'll leave the boys with Nicholas. It will be Nicholas's first time taking care of them alone, and it will also be my first time being away from the boys. But it's a good opportunity to start. I don't travel alone anymore!" Sarah's text read.

"Alright! Let's eat a Boston lobster roll and take a walk on Newbury Street!" I said, confirming our meet-up!

As I awoke the following day, jet-lagged and without a restful sleep, my heart filled with anticipation to walk around the city and explore every corner of my old-time memories. The search for a comforting cup of coffee beckoned me, as it had become an integral part of my daily routine. Eager to embark on a journey of reminiscence, I set off from the Back Bay area, allowing the chilly wind to guide my path toward the Prudential Center.

With each step, memories flooded my mind like whispers from the past. The towering high-rise buildings loomed before me, reminiscent of the skyline that had once been my backdrop. It had been years since I had laid eyes on these architectural marvels, and their grandeur evoked a sense of awe and familiarity. The rhythmic click-clack of my footsteps reverberated through the streets, harmonizing with the echoes of my memories.

Amidst the modern giants, there was this classic beauty of Boston with red brick buildings adorning the cityscape. Their timeless charm acted as portals, transporting me back to a different era. Each brick seemed to hold within it a story, a fragment of the city's rich history. It was as if I had opened a treasure trove of forgotten tales, letting them unfold before my eyes.

As I continued my solitary walk, the chilly wind whispered secrets in my ear. Finally, as I reached the Prudential Center, the city was slowly awakening from its slumber. The streets and malls were quiet, with many shops still closed, but amidst the tranquil surroundings, a familiar sight caught my attention in the central area of the shopping mall—a Blue Bottle Coffee shop.

Approaching the entrance, I found the space carefully crafted for the bustling morning crowd, preparing for a day of work. The Prudential Blue Bottle Coffee boasted a round bar with two espresso stations, four cold brew draft lines, and six drip coffee stations. The design of the shop seemed tailored to cater to the busy working individuals in the vicinity. Bright, natural light flooded the space, creating an inviting atmosphere. The interior embraced a Scandinavian modern aesthetic, featuring a communal table at its center and a scattering of benches and low stools around smaller tables.

My curiosity was piqued, and I couldn't resist the temptation to step into the queue and experience the offerings of this new addition. The aroma of freshly ground beans enveloped me as I watched the skilled baristas meticulously craft each cup of coffee with precision and care. The air was infused with anticipation, blending the familiar and the unknown. As the barista handed me my cafe latte, I took a moment to appreciate the artistry that had gone into its creation.

As I approached the counter to pay for my standard cup of coffee, a wave of surprise washed over me as I saw the price: over six US dollars. "Oh my God! When did Boston become so expensive?" I exclaimed inwardly. The sticker shock left me momentarily taken aback, prompting a mental comparison to the prices I had grown accustomed to in Spain.

Holding my cup of coffee, I found a spot strategically positioned at a long stretch of table by a large floor-to-ceiling window. I settled in, allowing myself to gaze outside and take in the view of the surrounding garden. Despite the bustling activity around me, there was a sense of tranquility and seclusion, as if I had found my private sanctuary within the busy café.

As I savored my cup of coffee, I thought, "Should I contact Katherine?" debating a lot.

"Hey, Katherine, I'm currently on a business-leisure trip for a few days. I apologize for not informing you earlier. I was wondering if you might have some free time to meet up?" I retrieved my phone and instinctively reached out to my long-lost best friend, sending her a text message without disclosing the main purpose of my trip.

Katherine and I go way back to our college days. We were introduced to each other through a mutual friend and instantly formed a strong bond. Throughout the years, we have become well-known as each other's best friends and travel companions. We took on countless adventures together, backpacking through Central America from Mexico to Panama. We experienced everything from thrilling "almost-drowning" cave explorations in Tulum, Mexico, to sharing beds with cockroaches in Antigua, Guatemala. In our twenties, we were fearless, climbing volcanoes in Ometepe, Nicaragua.

Katherine is a vibrant and energetic soul with a direct and opinionated nature. Her strong and dominant personality always leaves a lasting impression. She is an extraordinary woman who took on the responsibility of being the breadwinner for her family from a young age. Starting work as early as she could, while the rest of us were still figuring out our paths after college, Katherine was already excelling in her career and gaining valuable experience. Simultaneously, she pursued her college education, working diligently to complete her diploma as a full-time employee years later. I still marvel at how she managed to juggle it all.

She holds such a significant place in my life that she was the maid of honor at my wedding!

The decline of our relationship occurred during the arrival of my second child, coinciding with her wedding and bachelorette party. It was a period when I was battling depression, and my memories consisted of being confined to my room, cradling my newborn, and shedding tears every day. Unfortunately, I couldn't attend her wedding and failed to adequately explain the situation. As time passed, I gradually distanced myself from the relationship and everyone I knew.

During these past few years, apart from my crisis, Katherine also faced her own set of challenges. She yearned for a child, investing immense effort and resources into making it a reality. However, each attempt brought disappointment, one after another. As a result, she began to withdraw from the people she once knew, creating distance between herself and everyone around her.

We both have always been known for our assertive personalities, never hesitating to voice our desires and take action to fulfill them. It seemed as though we always knew what we wanted and had the determination to achieve it. We lived on our own terms, embracing our desires and making choices aligned with our innermost wishes. At least, we tried hard to maintain this image until life presented us with its own challenges and lessons to learn.

"We don't always get what we want, and we don't always know what we want!" Life was whispering to us both.

In addition to the joyful moments we have shared during our twenty-year friendship, there have also been moments of scarcity and pain. However, despite the things we did that bothered each other, we seemed to be in harmony most of the time, avoiding addressing any issues directly. Perhaps we were just too young to know how to navigate those feelings.

During the last few years of mindful living, I made an effort to declutter my relationships and let go of the past. I questioned whether it would be better to let my relationship with Katherine go or just let go of these hiccups within our relationship.

Without having a concrete answer, I felt an invisible force urging me to reach out to Katherine. It was as if something was compelling me to have an open and honest conversation, to address the issues we had faced in the past, and to share with her what had been going on in my life. I realized that it was essential for me to be there for her as well, to offer my support and understanding. This inner voice insisted that it was time to bridge the gap and reconnect with Katherine again, because deep down, I still cared about her and missed her very much. It was the pain and drama that I was suffering that kept me away from her.

"Oh my God, you're in Boston! Yes, of course I'm free. Let's meet tonight for dinner," Katherine texted me back almost instantly, exuding the familiar high vibrations that I had missed dearly. Instantly, any worries I had about her not wanting to meet washed away. She was still the same girl who would always extend her hand to welcome me anytime and anywhere, no matter what.

Katherine and her husband, Patrick, showed up at Eataly Prudential hours later. We navigated our way to the restaurant and ordered a glass of wine to accompany our dinner. There was no awkwardness or strangeness between us; we were simply overjoyed to see each other.

I didn't reveal the purpose of my visit being Brennan's wedding. I chose not to disclose it to Katherine, primarily because I carried guilt for not being able to attend her wedding. I didn't want her to feel I prioritized Brennan's wedding over hers. My intention was to protect her feelings and ensure our reunion was focused on reconnecting and strengthening our friendship.

We spent the next few hours delving into the events that had occurred over the years, and I openly expressed my guilt regarding my absence at their wedding. I shared the financial and emotional challenges I faced during that period, acknowledging that Katherine had put in tremendous effort to make me the happiest bride while I hadn't reciprocated in the same way. A wedding is a once-in-a-lifetime occasion with no retake, and that truth was difficult for me to accept and digest.

"Don't worry! Really. As much as I wanted you to be at our wedding, we understand you had just had a baby. Whether or not you were experiencing depression, you were supposed to be with your five-day-old baby!" Katherine and Patrick comforted me with their deepest understanding.

One dinner isn't enough to rekindle, so Katherine and I immediately arranged another private hangout without Patrick the following day, sitting in her car. It was a serene moment, with snow pouring outside, creating a peaceful ambiance. It felt like the perfect setting for what turned out to be the most open and honest conversation we had ever shared in our twenty-year friendship. During that conversation, Katherine bravely expressed her pain, which she had rarely done due to her strong personality. I, too, opened up about my struggles, which was uncharacteristic of me. Showing vulnerability had never been our strongest suit, but the challenges we faced over the years taught us that everyone carries burdens in life. It is our attitude and approach to handling those challenges that shape the outcomes we experience.

"Even though we don't speak to each other as often anymore, I want you to know that you will always have me, and I know you will always stand by me. I will plan my visit to Barcelona soon to be there with you. I'm sorry that you have to be all alone and so brave during these times," Katherine's words resonated deeply within me.

"I'm sorry I wasn't there for you during your most difficult time. And I'm grateful that we weren't heavily involved with each other the last three years. I was the kind of woman who constantly complained about life and believed that things wouldn't work out. I'm so glad my negativity didn't influence you," I responded with an open heart.

Of course, with social media being so prevalent nowadays, it's nearly impossible to keep things private. A few days after I returned to Barcelona from Boston, Katherine found out about the wedding, and I quickly explained the reason for not disclosing to her my main purpose of being in Boston. I felt guilty about not being able to contribute back to her wedding and didn't want her to feel that I prioritized my other good friend over her. Her response was, "Come on, no big deal! I know you care about me. Please don't get stressed over things like this. Move on and focus on your life." Her understanding reassured our strong relationship, and in that very moment, I realized that my struggle to accept myself for not being an attentive friend, and the pain caused by our past events were all irrelevant. It provided a sense of closure to that complex chapter. In my heart, I knew that if I were going into battle armed with weapons, Katherine would be the one – the only one – marching alongside me on the battlefield.

The Painful Relationship That Never Happened

Up until this point, I have mentioned Stefan, Cologne, and the diary that Caetano discovered. The story takes us back to a backpacking trip in Central America in 2010 with Katherine. It was during this trip that I met Stefan in Costa Rica. We were all in our late twenties and early thirties, full of energy and adventure. During that trip, Stefan and I grew closer. We spent much time together, doing activities as a pair, like ziplining and scuba diving. Little by little, every day, the distance between us diminished, and I developed romantic feelings for him. However, due to my commitment to Caetano and having moved to Brazil at that point, I suppressed these feelings, and we never crossed the line or acted upon them. I kept these feelings to myself without even mentioning them to anyone.

After weeks of journeying, on our last day in Antigua, Guatemala, we were at a hidden bar recommended by the locals, along with our backpacking friends, including Katherine. The bar was divided into two separate spaces by a wooden arch door that stood about 150 cm tall. While most people were gathered on the primary side of the bar, Stefan and I ended up sitting on the other side, just the two of us, engrossed in a playful game of hand slaps. It was during one of the turns, as it was my chance to strike his hand and anticipate his attempt to evade, that something unexpected happened. Instead of evading, he turned his hand around and caught mine. In that fleeting moment, time seemed to stand still. We locked eyes, understanding that this was our last night together, and if there was anything to be said, it had to be at that moment. However, before any words could be spoken, Katherine entered through the arch door, searching for me. Stefan and I instinctively pulled our hands apart without uttering another word.

Six months after the backpacking trip, as I was moving back to Taiwan from Brazil, I made a stop in Europe. Whether it was intentional to create an opportunity or purely coincidental, Stefan invited me to visit Cologne. Without hesitation, I told myself, "Yes!" I wanted to see him and have closure between us. It was a way for me to move forward, as I was on my path back to Taiwan with Caetano, ready to build a life together forever.

I tried to convince myself that my encounter with Stefan during that trip was nothing more than a fleeting moment, a beautiful romance that would never grow into anything real. After all, my life was in Brazil, committed to Caetano. In an attempt to move on, I poured my feelings onto the pages of my journal, expressing them explicitly, and then buried them deep within a drawer, just like how I buried my feelings that I planned not to revisit.

On that day in Cologne, Stefan took a day off from work and arrived at the train station to receive me. I still remember the warmth of that long hug, his gentle sway, and the piercing blue of his eyes. As we left the train station, the magnificent Cologne Cathedral appeared. He even suggested climbing up the tower, which under normal circumstances, I would have gladly done. However, with less than twenty-four hours to spend together, I knew time was precious, and I wanted to make the most of it with him, not waste time catching my breath!

He guided me to a plaza while we waited for Christof, another backpacking friend. With his help, Stefan and I took a photo together and shared it privately with Katherine. I am glad that the lack of 4G connectivity prevented me from seeing what was happening in the online world until the next day when I was finally connected. It turned out that Katherine had posted the photo sent to her on her Facebook page to share the happiness in this reunion, and Caetano had found out, which led to an endless stream of text messages.

Toward the end of the day in Cologne, Stefan and I shared moments and conversations on the serene space of his apartment balcony. We managed to connect without crossing any lines, just like we had done before. Standing side by side, sipping our tea, with all the opportunities to express ourselves, we didn't take them.

As I was leaving Cologne, I pondered whether the weight of letting Stefan go without saying a word was heavier, or if it was the impending return to reality with the task of dealing with Caetano's broken heart that I found out about that morning as I woke up. I had chosen to stand by Caetano's side, and I knew it would be the last time we would see each other. However, little did I know that this wound was deeply embedded in Caetano's heart, which had never healed in our relationship. No matter how much I tried to explain to him, he simply couldn't seem to move on from it.

Furthermore, almost a year after we had settled down in Taiwan, there came a day while I was working when I received a stream of text messages and images from Caetano. He discovered my journals and read everything I had explicitly written about my feelings for Stefan. Caetano typed out phrases verbatim from my journal and sent them to me as a reminder of what I had written.

In an effort to repair my marriage, I took drastic measures. I deleted all contacts from Stefan, apologized, changed jobs, moved cities, and publicly announced our wedding, emphasizing our commitment to each other. I did everything I could to help us move on. Unfortunately, even after ten years, as our marriage was coming to an end, I was still apologizing for my past behavior and the pain I had caused him. It became evident that he had never truly forgiven me. The truth is, I had barely spoken to Stefan since my time in Cologne, and yet his presence lingered in the shadows of our relationship.

Fast-forward to 2020 when COVID hit, I thought about Stefan working in the hospital. I dug through old emails to retrieve his contact and sent him a message, asking, "How are you? I remember your work in the hospital. I hope everything is fine with you."

Stefan replied, "Yes, everything is fine at work. Unfortunately, I caught COVID on a ski trip and also broke my arms."

"I'm sorry to hear that. I hope you feel better soon and stay healthy," I responded, closing our conversation and moving on with my life as it was.

"Happy Birthday!" Four months later, right before I went to bed on my birthday, I received a message from Stefan. It was a particularly delicate time, as it came only weeks after I had begun my journey to start a new life after the separation, and I was trying to move on with a fragile heart and a weakened mind.

It's hard to put into words how I felt when I saw the message. It wasn't a feeling of wanting to dive into his arms immediately. Instead, it was the realization that he was literally the only person I knew in Europe since COVID had closed down the borders. I was thrilled that someone remembered me and might be there to help me somehow, even if it was just by listening to me talk for ten minutes.

"Thank you! How are you?" I replied, feeling surprised with a glimmer of hope when the text came in.

"I'm fine, traveling to Austria now," Stefan quickly responded.

"We should find time to talk," I invited to set up a conversation.

"Yes, I will be in Austria this week. Let's talk next Thursday," he confirmed, sending me a photo of himself in Austria.

"Are you dating or married now?" I couldn't help but confirm his relationship status first.

"No girlfriend, no wife," he said.

"Talk to you next week," I confirmed, sending a few smiley emojis back.

On that Thursday, he disappeared, and I was ghosted. We never spoke again.

Of course, it was a heartbreaking experience. After everything I had been through, it felt like being ghosted by someone

I had placed such high hopes in for support, only to have them suddenly disappear, was the last thing I needed.

"I don't deserve this," I thought. "The least you could have done is to show me some respect. Sending me a text saying you couldn't make it or even saying you didn't feel like talking to me would have been far better than ghosting." My mind filled with frustration and disappointment.

In order to move on from it, I made a conscious effort to remove his emails and contacts, trying to declutter my relationship with him. I had convinced myself that in a world where self-worth matters, it was painful, but it had to be done.

It has been three years since that supposed-to-happen video call, and I believe I have moved on. At least Stefan no longer occupies my thoughts, neither through myself nor Caetano.

Interestingly, the Universe seems to send subtle signs to test me, as if it wants to ensure that I have truly buried those feelings or moved on from them. Sometimes, it's a Facebook reminder of a photo taken in Central America, and other times, he appears in my dreams out of nowhere. When the Universe is putting me to the test, his name pops up on and off, anywhere and everywhere. Even when I scroll through my phone, like checking out public feeds on Instagram, my first sight lands on Stephan, and just three seconds later, as I continue scrolling, I come across another Stefano. It's as if the Universe wants me to check in with myself, see if I have confronted and worked through those feelings, and finally find peace within me.

At the beginning of decluttering these toxic feelings, my mental talk often went like this:

Me: Oh, I wish we could have a chance to talk it out. Even if we can't be friends, at least I could get proper closure.

My mental talk: See! Now that's your problem. You are wishing too much, and in fact, you already got closure when he ghosted you. You gotta stop wearing your wishbone where your backbone should be.

Combining myself and my mental talk: Miss him, think about him, talk about him, and then drop it. You are just afraid to accept the stubborn decision you made before because it was too hard to swallow. Stop using Stefan to block that door of freedom. LET IT GO! Make space for the future. The Universe needs an empty doorway to send you someone even more impressive.

My mental talk continued: I must accept that time will never rewind for me to discover his feelings. I have to accept that I did not act on my feelings and, therefore, acknowledge that this invisible relationship will never have a chance to mature. On top of that, I have to accept that I will never find out why he chose to disappear.

Then, I made a conscious dialogue: "The closure lies within me! It is my call!"

Fifteen years ago, I chose to confine myself within the boundaries of a moral compass, suppressing my own voice deep within. This experience had a detrimental impact on my well-being and marriage. If I had been honest with myself and told him how I felt, even if we had still chosen to move on with our lives the way they were, it would have been better than saying nothing and doing nothing. In the process of acceptance, moving on from my story with Stefan has been one of the hardest things I have had to do. Every time the Universe puts me to the test, I find myself back in this swirling mental talk for a few days, feeling stuck!

Through mindfulness practice over the years, I slowly accepted the flawed decision I had made and the broken story that I had experienced through that decision. By coming to the present moment, I stopped letting the past and future control my life, gaining a deeper knowledge about myself and my feelings. I became fully aware that Stefan was merely a piece of my past, a lesson I had to learn, and he had always been this imaginary persona with whom I had never really spent time but had carried a burden for over ten years. Stefan is like a figure or a situation where it feels like heavy clouds from the past that just never healed.

Regardless of whether it was my marriage or Stefan, I needed to forgive who had hurt me and break free from the fear, suffering, and anger that chained me to the past, because those emotions were holding me back from living freely. They were holding me back from venturing into new territories. They were holding me back from being who I was meant to be. I needed to use my smarts and strength to let go.

As mindfulness practice teaches us, "If it's meant to be, it will be."

My Journey of Mindfulness

I began my mindfulness practice with yoga as a way to rebuild my life during the challenging period of my divorce. Initially, my primary intention was to find relief from the pain I was experiencing and to counter the negative self-talk that filled my mind. During those ninety minutes of practice, I made a conscious effort to stay present and focus on the physical postures rather than getting caught up in my emotional turmoil and the issues I was dealing with.

Through the combination of yoga and meditation, I gradually started to experience a deeper understanding and acceptance of myself. I realized that each day on the mat was different, and while I might excel in my yoga practice one day, the next day might not be as smooth. However, I learned to accept these variations, listen to my body, and understand that not every day would be the same. This realization expanded to my life, allowing me to raise self-awareness without judgment, cultivate self-compassion, and let go of the need for perfection.

As I continued my mindfulness journey, I noticed a profound shift in my emotional state during the divorce process. Anger slowly dissipated, and the disappointment I felt toward myself began to fade away. Through my practice, I developed the ability to detach myself emotionally from the challenging circumstances I was facing. This detachment enabled me to approach the divorce with greater clarity and inner peace.

Mindfulness has proven invaluable in helping me navigate critical moments, such as sitting in the cafe with Caetano during our final chat about the divorce agreement. Despite the challenging situation, my dedicated mindfulness practice allowed me to approach the experience with remarkable calmness and openness. In the face of uncertainty, I found the ability to stay present and focus on the necessary actions rather than succumbing to anger, panic, or fear.

Through my mindfulness practice, I learned the importance of embracing the present moment as it unfolds, without resistance, expectation, or judgment. This acceptance allowed me to let go of the need for control and trust in the inherent intelligence of the Universe. No resistance to what is, allow the present moment to be and accept the nature of all things. Let it flow! I'm sure the Universe has got it covered for me.

Identification with the Mind

In life, many people tend to attach their sense of self and personal identity to their thoughts, beliefs, and mental constructs. This entanglement with the narratives created by our thinking mind can overshadow our true essence.

However, mindfulness offers a powerful tool to cultivate an active and non-judgmental awareness of the present moment. We can disengage from the incessant mental chatter by directing our attention to thoughts, feelings, and the environment without becoming overwhelmed or attached. Through this process, we begin to recognize the transient and impersonal nature of our thinking processes.

Practicing mindfulness can be initiated through simple techniques such as observing the breath, paying attention to bodily sensations, or fully being present ourselves in everyday activities. As we detach from our thoughts, we gain a deeper understanding of ourselves and the world around us. This allows us to access a state of mind where clarity, intuition, and wisdom reside. We become the "observer" behind our thoughts rather than the "judge."

Presence and Stillness

Presence, in its essence, is a state of complete attention and awareness of the here and now without being consumed by thoughts of the past or future. When we practice presence, we can experience life directly as it happens, without being hindered by expectations. We liberate ourselves from mental preoccupations and distractions by fully engaging with our surroundings, experiences, and relationships. It is a practice of "being in the flow."

On the other hand, *stillness* refers to a state of inner calm and tranquility, where the mind is quiet and free from incessant thinking. It is a state of non-resistance and non-reactivity, allowing us to access a deeper level of consciousness beyond the noise of the thinking mind. In moments of stillness, we connect with a sense of inner spaciousness, peace, and clarity that enables us to see things with greater clarity and wisdom.

Both presence and stillness have played a critical role in my personal growth and healing over the last few years. They have become essential tools that I use to connect myself to the world around me. Through cultivating presence, I have learned to savor each moment, finding joy in the simple pleasures of life. I have discovered that my interactions with others become more meaningful when I am fully present, and I feel a deeper connection with them.

Similarly, practicing stillness has allowed me to find inner peace and balance during life's challenges. It has been a refuge during times of stress and uncertainty, helping me to navigate complex emotions with grace and equanimity. By cultivating moments of stillness, I have tapped into a wellspring of inner strength and resilience that has supported me in my journey of self-discovery.

In combination, presence and stillness have become anchors that ground me in the present and nurture my overall well-being. They serve as powerful reminders to slow down, breathe, and savor the beauty of life. I have found a greater sense of harmony and fulfillment by embracing these key elements in my daily practice.

Time: Past, Present, and Future

In mindfulness practice, it is essential to recognize the significance of time as a tool rather than the focus. The past holds valuable experiences that can help us avoid recurring errors, while setting goals creates mental images that guide us in taking appropriate actions based on our predictions. However, it is crucial to understand that any planning, learning, or pursuit of goals can only be executed in the present moment—in the now.

Mindfulness enhances self-awareness, allowing me to understand better my thoughts, emotions, and behaviors in real time. By integrating lessons from the past, I align my values and make skillful and conscious decisions, avoiding repeated mistakes. This heightened awareness enables me to focus on the present situations, the signs, and guidance rather than fixating on the outcome.

Being grounded in the present empowers me to take steps toward my goals, adapting with ease and grace as needed. By aligning with the present moment, I can consciously progress toward my goals without stress and anxiety, manifesting higher vibrations and attracting positive outcomes through the law of attraction. Embracing mindfulness in my daily life empowers me to trust in the process of the Universe, knowing that everything occurs in divine timing.

Aligning my thoughts, feelings, and actions with my true self and higher purpose is essential. I set clear and positive intentions for what I want to manifest in life, using the power of visualization to create a mental image of my desired reality and feeling the emotions associated with achieving it. Taking mindful action toward my goals, following my intuition, and staying present in each step of the journey leads to more authentic and desired outcomes.

Don't Let Ego Eat You Alive

In mindfulness practice, exploring the concept of ego is essential. The ego, often seen as the sense of a separate self or the identification with thoughts, beliefs, and personal narratives, can be a significant source of suffering. By observing and investigating the ego, we aim to understand its influence and eventually transcend its limitations.

The ego tends to create a strong sense of self-importance, leading to the attachment to outcomes and judgment of oneself and others. It constantly seeks validation by comparing and contrasting experiences to uphold its self-image. This attachment can result in various forms of suffering, such as anxiety, dissatisfaction, and conflict in relationships.

In the past, I indulged in material possessions and lived a wasteful lifestyle, all attempting to impress others. The person I presented to the world was the one my parents and boss wanted me to be, but it wasn't the real me. I felt trapped in a marriage that didn't work, accumulating emotional pain and living with negativity throughout my life. This negative energy, rooted in unresolved emotional traumas and childhood issues, triggered unconscious behaviors that affected every aspect of my life.

Through mindfulness practice, I realized how my ego was intertwined with these negative emotions, continuously feeding off my identification with it. I began to observe my emotional patterns and recognize when they were activated. Mindful breathing and cultivating mindfulness helped me gain clarity without judgment. As I delved deeper into my consciousness, I started to observe ego-driven thoughts and emotions without getting entangled in negative self-talk and narratives. This led to inner transformation and liberation.

When faced with hurtful words from Caetano, I used to react impulsively with anger. Through mindfulness practice, I learned to read those texts without immediate reaction. I could respond with calmness, not getting entangled in his negative energy.

Remember that mindfulness is an ongoing practice that requires consistent effort and dedication. Staying committed to the practice and making mindfulness a part of our daily lives is crucial for lasting transformation and growth.

Letting Go of Resistance and Embracing Surrender

As I began my journey of recovery from a broken marriage and started a new life in Spain, I realized the importance of letting go of resistance and surrendering to the present moment. Instead of struggling with the Universe, filled with negative thoughts and emotions, I chose to surrender and accept what was happening in my life. By doing so, I stopped fighting against the circumstances and let go of feelings of dissatisfaction and frustration.

To release the mental and emotional burden that weighed me down, I detached myself from my preferences, expectations, and desires. This way, I didn't create a gap between reality and my mental projections when things didn't align perfectly. Letting go of resistance allowed me to shift my focus from wanting things to be different to embracing the present moment as it was. When challenging situations arose, I learned to observe them without labeling or identifying with them, viewing them instead as lessons to learn and adopting a solution-oriented attitude.

Surrendering doesn't mean giving up personal will or being passive in life. Instead, it involves letting go of the egoic need for control and surrendering to a higher intelligence inherent in the present moment. In this state of surrender, I found deep peace, freedom, and alignment with the natural flow of existence. It allowed me to trust the blossoming of life and be guided by the Universe, recognizing signs and taking the following steps without resentment.

Acceptance of the present moment, including any challenges or difficulties, became a key to finding peace and attracting positive outcomes. By letting go of attachment to specific outcomes and trusting in the flow of life, I began to understand that the Universe provides what is best for me.

In my mindfulness practice, I also learned to recognize the tendency to dwell on the past or become overly focused on the future. Dwelling on the past led to regrets and resentments, while excessive focus on the future brought anxiety and fear. True peace and fulfillment can only be found in the present moment. Letting go of excessive attachment to the past and future allowed me to fully experience the richness of the present and break free from the cycle of suffering.

Practicing detachment further enhanced my ability to find contentment within myself, detached from the need for external validation. This newfound inner peace allowed me to attract positive experiences and live authentically. Through mindfulness and surrender, I discovered the transformative power of embracing the present moment and trusting the journey that the Universe has in store for me.

100-Day Gratitude Journal

Gratitude is a powerful practice that I engage in regularly to shift my focus from lack to abundance and embrace the positive aspects of life. By cultivating emotions like joy, love, and compassion, I can transform my old negative mindset, elevating my vibrational energy and attracting positivity into my life.

Practicing self-compassion and self-love has been instrumental in acknowledging my worthiness, allowing more love to flow into my life. Embracing positive affirmations has reprogrammed my subconscious mind, breaking free from limiting beliefs and opening doors to attract positive experiences.

In my relationships, mindfulness plays a significant role, allowing me to communicate with presence, empathy, and understanding, thereby fostering harmonious and supportive connections.

To raise my vibrational energy and establish inner alignment with my true authentic self, I have learned to trust the process and have faith in the law of attraction. I firmly believe that the Universe is abundant and holds everything I desire, working in harmony with my intentions to manifest a life filled with fulfillment and joy.

Chapter 4:
Your Vibe Attracts Your Tribe

"The best people to surround yourself with are the people that bring out the best in you."

- Jay Shetty

Embarking on the journey of single parenthood naturally led me to seek out and attract single parents. Eventually, you form your tribe as a support system. The shared experience of raising children on our own forged a deep bond among us, a connection built on empathy, understanding, and unwavering support.

Within our single-parent tribe, we could relate to one another's triumphs and struggles, knowing firsthand the challenges and joys that accompany this unique path. Whether it was navigating co-parenting arrangements, managing the day-to-day responsibilities of parenting solo, or simply needing a shoulder to lean on during tough times, our tribe became an invaluable source of strength. In this safe space, we found understanding hearts, compassionate ears, and steadfast support that helped us heal and grow.

"We need to fix your German situation. We should arrange some German dates for you to get over it," Tina joked, lightening the mood after hearing about my fixation. "Trust me, if you're envisioning a romantic figure in your writer's mind, Germans are often ranked as some of the least romantic people in the world. Girl, it is probably better to leave fantasy as a fantasy."

Tina, an American, had entered my life through Maggie after our trip to Avignon. She was enjoying her life in Bodensee, Germany, before she decided to uproot her life and relocate to Spain with her boyfriend, Ben, who happened to be a single father too, was nothing short of bold. The love between Tina and Ben had flourished in Germany, but due to Ben's co-parenting arrangement in Barcelona, their lives became a constant dance between Spain during the school year and Germany during the summer and winter breaks. Tina's untiring determination to pursue her love and embark on this adventurous journey left me in awe of her bravery.

"Let me search through my contact list and see if I have any German friends who can set you up for a date. Since I worked in a German company, maybe we can do something about it," Kenan chimed in, eager to contribute.

"Guys, guys!" I interjected, laughter bubbling up within me. "My life is perfectly fine. I'm not desperate for love. I don't need a date, and also, I'm not obsessed with Germans. My real obsession lies in the fact that I didn't listen to myself, which caused my regret. Let's not twist the whole thing!"

We all joined in the laughter, realizing how lighthearted and comical the conversation had become. "Kenan is the one searching for a date, not me," I added, playfully trying to shift the subject of attention toward him.

Kenan, one of the very first people I met in Barcelona, quickly became a close friend and confidant. Our relationship had an interesting beginning, as we went on a series of "dates" before silently agreeing that we were better off as friends. Kenan, a devoted single father from Turkey, likes to joke that he is still searching for a date, as of the day I informed him about writing a book about our stories.

Over the years in Barcelona, we have cultivated a special bond deeply rooted in our shared experiences. Kenan's journey has been nothing short of fascinating. Having previously lived in the United States as a student and later residing in Brussels before settling in Spain, he carries a wealth of international experience. Language learning is one of his remarkable passions, and he has achieved fluency in several languages, including French, Spanish, English, and Turkish. Now, he has started learning Catalan, further enriching his linguistic repertoire.

As Tina inquired about the potential sparks between Kenan and me, I reiterated with a playful tone, "Oh, no, Kenan and I are the kind of friends where nothing will happen if you leave both of us alone in the apartment for days."

Between Kenan and I, we could openly discuss various aspects of our lives. We could talk freely about our dating experiences, sexual preferences, spiritual practices, and parenting styles without fear of judgment. Our conversations flowed effortlessly, and we even exchanged valuable travel tips, further solidifying our connection. It was comforting to have someone with whom my thoughts aligned on multiple topics, fostering a sense of understanding and acceptance between us. I treasure our friendship with him immensely. What sets our bond apart from others is that out of all the men I've met since in Barcelona, I feel most like myself when I'm with him. I can freely discuss any uncertain subject, and he listens with full attention. His experience as a single father enables him to empathize and understand my thoughts and feelings.

With Kenan, there's no need to calculate my efforts or worry about imbalances in give and take. Our relationship is characterized by a natural and authentic balance and, above all, genuine care for one another that provides a sense of security.

I vividly recall the early months of getting to know Kenan, which coincided with a period when I was still adjusting to life after separating from my ex-husband. During those initial few months, I mostly retreated into my own cocoon, often hesitating to venture out at night, preferring the comfort of my home. I had established a strict routine, almost to the point where Kenan playfully remarked that if I were to meet a new date, the Amazon delivery guy would be my only chance, considering my preference for staying home.

Sant Jordi

Sant Jordi is one of my favorite days in Catalonia. Sant Jordi, also known as Saint George's Day, is a significant cultural and traditional celebration in Catalonia. It takes place annually on April 23 and holds both historical and legendary significance. The origins of Sant Jordi date back to the medieval era. According to legend, Sant Jordi (Saint George) was a Roman soldier who valiantly fought against a dragon to save a princess and the people of a town. It is said that from the dragon's blood, a rosebush bloomed, and Sant Jordi plucked a red rose, which he gifted to the princess. This tale became a symbol of chivalry, love, and bravery. Over time, Jordi's Day became a way to honor both the saint and the legend associated with him.

On Sant Jordi's Day, the streets of Catalonia come alive with vibrant festivities. It is often referred to as the Catalan Valentine's Day due to the tradition of exchanging gifts between loved ones. Men typically give women a red rose, symbolizing the romantic gesture of Sant Jordi offering the rose to the princess. Women, in turn, give men a book inspired by the coincidence of April 23, also the anniversary of the deaths of renowned writers William Shakespeare and Miguel de Cervantes.

Bookstores, flower stands, and street vendors fill the streets, creating a colorful and festive atmosphere. It is a day of love, literature, and culture, where people of all ages browse and purchase books, explore Catalonia's literary heritage, and enjoy the beauty of roses. Sant Jordi has become a cherished celebration that highlights Catalan identity and creativity.

Living in a small town 15 km away from Barcelona's city center, away from the major tourist hubs, I have the privilege of experiencing a unique perspective on Sant Jordi's Day beyond just romantic couples. This special day unfolds with a beautiful tapestry of love expressed in various forms. It goes beyond traditional relationships, as I witness fathers giving roses to their daughters, sons presenting books to their mothers, and friends exchanging heartfelt gifts. Love permeates the air, revealing its multifaceted nature. This diverse and dynamic display of affection makes Sant Jordi's Day particularly enchanting and romantic to me.

Meeting Kenan and heading to Plaça de Catalunya for my first Barcelona Sant Jordi experience since moving here was exhilarating. As I stepped out of the metro station, I was instantly overwhelmed by the sheer number of people flooding the streets before me. Having experienced the bustling atmosphere of Times Square in New York during the New Year countdown, I thought I had witnessed the pinnacle of crowds. However, my first Sant Jordi in Barcelona proved me wrong. The sheer magnitude of people gathered in one area at once was shocking.

The crowd seemed to stretch endlessly, reaching as far as the eye could see, extending all the way to the end of Passeig de Gràcia. The city had taken extraordinary measures to accommodate the throngs of visitors, closing off blocks and creating a sprawling public "bookstore" for book lovers to lose themselves in. It was an impressive sight, an expansive sea of people weaving through the streets with a shared enthusiasm for the occasion. The energy was infectious as everyone joined in the celebration of love and literature, making it a truly memorable experience.

However, personally, I have never been good at dealing with big crowds. Seeing this overwhelmed crowd somewhat diminished the romantic atmosphere that I had anticipated for this special day in the center of Barcelona. The sheer volume of people made it challenging to embrace the intimate and sentimental aspects of Sant Jordi fully. The constant hustle and bustle, the jostling and maneuvering through the masses, somewhat detracted from the tranquility and enchantment I had experienced in my town.

Despite feeling a bit overwhelmed, I still appreciated the vibrant energy and the spirit of celebration that filled the air. Book signings by renowned authors attracted eager readers, who patiently waited in line for their turn to meet their literary idols. The atmosphere was electric with anticipation and literary enthusiasm. It was heartwarming to witness people expressing their love and affection in various ways, sharing the joy of giving and receiving books and roses.

As I approached Kenan and his two boys, they extended a rose to me together, their gestures filled with warmth and thoughtfulness. It was an adorable moment. This rose held special significance for me as it was my first Sant Jordi rose, making it all the more memorable. Kenan's boys were incredibly sweet, their innocence and kindness shining through.

Kenan's children were older than mine, so we didn't typically arrange playdates due to the age difference. However, Kenan's experience as a parent often offered me invaluable support and insight. He was always there to lend a helping hand, whether it was guiding me through speech therapy, assisting with managing sibling conflicts, or providing emotional training for our children. One of our children, who was introverted and less inclined to express themselves, particularly benefited from Kenan's expertise and understanding. His advice and understanding were a great source of comfort and guidance for me as I navigated the challenges of parenthood.

When the school informed me that my younger daughter needed speech therapy lessons, I immediately concluded that something was wrong with her. In those moments of worry and self-doubt, Kenan was always there to offer support and encouragement. He understood parenthood and reminded me not to compare my child to others. Kenan reassured me that as long as my daughter was making an effort to improve, progress would come little by little. He reminded me that children have their own unique pace in their journey, and giving them the time and space to grow at their own pace is essential. With his wisdom and reassurance, I approached my daughter's speech therapy with a more patient and positive mindset, allowing her to progress and develop at her speed.

Three months after my kids' therapy began, I recall a conversation with Mia, a single mother by choice. She exuded confidence, was always impeccably dressed, and expressed herself clearly. Mia was also advised to send her daughter to a therapist to enhance her speaking skills. When the school shared the same recommendation with me, I immediately spiraled into a guilt-ridden state, questioning my parenting abilities. Without hesitation, I signed up for the therapy as suggested by the school.

However, Mia approached the situation with confidence. She confidently stated, "I am a dentist, and I understand that my child's age is a crucial period for developing their oral skills.

They need time to explore and understand how to use their mouths. It's a process, and she will be just fine. Moreover, this is the year when children learn the pronunciation of all the letters of the alphabet, and I trust that the teachers are well-equipped to guide them through this stage since it's a part of their training for this specific grade."

Her words resonated deeply with me. I lacked the self-assurance to make the same choice for my child. However, Mia's influence and perspective had a profound impact on me. After thoughtful consideration, I decided to cancel the therapy after three months. It was liberating to trust my instincts as a parent and believe in my child's natural development, allowing her the time and space to grow and learn at her own pace.

Mia's confidence became a catalyst for me to re-evaluate the situation and make a decision that aligned with my own beliefs and instincts as a parent. I am grateful for her influence, which ultimately led me to trust in my child's development journey and nurture her progress with confidence and patience. It was a significant moment of empowerment, recognizing that as a parent, I have the wisdom to guide my child and make choices that resonate with our unique circumstances and values. From then on, I approached parenting with a newfound sense of trust and assurance.

Kenan exemplified the kind of friend who wholeheartedly embraced me and welcomed me into his life. He created a safe space where I felt comfortable expressing myself. It took some time for me to open up and share my personal life with him, but

Kenan's constant encouragement nudged me to speak up. He often said, "Why don't you say something?" His words served as a gentle reminder that I had a supportive friend who genuinely cared about me. With Kenan by my side, I felt heard, understood, and valued in our friendship.

Moreover, Kenan was acutely aware that I would be in Barcelona without any family besides my two children, and he understood the years I had spent away from my own family. He was the kind of man who went out of his way to create meaningful connections. One particular instance stands out vividly in my memory. Gathering a group of seven men, Kenan organized a trip from the bustling center of Barcelona to a quaint town located forty minutes away. The purpose? Simply to spend time with me before each of them went on their respective journeys back home for Christmas. It was a gesture of genuine friendship and support that touched my heart deeply. In that moment, I felt an overwhelming sense of gratitude for having someone like him in my life. His willingness to go the extra mile, both figuratively and literally, just to be in my company was a testament to the strength of our friendship. During that remarkable period, I had the privilege of forging deep bonds with a few of Kenan's beloved friends.

First was Thomas, a single father from Belgium. He had made Spain his home for nearly fifteen years. What charmed me about him was his seamless transition from being a lawyer to effortlessly embodying the roles of an official professional translator and an intrepid globetrotter. His extraordinary talent for taking exhilarating journeys while keeping to a modest budget exemplified his genuine passion for adventure and his dedication to experiencing the world in all its glory. He would sing one of the most iconic songs, '月亮代表我的心' *(Yuè Liàng Dài Biǎo Wǒ De Xīn)*, which means 'The moon represents my heart,' the first time we met.

I don't see Thomas often, as he is always on the road, but whenever we have time together, he always shares his most recent travel experience. One vivid, memorable moment is his bus travel experience in Sicily, Italy. He animatedly described the peculiar rhythm of life there, where delays and detours became part of the norm. Amidst these unexpected pauses, the bus driver would casually halt in the middle of the road, engaging in lively conversations with locals. These spontaneous interactions embodied the essence of Italian culture, where time took a back-seat to the profound connections forged in the present moment. Thomas often said, "Embrace the flow without expectation, for it is in these moments that true magic unfolds." The enthusiasm in his eyes as he shared the story was contagious.

He is the kind of man who would go on a wild mountain hiking adventure alone, carrying only a small backpack (complete with wine) and a simple tent, ascending to heights of three thousand meters. He passionately expressed, "The truth is that nothing compares to the comfort of a bed. Yes, the wilderness may bring cold nights, startling noises, bugs, and more. However, amidst all that, there's an indescribable feeling of freedom and purity in the air, bathed in the beauty of natural light. And, last but not least, it serves as a mental and physical reset when you return to the bustling city of Barcelona." His description was a testament to his adventurous spirit and appreciation for the untamed beauty of nature. On a lighter note, Thomas has a romantic side; he would use the word *lunatic* to describe.

Thomas is an exceptional individual whose positive energy is truly infectious. He would excitedly show me photos of his adventures, like the iconic Din Tai Fung restaurant at the Dubai airport, and his enthusiasm never failed to brighten my day. Another time, he proudly wore a pair of shoes labeled "Made in Taiwan" that he had bought several years ago during his visit to my hometown, Tainan City. It was a heartwarming gesture that reminded me of our shared connection.

Thomas's kindness knows no bounds; he always goes the extra mile to make others feel special. During his visit to my town with Kenan, he presented me with a glass of wine, saying, "I'm sure you don't have Christmas presents from Santa." His empathetic words showed his understanding, as a single father, that being far from family and friends, my children and I might not have received the usual gifts during the festive season. Thomas's thoughtfulness and genuine care for others shone through in every interaction, leaving a lasting impression on those fortunate to know him.

Additionally, I had the pleasure of meeting Rémi and Gigi, an extraordinary couple whose love transcended borders and brought them together in Barcelona. Rémi, originally from France, possessed gorgeous greenish eyes framed by a thin blue circumference. His gaze captivated me whenever he spoke, his strong French accent adding enchanting charm to his words. Gigi, hailing from Turkey, was a quiet and reserved individual, often sitting at the table attentively listening to everyone around him. Unless you turned to him directly, you might not hear his voice. Both Gigi and I were known for being somewhat guarded and slow to open up, which is why it took nearly a year for us to develop a closer bond.

Rémi and Gigi also visited my town to spend time with me. They are my fun net, the ones with whom I can share almost anything on my mind, and they will always respond with a supportive laugh, free from judgment.

"What was the last movie you watched?" Rémi asked as we sat at the bar, sipping our beers.

I chuckled and replied, "*Sexo y Lucia,* because I want to practice Spanish and still watch porn."

Rémi is a masculine man from Southern France, while Gigi is a younger, slender Turkish man. Their beautiful love story began when they randomly met on a trip. It seemed like destiny had a hand in their relationship, as both of them found jobs in Barcelona after conducting a long-distance relationship for a while. Eventually, they both decided to move in and settle down together in Barcelona, after only meeting in person twice.

Between Rémi and Gigi, Rémi is more outgoing, while Gigi tends to sit at the table quietly, listening to our conversations without saying much. Rémi's open personality makes it easier to get to know him, while with Gigi, our relationship deepens through subtle gestures. I remember one time we met after knowing each other for almost six months. As Gigi approached me upon his arrival, he embraced me with his warm smile and gentle demeanor. Instead of letting go immediately, he held on for an extra three seconds as if savoring the joy of seeing me. Our bodies swayed ever so slightly in sync, a subtle gesture that spoke volumes. With a smile, he looked at me and asked, "How are you doing?" In that instant, I knew we had become true friends who had connected in each other's hearts. I am no longer just "Kenan's friend," but I have also formed a genuine connection with Gigi.

Listening to Rémi and Thomas speaking English is akin to conducting an orchestra. Rémi carries a distinct French accent, giving his sentences a light and floaty quality. The way he pronounces words adds a certain elegance and grace to his speech, and he has a soothing tone of voice that feels like a feather dancing in the air—light, pure, and without force. On the other hand, Thomas's accent has a more robust and muscular quality. Each word he utters carries a punch, delivering a powerful and emphatic impact. Together, their contrasting accents create a harmonious blend of sounds, adding depth and richness to their conversations.

Rémi and Thomas, culturally just one border away from each other as French and Belgian, have remarkably different approaches to managing their lives. I vividly remember a passionate statement from Rémi, expressing his readiness to retire and embrace a life of leisure. On the other hand, with his lawyer's nature, Thomas would engage in thought-provoking debates on how one can retire while maintaining a sense of purpose. He believed it could be detrimental to one's self-esteem not to engage in something meaningful actively. Our careers often shape our identities and play a significant role in defining who we are. However, Rémi held the perspective that after years of hard work, he yearned to spend his time leisurely, savoring a beer by the Costa Brava, indulging in books, and pursuing further education based on his interests.

Thomas, inquisitive as ever, asked, "How can one do nothing and still feel fulfilled?"

Rémi, true to his French nature, responded, "By doing nothing, I am doing something." With that, I love and embrace Rémi's approach to life!

Even when it comes to the question, "What is the most popular Christmas market in France?"

Rémi would proudly say, "Colmar." At the same time, Thomas would confidently counter the answer with, "Strasbourg," having lived in Belgium and experienced life in France.

These moments always brighten up our group atmosphere and remind me of our differences and similarities.

"Do you have kids this week?" is the most common question to start our conversation. Tina says, "Wanna gang up for a drink?"

Regardless of our diverse backgrounds and the reasons that brought us to Barcelona, we all share a common passion: travel. Our conversations naturally revolve around our travel plans, visa issues (due to our expat background), retirement dreams, envisioning the future for our children, and contemplating life once they leave the nest. However, it is travel that truly binds us together; it is the heart of our discussions.

From inquiring about each other's upcoming holiday destinations to sharing our plans for Christmas, Easter holidays, and summer vacations, talking about travel has become a regular occurrence among us. We even make time to travel within Catalonia together, exploring the beauty of the region. The excitement of discovering new places, immersing ourselves in different cultures, and creating cherished memories fuels our bond and plays a significant role in our interactions. We eagerly exchange recommendations, delight in each other's stories of past adventures, and enthusiastically await the next opportunity to go on a new journey together.

Within this close-knit circle of friends, travel is more than just a hobby; it is a shared philosophy of life. Through our shared experiences on the road, we grow closer, deepen our understanding of one another, and build lasting connections beyond the boundaries of geography and culture.

Observing the single parents within our tribe, it becomes apparent that each of us is progressing at our own pace and navigating different stages of our healing journeys. It's especially noteworthy that we all have been divorced for a different amount of time. However, we all went through a similar path of navigating healing emotions, from sadness, disappointment, and broken hearts to feeling lost. Coming from diverse backgrounds, we naturally have varying parenting styles as well.

Through countless conversations, we realized that every single parent had endured their unique hardships along the way. Some had found themselves relegated to the couch, grappling with the painful knowledge of their partner's infidelity. Others had weathered abusive relationships, the scars of which still lingered. There were tales of financial struggles, where the weight of life's demands seemed insurmountable, yet they pressed on with unwavering determination. I recall one particular story of a brave soul starting the single parenting journey with nights spent on nothing more than an air mattress in the barren expanse of an empty apartment.

Although Rémi and Gigi were not directly navigating the challenges of single parenting, they faced a different set of hurdles as a gay couple. Every day, they had to confront the judgment and prejudice of those who couldn't accept or understand their relationship, especially considering that one of them hailed from Turkey. In this country, same-sex relationships were not openly discussed.

Their lives were marked by a constant need to conceal their true selves from old friends and their families. They grappled with the absence of support and acceptance from loved ones, often leaving them feeling isolated and vulnerable. The weight of societal expectations and the fear of being ostracized became a constant presence in their lives, creating an additional layer of complexity and emotional strain.

However, despite the struggles and drama we have experienced, none of us present ourselves as victims. The situations we have encountered could have easily led us to engage in the blame game or point fingers at others. However, we have consciously chosen not to let our circumstances define or hold us back. Instead, we embrace our roles with strength and resilience.

We acknowledge that life often presents us with challenges, but we are determined to face them head-on. Our primary goal is to create a fulfilling and joyful life for ourselves, our children, and our partners. We share a collective empowerment mindset, recognizing the immense potential for personal growth and development that single parenting offers. Our camaraderie fuels us to continue thriving, defying societal expectations, and embracing the opportunities that lie ahead. We are united in our refusal to be defined by our challenges, choosing instead to forge a path of resilience and triumph as we navigate the complexities of not being the norm in society.

Love Is a Choice, a Decision

When I first met Kenan, he was already involved in a semi-serious on-and-off relationship that spanned several years. On the other hand, Tina and Ben have found love once again and are eager to move forward from their previous relationships. As for Thomas, he adopts a deliberate approach to dating, taking his time to truly get to know a person. He believes in investing time (could be six months or longer) to establish a deeper emotional and physical connection. Kenan and I have often discussed the potential dilemma of discovering sexual incompatibility after investing a significant amount of time. Would one be willing to accept it or continue the relationship despite this mismatch?

It's been nearly four years since my separation, and I'm surprised at how long it's taken me to consider diving into another committed relationship. In the past, after ending a long-term relationship, it usually took me about a year after a break-up to enter another serious relationship. But this time, the process has taken much longer than I expected. The past situation and painful experience I endured kept me blocked and hesitant. I wanted to take the time to internalize my feelings and realign myself, which led me to cut off negative situations, toxic friendships, and situationships. As I re-evaluated my living style, I realized I also wanted to approach my relationships more minimally.

Looking back at my past years, I was always surrounded by many people, constantly receiving messages on my phone, and being involved in numerous directions. I would spread my energy across different things and people, leaving little room for a deeper connection with key people and myself. But I've learned that focusing on quality over quantity is essential. British evolutionary psychology professor Robin Dunbar's famous study, known as "Dunbar's number," highlighted that each individual's suggested social network has an average maximum of 150 people, of which only about five can have close interactions. To use my love, time, and effort effectively and wisely, I now prioritize the people who genuinely care for me, make me feel good, and help me grow.

As I sought to minimize all aspects of my life, I began to recognize the significance of creating meaningful and profound connections with those who truly matter. By adopting a more minimalist approach to my relationships, I want to cultivate deeper and more authentic harmonies that will stand the test of time. Therefore, at this moment in my life, I find comfort in casual relationships. Whether it is due to fear or simply my desire to avoid complicating my relationships, I feel it's crucial for me to focus on myself and my personal growth. This period of self-discovery will allow me to fully understand what I truly want and need in a committed relationship, ensuring that when the time comes, I am ready to embrace it with an open heart and a clear mind.

"Within the deepest truth is the realization that even if I would like to fall in love, the amount of fear I carry with me has blocked me from experiencing it fully. I feel uncertain about how to love now. I once read that love is a decision, a willingness to give unconditionally. With that theory in mind, I often find myself calculating and measuring the effort, as well as deciding if I want to love someone, unlike my previous experiences, where I could easily fall in love romantically as soon as I clicked with the person and pour myself out right away without hesitation," I explained my feelings, sitting with my tribe, sipping Clara beer.

"Imagine a thrilling journey on a motorbike with two people, embarking on an adventure of a lifetime. At the beginning of their ride, there might be some hesitation and fear about what lies ahead, uncertainties about the path they'll take, and the challenges they might encounter. But as they ride together, side by side, they start to build trust and connection with each other," Tina explained. "The theory of being brave to love is like riding that motorbike. Love requires courage, just like taking on an open road with twists and turns. It involves vulnerability, as both individuals open themselves up to each other, exposing their true selves without barriers. It's about being willing to ride through uncertainties and difficulties and facing the unknown with bravery and resilience. When they ride together, they support and complement each other, finding strength in unity. They communicate and listen, ensuring they are on the same page and understanding each other's needs and desires. The motorbike journey becomes a dance of two souls in sync, navigating through life's challenges and cherishing moments of joy and connection." Kenan, Rémi, Gigi, and I listened carefully as Tina continued, "Being brave to love means acknowledging the risks and potential heartaches that may come with it, yet choosing to embrace the journey anyway. It's about taking that leap of faith, knowing that love is worth the ride, regardless of the destination. The two riders recognize that they might encounter bumps along the way but are willing to face them together, finding strength in their bond. As they ride together, their trust and connection deepen, and they become each other's pillars of support. They experience the freedom that comes with opening their hearts and allowing themselves to love and be loved fully. It's a shared adventure where they both contribute to making the ride exhilarating and meaningful."

"Is it too crazy for me to consider staying in casual relationships before committing to someone and even contemplate exploring an open relationship once I'm committed?" I inquired, a mischievous grin spreading across my face.

"Girl, you can be as casual or open as you want. Heck, if you want to juggle multiple men simultaneously in one night and it brings you joy, so be it!" Tina responded, her nonjudgmental support shining through. We burst into fits of laughter, unable to contain our amusement. Tina had always been that friend who wholeheartedly embraced my happiness above all else.

"Oh! The idea of having multiples in one night is interesting!" Kenan exclaimed, the humor of the situation washing over us.

Our laughter always reminded us of the bond we had formed within our tribe—a bond characterized by unfiltered conversations and an acceptance of each other's quirks and desires. The freedom to openly discuss unconventional relationship dynamics without fear of judgment was a testament to the depth of our friendship and the genuine connections we had nurtured. It is fascinating to witness the diverse paths we traverse within our tribe, acknowledging our individual choices in pursuit of happiness, personal growth, and meaningful connections. Our discussions are filled with shared experiences, insightful perspectives, and thought-provoking questions, which contribute to the tapestry of our collective support system.

The Safe Habor of Female Wisdom

Besides my single-parent tribe, my relationship with Victoria has grown in the past few years. Along the way, I connected with other incredible women through her, like Maddy, Marinus, and Claudette, who were all former models. They became my trusted advisors in the world of fashion, teaching me the importance of authenticity and feeling comfortable in my skin. The best beauty is the natural beauty from within, even without relying on makeup. (But let's be honest, beauty and self-care go hand in hand. It's important to practice self-care, eat mindfully, and exercise, and we all do that!) Their influence helped me break free from societal expectations and embrace my true self.

It's not just their fashion sense that sets them apart; the self-assurance they exude serves as a powerful inspiration for me. Victoria, a professional model, radiates a remarkable sense of confidence. She is definitely not a Christian Dior kind of girl with a romantic and dreamy style. Instead, Hermès's sleek and sophisticated aesthetic perfectly complements her elegance and timeless appeal. She knows her dreams and isn't afraid to speak her mind. She is exceptionally generous and always gives her undivided attention when we need it. I can always count on her support whenever I have questions or doubts. She goes above and beyond to be there for her friends. Her favorite topics range from astrology to energy, fashion to food. To top it off, she has an extensive collection of delicious and healthy food recipes.

Marinus, originally from Russia, is now Spanish. She married a German who recently relocated to Switzerland. She visits Spain with her two young children every couple of months to enjoy the sunshine. She is truly a supermom. I have never witnessed such calmness in a mother. She effortlessly joins our regular lunch meetups, maneuvering a baby stroller with one hand while holding her three-year-old son with the other. There's no sign of stress or panic. It's like magic how she maintains such a tranquil and peaceful demeanor at all times (while still looking gorgeous!) If you're feeling stressed, just take a deep breath and look at Marinus. I'm sure you'll instantly find calmness in her presence.

Next is Claudette, from Germany, who has always been a nomad. During her transition from modeling to becoming a psychologist, she successfully managed to balance work and study. Currently, she devotes herself to helping those in need in a hospital setting. Claudette is the perfect companion if you ever feel tense and need aimless wandering. She actively seeks love and embraces it openly. Her courageous spirit is truly inspiring.

Maddy, a Swedish mother with a daughter close in age to my own, stands out as an exceptional individual. As the founder of a real estate company, she exemplifies the ability to set high standards, work diligently, and achieve her goals. Maddy possesses an entrepreneurial spirit and fearlessly embraces new challenges. I love it whenever she talks about property-related subjects; her seriousness is evident as she uses her finger gently and expertly to push up her glasses at the bridge of her nose, sharing her deep knowledge and insight.

If we were all walking through the scariest haunted house at Universal Studios, I could imagine Maddy fearlessly leading the way, with Victoria at the end, ensuring everyone stays together. The rest of us would carefully advance, feeling protected by their presence. Each of us has a unique eye color, ranging from dark brown and yellowish-green to bluish-brown and greenish-blue. We all have stories and personalities, and I have much to learn from them. They have become my safe harbor of female wisdom.

Each of us has our unique relationship dynamics and carries different stories. Victoria, for instance, is the type of person who isn't afraid to take the leap and move in with her partner just a week after meeting. Despite the ups and downs, they are now happily building their life together. On the other hand, Maddy decided to relocate from Sweden to Barcelona with her partner. They have since become parents to a beautiful daughter, experiencing the joys and challenges of family life.

Claudette, a divorcee without children, holds a strong belief in love. She approaches relationships passionately and always strives to see their positive aspects. Marinus, a mother of one toddler and one newborn, faces the challenges of her husband's busy working schedule. Given the high cost of living in Switzerland, hiring a full-time nanny is not economically feasible for them. Despite this, Marinus handles everything with an admirable and positive spirit. I am genuinely amazed by how gracefully she manages it all!

As for myself, I am a divorcee with two children. While being unsure about love, I remain open to exploring new possibilities. I have chosen not to uproot my children and merge with someone else's life but instead, focus on creating a stable environment for the three of us as a family. This approach feels right for me at this moment in time.

We, Victoria, Maddy, Claudette, Marinus, and I, have unique circumstances and have chosen a path that aligns with our circumstances and desires. Despite our differences, we support and respect one another's choices, understanding that love takes various forms and evolves differently for each individual. Together, we form a supportive and understanding community that uplifts and empowers one another as we navigate our journeys of love and life.

Of course, our love life is far from perfect, and each of us carries our own set of challenges in our unique ways. While we recognize that the solutions to these challenges ultimately lie in our own hands and are within our control, we have become a source of support for one another whenever these issues arise. We can openly discuss our experiences and offer a listening ear and understanding.

I can openly share the details of my agreement process, even being vulnerable, something I didn't usually do in my pre-COVID life. Victoria may describe the stress she feels in search of a harmonious partnership. At the same time, Maddy and Marinus often discuss their challenges within their marriages, seeking guidance and perspectives from one another. On the other hand, Claudette grapples with doubts about her life path and may sometimes feel lost. We provide her with support and encouragement to navigate these uncertainties.

We each have our own set of requirements and priorities. In our friendship, we have created a safe space where we can openly discuss our challenges. We offer empathy, advice, and a listening ear, knowing we can rely on one another for support and understanding. Together, we navigate through the complexities of life, offering strength and encouragement when needed.

"Are you following Johnny Depp's trial?" I asked during our regular lunch gathering at our favorite backyard kitchen, Honest Green. "I'm keeping up with it every day. It's like a gripping drama series, even better than anything on TV right now. It feels so real, like witnessing a real-life drama taking place, revealing the complexities of the Me Too movement," I added.

"Exactly. I support helping victims, but I have my doubts about the Me Too movement. It seems like it has become a platform for a few celebrities to make claims," Victoria expressed. "Let's rewind our memories to when those assaults happened. I felt sorry for the victims, but the Hollywood industry is not so different from the modeling industry. It's a known reality, and entering the industry was their choice."

"Moreover, when the assault occurred, they had the choice to fight back or surrender. But now, twenty years later, these celebrities have achieved fame, won awards, and enjoyed a luxurious life, and suddenly come out as victims. Oh, come on! There are women out there who faced rejection head-on from these monsters, got canceled, lost jobs, and were forced to leave the industry. Those women who truly suffered without a choice were not adequately protected. The media attention turned it into a show for a few select celebrities. It just doesn't feel right," she added.

"I was one of them who said no in my early modeling years. You don't hear anything back for a while. Being so young in your twenties, having to face the consequences of that no, you had constant self-doubt about whether it was worse to give your body to a producer and photographer or lose a career altogether. It was really in the later years that I was so glad that I dared to say no," Victoria shared her own experiences with conviction.

It was intriguing for me to delve into Victoria's perspective on this topic. She highlighted the truth and depth of the situation, which I, like many others, had overlooked while focusing on the celebrities' stories. She was right in pointing out that there are individuals who have lost everything by saying no, and their stories deserve consideration. On the other hand, there are people for whom the cost of saying no is too high, risking the sacrifice of their dreams.

As someone who has experienced assault in a public place, I have also found myself in moments where I didn't know how to navigate such situations. Beyond feeling shocked and my heart racing, the rest of my body seemed to go silent. It's essential to recognize the complexities and nuances of each person's experience, as well as the courage it takes to share these stories.

I often gained valuable insights from Victoria's perspective through dialogue like this, as it holds its own truth within the larger narrative. Our conversations were characterized by mutual respect and viewpoints, acknowledging that these complex issues demand careful consideration and a nuanced understanding. It was a reminder that there is often more than one side to a story, and through open-minded dialogue, we can broaden our perspectives and deepen our empathy for others. Engaging in such discussions with my friends allowed me to grow and evolve as an individual, fostering a greater appreciation for the diversity of human experiences.

Through my limited experiences in the modeling industry, a significant portion of my knowledge came from watching reality shows like *America's Next Top Model* and tuning in each year for the Victoria's Secret Fashion Show. It is safe to say that I didn't have a deep understanding of the modeling industry. Nonetheless, it has always fascinated me to hear some of the stories of these girlfriends.

"I could write a book about the flaws of the modeling industry," Maddy said.

"I encountered a prevailing perception that models constantly engage in unhealthy behaviors, particularly related to their eating and drug habits. I even heard a disturbing story about a manager criticizing an already-skinny model for looking too big and suggesting she use cocaine to control her weight. Every aspect of this story felt disheartening and haunting to me. I wouldn't want my daughter exposed to it," I said.

"In addition to body type, the youth appeared to be a critical factor for women in securing modeling jobs. Unfortunately, this belief seems to stem from the stereotypical portrayal of models in the media, especially in the early days, where extreme thinness is often depicted as the epitome of beauty. I was offered a Botox treatment to tighten my skin at age twenty-five," Maddy shared.

"What you heard from the interview on television about the drugs and party scene in the modeling industry is true. The unhealthy nature of the industry that you've heard of is real. Models are often expected to be socially active, with constant networking, and these gatherings can involve alcohol, sex, and drugs. Within these social activities, models may potentially meet photographers or clients who can boost their careers. Unfortunately, if you're a model who doesn't engage in extensive networking, the likelihood of landing jobs diminishes greatly. The boundaries within the modeling industry are just as blurry as they are in Hollywood," Victoria added.

"We were subjected to meticulous measurements, with every centimeter of our bodies being scrutinized," Maddy explained, demonstrating how they would measure the distance from the neck to the ear or assess head size. "Models were constantly aware of their body measurements, monitoring themselves daily to weekly."

"The whole experience of not eating meant two yogurts a day. I've been there, done it! And I'm never going back," Victoria candidly described her past experiences as a young model, acknowledging that she, like many others, sought attention, battled with self-doubt, and engaged in actions to please others.

While it is true that the fashion industry has faced criticism for promoting unrealistic beauty standards, my interactions with these friends also made me realize that such generalizations are becoming outdated. Models, like individuals in any other profession, are starting to welcome a variety of shapes, colors, sizes, and backgrounds. Many, including Victoria, prioritize their health and well-being by maintaining a balanced lifestyle and following a nutritious diet.

"It takes experience and time to accept our bodies and looks," Victoria commented. "And now, the industry values more than just external beauty. They emphasize the importance of inner beauty as well. I've been interviewed for shooting, requiring me to make a video of engaging in the hobbies that nourish me. So I filmed myself cooking granola two days ago." We all laughed together teasingly, joking about the added effort required to secure a job in the industry nowadays to embrace the shift toward a more inclusive and holistic approach to beauty.

"There are cases where you can be unbooked just five seconds before the show. After all the anticipation, hard work, and preparation, it can be devastating for a model to accept that the designer decided to remove them simply because the look didn't feel right. It's as cruel as it sounds." The ladies continued sharing some stories.

"Hell no! After two months of hard work, if they try to stop me right at the entrance of the Hermès fashion show, I'm gonna be like, 'Shut up!' and walk right in," I responded jokingly, making a gesture with my hand to symbolize shutting down the designer's decision.

"It happens all the time. Maybe I should do that, and that's how people get really famous nowadays with a viral video," Victoria added with a hint of sarcasm.

"Yeah, yeah! And then that outfit becomes the best-selling item," Maddy chimed in. We all burst into laughter, recognizing the absurdity and heartbreak that can come with such experiences.

Body Image in Childhood

Growing up in a Taiwanese community, it was common to have relatives, aunts, or even mothers who wouldn't hesitate to point out what was wrong with your face and body. As an Asian woman, self-doubt seemed to be an ingrained part of life. In South Korea, parents would even go as far as paying for their children's cosmetic procedures to celebrate their graduation from high school and entrance into university. Thailand, particularly its metropolis, has seen a rise in the number of beauty clinics. Taiwan's medical aesthetic market continues to grow steadily, with anti-aging treatments being one of the most sought-after procedures.

"I'm that Asian girl who never found the right shoe size while shopping in Taiwan because I'm taller than the average Taiwanese girl, with bigger feet. They don't usually make my size. I grew up being told I had big feet," I explained. "So to make them look smaller in order to fit my low self-esteem, I would buy shoes half a size smaller and live with painful feet. It was a part of my life for years."

"I lived in a society where people would politely greet you by commenting on your appearance. 'Long time no see. You are looking good. Have you lost weight?' This societal focus on weight made me and most girls very conscious. We are constantly educated about watching our weight, and it wouldn't be surprising to hear people comparing their body mass index (BMI). Can you imagine that weight management supplements remain one of the top consumer products in the Taiwanese market?" I added, highlighting the pressure on physical appearance in such an intense culture.

"Other than being judged by our appearance, we constantly compared ourselves with others. I remember growing up, every semester during exams, the school would announce the rankings of each student from first place to last, publicly displaying their names on the announcement board in the school hall. This was one of the cruelest things to experience as a young kid. I mean, thanks for telling everyone I suck!"

"If students scored 95 out of 100, they would more likely be punished or criticized for the five missing points rather than being applauded for the hard-earned 95. It's sad to say, but that was our reality and part of our childhood trauma. The constant pressure to be perfect and the fear of not meeting expectations left a lasting impact on me, making me feel like I was never good enough."

"Sweden ranked people, too, and that's just way too much. Now that I am a mother, I often practice self-affirmation with my daughter, making sure she understands she is who she is, and we strive for improvement and progress, not perfection," Maddy agreed.

"In Lithuania, once the school day was over, that was it. You either learned or you didn't. There was no ranking at all," Victoria added, giving us a sense of liberty!

Spending quality time with these ladies always gives me a different cultural perspective on how we grew up and how it shapes our beliefs today. In the company of these incredible women, I have learned to redefine beauty for myself and others.

It is a holistic concept encompassing physical, emotional, and spiritual well-being. It involves cultivating inner beauty, nourishing the soul, and embracing beauty in every moment and every person we encounter.

Living in Barcelona has been a transformative experience that further enhanced my understanding and appreciation for individuality and personal expression. Barcelona is renowned for its open-mindedness and cosmopolitan vibe, while still holding onto its traditional Catalan customs. It is a city where diversity and uniqueness are celebrated, allowing people to be themselves authentically.

As I walked the streets of Barcelona, I noticed the stark contrast to the beauty standards I had grown accustomed to. Here, women didn't feel pressured to wear premium brands or adhere to a specific style dictated by society. Instead, they confidently embraced their individuality, freely expressing themselves through fashion choices without being overly concerned about judgment or societal norms.

With the influence of Barcelona, I underwent a profound transformation in my attitude toward beauty and body image. The vibrant city inspired me to embrace my unique style, express myself authentically, and break free from the chains of arbitrary beauty standards. For the first time in my life, I was able to silence the constant inner dialogue of self-criticism. Thoughts like "I'm too fat" or "I need to be on a diet" no longer consumed my mind. Instead, I developed a newfound appreciation for my body, flaws, imperfections, etc.

Therefore, rather than idolizing the "perfect" body types depicted in Vogue magazine, I have expanded my understanding of beauty to encompass more than just physical appearance. I have shifted my focus toward self-care, self-love, and nurturing both my body and mind.

True beauty lies in self-acceptance and self-love. It is about being comfortable in your skin, embracing flaws, and nurturing a positive body image. The confidence that radiates from within when one recognizes one's worth and appreciates one's beauty is truly empowering. Beauty goes beyond external factors; it is about uplifting others, spreading kindness, and making a positive impact in the world. It is the ability to empathize, support, and empower those around us. True beauty is reflected in how we treat others with respect and compassion, embracing inclusivity and celebrating the beauty in diversity.

Although this concept may seem obvious to many, in reality, it can be easy to forget amid the pressures of society and the constant comparison to unrealistic standards. However, when we shift our focus from external appearances to inner qualities and our impact on others, we begin to understand the true essence of beauty.

This journey of self-discovery and acceptance has been a transformative experience, and I'm thankful for the wisdom and insight gained from these remarkable women and the city of Barcelona. We celebrate beauty in all forms and encourage each other to embrace our uniqueness. As a result of this transformation, it has not only encouraged me to be true to myself but has also inspired me to extend these beliefs to my children. When I engage in affirmations with my daughters, I genuinely express the true essence of being "beautiful" from the depths of my heart. I hope to guide them away from the narrow beauty standards I struggled with from a young age. I want them to wholeheartedly embrace their uniqueness, letting go of the damaging habit of comparing themselves to others and harshly judging themselves. I want them to live with an open mindset, recognizing that the perceived flaws they may identify today could become their greatest assets in the future and understanding that true beauty radiates from within—an individual's ability to exude love and kindness toward others. No beauty shines brighter than that of a good heart.

Barcelona Fashion Week

"Hey, ladies! I have tickets for you to attend Barcelona Fashion Week. Here are the schedules," Victoria texted us excitedly.

Eager to witness the glamour of the event, Maddy, Claudette, and I arrived at Hospital Sant Pau a good twenty minutes before the show was set to begin. As we approached the entrance, I was fascinated by the magnificent UNESCO World Heritage site, the Modernist architecture of Sant Pau. The ornate details and grandeur of the building surrounded us, creating an atmosphere of awe and anticipation.

Stepping through the side door, we were greeted by the scent of lavender lingering in the air, adding a touch of serenity to the bustling energy of the venue. We made our way toward the heart of the hospital, where the welcome open bar and DJ booth were strategically placed in the center of the open space.

The vibrant music and lively chatter filled the air, setting the stage for a fashion experience. Surrounded by the stunning architecture, I felt privileged and excited. The combination of the historical backdrop and the contemporary fashion setting created a unique and enchanting ambiance. It was a true fusion of old and new, tradition and innovation.

As we mingled with fellow fashion enthusiasts and industry professionals, the anticipation continued to build. We could feel the collective energy and passion for fashion pulsating through the venue. The atmosphere was electric, filled with a palpable sense of creativity and style.

It was my first time attending fashion week, and I noticed how people had put so much effort into their outfits to showcase their best selves. In fact, some of them went above and beyond, turning their attire into works of art. As I looked around, I couldn't help but wonder, "Did you come here dressed like that?" The level of creativity and expression was truly remarkable. It was as if the arena had transformed into a vibrant venue, with each individual making a bold statement through their fashion choices. From avant-garde ensembles to extravagant accessories, there was an undeniable sense of artistry and individuality in every corner.

It was inspiring to witness such sartorial confidence. People had embraced fashion as a means of self-expression, using it to communicate their unique personalities and perspectives. The diversity of styles was a testament to the limitless possibilities that fashion offered. As I observed the attendees, I admired the courage it took for them to step out of their comfort zones and experiment with unconventional fashion choices. It was a celebration of individuality, a reminder that fashion is not just about following trends but expressing oneself authentically.

Approaching the show time, we stood in line, holding our invitation barcodes ready alongside other participants, making our way into the venue. As we entered, the atmosphere transformed into a mysterious ambiance, with dim lighting and an enchanting red glow. As we stepped into the fashion sanctuary, three parallel walkways stretched out before us, each adorned with neatly arranged chairs on either side. The media space was in the heart of the venue, at the back of the central walkway. It was a hub of activity, with professional cameras capturing every angle and journalists preparing to document the fashion extravaganza. The presence of the media added to the anticipation and excitement that filled the air.

We took our seats shortly after scanning the environment, and the background music began to play, setting the mood for the upcoming show. The beats and melodies reverberated through the space, creating an energetic and captivating ambiance. The music served as a prelude to the fashion spectacle that was about to ensue before our eyes. The combination of the lighting with red hues and the upbeat music created a sense of anticipation and intrigue. We eagerly awaited the start of the show to catch a glimpse of our beloved Victoria!

The lights dimmed, the venue became pitch dark, and the music changed. Seconds later, Victoria gracefully emerged from the main entrance in a black sleeveless top that showcased her beautiful collarbone and shoulders. She paired it with a high-waisted, lace-like long skirt, her hair neatly bundled up and sporting minimalist natural makeup. As she calmly walked past the three of us, a sense of pride washed over us.

Within the fashion show, there were no limitations in size, shape, or ethnicity. In fact, through careful observation, I noticed that the designers sought to celebrate a mosaic of diversity. The runway showcased a variety of models, including plus-size individuals, women with freckles, individuals with diverse skin colors, and people from various backgrounds. The collection of unique profiles highlighted the beauty that comes from embracing one's features, inner strength, confidence, and self-expression. It was a vibrant display of the richness and inclusivity of human diversity.

The sensation of standing within a historic UNESCO World Heritage building, absorbed in a show that embodies creativity and the future, was indeed a blessing.

Flamenco Show at the Palau de la Música Catalana

As I stood outside Palau de la Música Catalana, marveling at its breathtaking architecture with Tina, I couldn't contain my excitement for the flamenco show that awaited us inside. Watching a performance like this had always been a dream of mine, but I wanted to share this experience with the right person—one who would genuinely appreciate the talented performers, the soul-stirring music, and the stunning beauty of the venue. I didn't just want someone to accompany me; I longed for a companion who could immerse themselves in the magical moments alongside me.

Sure, I could have gone to the show any time, but there was something special about waiting for the right moment and person to share it with. And that moment had finally arrived with Tina by my side, sharing experiences with someone who understands and values the same things. It was more than just attending a show; it was about forging a deeper connection through a shared appreciation of art and culture.

As we stood in line outside Palau de la Música Catalana, a sense of excitement and anticipation filled the air. The line snaked its way along the exterior of the building, with a diverse group of people eagerly awaiting their turn to enter the main hall. Conversations buzzed around us, creating a lively atmosphere as we exchanged smiles and shared our anticipation for the upcoming show.

Finally, it was our turn to ascend the grand staircase leading us into the heart of the Palau. The stairs, adorned with intricate carvings and ornate details, carried us closer to the magic that awaited inside. As we made our way up, the soft glow of the warm lighting added a touch of elegance to the surroundings, enhancing the sense of anticipation. Passing through the majestic doors, we were greeted by a breathtaking sight. The main hall of Palau de la Música Catalana revealed itself in all its splendor.

"My last time here was during COVID, and it was all quiet. The atmosphere now feels like COVID never happened," I told Tina. As we stepped into the main hall, a sense of wonder washed over Tina, as she took in the intricate details surrounding us. Excitedly, Tina and I instinctively took out our phones to capture the beauty of every corner.

As we explored the hall, we looked up at the ceiling of Palau de la Música Catalana together, and we were immediately mesmerized by the exquisite arrangement of lights suspended above us. I pointed to the ceiling and took the opportunity to share with Tina what I had learned during my previous visit, explaining the significance of its design.

Remarkable Palau de la Música Catalana was designed by the renowned architect Lluís Domènech i Montaner. It stands as a true architectural gem and was recognized as a UNESCO World Heritage Site in 1997. The concert hall of the palace, with a seating capacity of approximately 2,200 people, boasts a unique feature—it is the only auditorium in Europe illuminated entirely by natural light during daylight hours. The ceiling of the main hall is a masterpiece in itself, showcasing a stunning skylight that allows natural light to filter through during the daytime, bathing the entire space in a soft, ethereal glow. This skylight is adorned with an intricate stained glass canopy, thoughtfully crafted by Antoni Rigalt i Blanch, which serves as the centerpiece of the ceiling. The centerpiece is an inverted dome in shades of gold surrounded by blue, suggesting the sun and the sky. A choir of young women surrounds the "sun" in the stained-glass skylight.

"Ben was here enjoying a show years ago, too, and he mentioned the ceiling lights in the main hall are stunning," Tina shared, her voice laced with humor as she imitated Ben's unique blend of German-English. She continued, "He said the ceiling light is inside out, upside down. You get a sense of how we communicate?" We chuckled at the thought of Ben, his words capturing the quirkiness of the situation.

The idea behind this sensational ceiling design was to infuse the hall with natural light, creating a harmonious connection between the interior and the outside world. The use of stained glass allows the light to cast a kaleidoscope of colors, symbolizing the richness and diversity of the cultural heritage of Catalonia.

During our evening visit to the Palau de la Música Catalana, the stunning canopy of lights was illuminated, creating an ambiance that was nothing short of enchanting. The arrangement of the lights was thoughtfully made, ensuring that each fixture complements the overall design and enhances the beauty of the space. The lights seemed to hang in perfect balance, resembling graceful petals gently floating in the air. The interplay of light and shadow added depth and dimension, creating a dynamic visual spectacle that impressed all who entered the hall.

Unlike a traditional theater, the hall's design incorporates massive sculptures flanking the stage, making the use of scenery nearly impossible. This emphasis on the musical experience is further enhanced by the presence of a noble pipe organ gracefully adorning the apse-like area above and behind the stage. Despite this grandeur, the hall is not a church but a space dedicated to celebrating music and artistic expression.

We eagerly took our front-row seats and turned our attention to the stage. It was a sight to behold, perfectly set for the mesmerizing flamenco show that was about to take place. A large wooden board stood at the center of the stage, polished and gleaming under the spotlight. It was the heart of the performance, the platform on which the dancers would showcase their incredible skills and fiery passion. The board's surface hinted at the countless hours of practice and myriad performances it had witnessed.

Behind the neat row of wooden chairs on the stage, a percussion set patiently awaited, ready to contribute its rhythmic beats to the vibrant soundscape of the flamenco performance. However, it was not just the performers who graced the stage; behind it was an eye-catching semicircle featuring the depictions of eighteen young women, fondly known as the "muses." These figures were a beautiful fusion of artistry, with their upper bodies sculpted by Eusebi Arnau and their lower bodies adorned with vibrant mosaics crafted by Lluís Bru. The women's upper bodies gracefully protruded from the wall in a monotone fashion, while their lower bodies came to life through the intricate and colorful mosaic work. Each woman was artistically portrayed playing a unique musical instrument, and they were elegantly attired in different skirts, blouses, and headdresses, all boasting elaborate designs.

As the lights bathed the stage in a warm and enchanting glow, the backdrop behind the performers was illuminated in a rich red hue. This choice of color created a dramatic contrast against the wooden elements and brought a sense of intensity and passion to the entire scene. The red light seemed to symbolize the raw emotions and fierce energy that would soon fill the air. The anticipation in the air grew as the show was about to begin. The lights in the grand hall dimmed, casting a soft glow over the audience. It was a moment of quiet anticipation, and then the enchantment began.

Two singers, one female, and one male, took their positions behind the microphones. There was no music accompanying them, just the pure and soulful resonance of their voices. Their heartfelt melodies filled the air, carrying the essence of Flamenco through the hall. The music was passionate, evoking a range of emotions from joy to sorrow, with intricate melodies and haunting vocals that echoed through the space. And then, from the backstage door that connected to a low set of stairs on the stage, three beautiful Flamenco dancers made their entrance. Their stunning Flamenco attire immediately caught the eye, adding an extra layer of visual splendor to the performance. They wore traditional Flamenco dresses, known as *trajes de flamenca*, which were characterized by their vibrant colors and ruffled layers. The dresses flowed gracefully as the dancers descended step by step, enhancing the visual spectacle of their movements. The vibrant hues, such as fiery reds, passionate blacks, and vibrant blues, added to the overall dynamism and intensity of the performance. The dancers' dresses were adorned with intricate details, from delicate lace trimmings to ornate floral patterns. The ruffled sleeves and flowing skirts of the dresses accentuated their every movement, creating a sense of drama and flair. The dancers' attire exuded a sense of tradition and elegance, embodying the spirit of flamenco.

As the performance progressed, the three dancers split into two groups. The most senior dancer took the center stage, commanding attention as she started a mesmerizing solo performance again and again. Her every movement was infused with years of experience and mastery, captivating the audience with her artistry. Meanwhile, the other two dancers formed a seamless pair, their movements perfectly synchronized as they danced harmoniously. Their chemistry was evident as they effortlessly complemented each other's steps and gestures, creating a stunning visual display of unity and coordination.

As the music swelled, the leading guitarists and the violinist joined the stage with the vocalists, ready to infuse the air with the soul-stirring melodies of traditional flamenco music. And then it began—the rhythmic clapping of the traditional flamenco music, known as palmas. The sound reverberated through the hall, creating an intoxicating pulse that resonated deep within the hearts of the audience. Each clap echoed with power and precision, adding a layer of percussive brilliance to the already enchanting composition. The clapping of palmas in traditional flamenco music was not merely a technique but a language spoken through hands and hearts. It evoked a sense of joy, passion, and collective celebration, connecting performers and audience members in a profound and unspoken understanding. The melodic notes intertwined with the dancers' movements, and the music filled the hall, weaving a tapestry of emotion and rhythm that enveloped the audience. The percussion instruments added a vibrant pulse to the performance, enhancing the energetic and passionate atmosphere.

As the dancers took the stage, their artistry seemed to transcend time. Every movement they made seemed enchanted, drawing the audience's attention and evoking deep emotions. Mesmerized by their skill and passion, the spectators were wholly engrossed, their eyes fixed on the enthralling performance. The room fell into a hushed silence, as if every person held their breath, afraid to miss even the slightest nuance. In that moment, being in the present was paramount. There was no space for any other thoughts; my entire focus was on the intricate beats and movements unfolding before me. Riveted by the performance, I lost myself in the rhythm, swept away by the magic of the dancers' artistry. In this shared experience, time seemed to stand still, and the world outside the stage faded away, leaving only the rivetting performance and the powerful emotions it evoked.

The dancers' feet became instruments, pounding the floor with incredible precision and power. The sounds of their steps resonated perfectly with the music, creating a symphony of rhythm that enveloped the space. It was a thrilling auditory experience, the beats pulsating through the air and reverberating in the hearts of the spectators. Their hands gracefully gestured, conveying a story of love, longing, and deep emotion. As the dancers moved, their fingers delicately held the castanets, ready to unleash their rhythmic magic. Castanets are percussion instruments made of two small concave shells, traditionally made of wood or fiberglass. The dancer holds one castanet in each hand and uses their thumb and fingers to rhythmically strike the shells together, producing the characteristic clicking sound. With each flick of the wrist, the castanets clicked in perfect synchrony with the music, punctuating the air with their distinctive sound.

The dancers' skillful manipulation of the castanets, combined with their intricate footwork and expressive movements, showcased their exceptional talent. Every arm movement and facial expression connected profoundly to the music, the clapping, and the melodies. It was as if their bodies were translating the melodies and rhythms into a language understood by the heart, evoking a range of emotions within the audience. As I watched their performance, my body responded with goosebumps, repeatedly experiencing the powerful energy emanating from the stage. Sitting next to me, Tina was equally captivated and remained motionless throughout the performance.

As the performance approached its grand finale, a hushed excitement filled the air. The lights dimmed, and one by one, the performers were introduced, their names resonating with an air of reverence. The singers, percussionists, guitarists, and violinists were all talented musicians who had poured their hearts and souls into this unforgettable evening. And the dancers were the embodiment of grace, passion, and artistry.

Gathered at the center stage, bathed in the warm glow of the spotlight, they took a collective bow, their faces radiant with a mix of exhaustion and exhilaration. The audience, moved beyond words by the sheer brilliance of the performance, rose to their feet in a standing ovation. The thunderous applause filled the hall, echoing with appreciation and admiration.

In that moment, time stood still. Goosebumps cascaded down my arms and legs, a tangible testament to the depth of emotions evoked by the dancers' mesmerizing artistry. It was a culmination of months, even years, of anticipation—the perfect alignment of music, movement, and shared experience. Amidst the standing ovation, I felt an overwhelming sense of gratitude—gratitude for being present in that magical space, surrounded by people who shared the same love and appreciation for this extraordinary art form. I was thankful for the company of Tina, whose presence by my side enhanced every moment. The energy in the room seemed to align with the spirit of the evening, as if nature itself was celebrating alongside us.

Every second spent in the Palau de la Música in the spellbinding world of flamenco served as a testament to the power of music and dance to transcend boundaries and touch the depths of our souls. It was an experience that surpassed my wildest expectations, leaving an indelible mark in my memories. I knew very well that this was a night worth cherishing, a story to be told for years to come.

As I reflected on the perfection of that evening, I felt a sense of fulfillment and contentment. It was everything I had hoped for and more—a symphony of emotions, a feast for the senses, a moment of pure magic. Grateful doesn't even begin to capture the depth of my appreciation for that beautiful evening. I was glad I had patiently waited, manifesting my wish, and the Universe sent me a perfect companion to share the night with. With Tina by my side, every moment became even more meaningful and unforgettable. Our shared delight in the performance and the exquisite beauty of Palau de la Música made the experience even more profound.

Nataly

It had been nearly a year since my unforgettable "marathon" hiking month with Nataly, and the passage of time had brought about significant changes in Nataly's life. She had found the love of her life, moved in with him, and was starting a new career path that she was still navigating with enthusiasm and determination.

Nataly possesses a graceful presence, standing slightly taller than me, her long blonde hair flowing freely. Her impeccable sense of style reflects her vibrant personality, as she always appears chic and put-together, effortlessly exuding confidence. On this particular day, we both arrived wearing white tops by a delightful coincidence. Nataly had paired hers with silky pink pants adorned with an enchanting aquarium print, adding a touch of whimsy to her ensemble. She approached me with her signature big smile, "Hey, Nataly, it's great to see you. It's been a while," I greeted Nataly as we met up in the town of Sant Cugat for our regular quarterly catch-up.

"Hey! You look beautiful and sharp!" Nataly responded with genuine sweetness, fully aware of my tendency to stick to the same jacket, pair of jeans, and those familiar white Camper shoes that I wear daily—almost like a signature look. I had bought at least three pairs of those shoes without ever changing my choice—the ever-repeating ensemble. However, that day, I decided to step out of my comfort zone and show up with a white top and a silky long skirt, paired with my one and only Camper white shoe. I neatly tied my hair up and put on light makeup, something I rarely do since I decided to embrace a more "naturalist" style.

Her compliment was like a breath of fresh air, making me realize how comforting yet limiting my fashion choices had become. The familiar outfit had almost become a safety blanket, preventing me from exploring new styles and expressing myself through fashion. I had grown so accustomed to my repetitive look that I hadn't realized how much I was holding back from experimenting with different clothing combinations.

"Thank you! I just returned from Dublin, and I must say, the people there really inspired me. Despite the challenging weather, they dress impeccably and exude confidence in their social interactions," I shared enthusiastically, providing a brief update on my recent travel.

Nataly has always been an incredibly motivated person despite not yet finding the perfect job. She's constantly searching for the right fit but never complains about the stress she endures at work. Nataly greatly values who she is and how much she can bring to the table. As we strolled through the medieval old town of Sant Cugat, the sound of our footsteps on the cobblestone, we kept an eye out for a cozy café where we could enjoy a cup of coffee before our scheduled lunch.

We randomly chose to enjoy our morning coffee at Somewhere. Upon walking in, the warm and inviting decor welcomed us. There was a large wooden communal table, uniquely constructed with recycled ancient doors from the restaurant, where a few people were seated with their laptops next to their coffees, followed by several more subsequent tables. We requested a table on the terrace in their adjacent patio, where cascading bougainvillea adorned the walls around and above us. The vibrant purple flowers were starting to bloom, signaling the arrival of late Spring, and the bright color of the bracts added to the charm of our morning chit-chat moment.

As we settled in, Nataly couldn't contain her excitement and immediately shared her big news. "I have changed to a new job," she announced with her usual radiant smile and positive attitude.

"Wow! Congratulations! That's amazing news! What happened to the previous job? How did you find a new one so quickly?" I responded eagerly, my eyes widening with excitement as I leaned in to hear the full story.

"I decided to leave the company. The work environment had become incredibly stressful, and it was taking a toll on my well-being. On top of that, my boss had a habit of yelling at the staff whenever he was tense. I simply didn't want to continue working with people who made me feel uncomfortable," Nataly explained.

I deeply admire Nataly for always being the captain of her own life, consciously steering the path she wants to take. In my experience, I've encountered many individuals, including myself back in the day, who would continue to work in jobs they dislike or remain in toxic work environments simply because they found comfort in stability or fear of change. Experiences could range from bosses yelling at co-workers, taking credit for their work, and demanding weekend non-paid hours to sixty-hour workweeks. Sadly, such situations have become all too common in the society I'm familiar with.

However, Nataly's approach is truly inspiring. She refuses to settle for an environment where her values are not recognized and respect is absent. Her determination and refusal to compromise serve as a powerful reminder of the importance of prioritizing self-love and seeking environments that foster growth and appreciation.

Nataly's determination goes beyond making bold career choices; she actively seeks personal growth by engaging with a motivational coach who guides her in cultivating a positive relationship with money and building a fulfilling life. She delves into LinkedIn, utilizing the expertise of a professional editor to guide her in maximizing the strengths of her profile. Additionally, she reaches out to her network to explore various opportunities and delves into comprehensive research to understand the potential of different careers.

Fearlessly embracing new opportunities, Nataly operates with a mindset that says, "This is not about what if, but about taking action." She is undoubtedly the kind of woman who acts when she senses it's the right time, embodying a proactive and confident approach to life. Her unwavering commitment to personal and professional growth is a testament to her resilience and determination, inspiring those around her to do the same.

As we savored our coffee, I was drawn in by Nataly's inspiring journey, and I felt compelled to share my recent news: "My divorce has finally been finalized. My kids and I can finally return to Taiwan after nearly four years without seeing family."

"How about your dating life?" Nataly continued to expand the conversation.

"It's been quite an adventure! I'm enjoying my casual relationships at the moment. I was kind of seeing this artistic Catalan guy on and off, followed by a super-tall Dutch fellow that I mentioned to you last year. But hold on to your seat, because here comes the exciting part! Next month, I'm jetting off to Italy to meet an Italian man I met online a few years ago. He's a San Francisco resident but turns into a globe-trotting Italian family man every summer. He invited me to Milan for the last two years, but I didn't feel right. However, this year, he's offering me Puglia, and I thought, why not give it a shot?" I shared some lighthearted news with Nataly.

"So it's not the man causing the trouble. It's the location he has chosen!" Nataly replied as we chuckled together, savoring the humor in the situation.

Alongside this personal milestone, I expressed my current challenge of facing banking issues with the e-commerce startup I had established a few years ago. Feeling somewhat adrift in my career path, I confided in Nataly, saying, "Growing up, my career and academic choices were always driven by what other people thought I should or wanted me to do. The main reason I left my regular office job was because I was never happy with that kind of schedule. In the last few years of experimenting with being a freelancer, although my financial situation wasn't at its best, my happiness and freedom were in the right place. I know this is the kind of life I like and want. But I must admit, my financial status was stable when I had a regular job. Nowadays, my money situation is always my main concern, and I am always seeking opportunities to hustle. So, at the beginning of the year, I edited my resume and considered starting to apply for office jobs again."

"However, I want to be a writer. I have always harbored a desire to write a book, which is something I've talked about for years. I'm in a moment of feeling so lost that I don't know what to do. How can I shift my focus from financial stress to finding motivation and creating the life I want?" I sought Nataly's feedback.

"No! Don't go back to a regular job, because you have already tried it for years and decades, and you know very well that's not the life you want! It didn't work! Don't put yourself back into that environment again!" Nataly quickly responded to my concerns. "Of course you are a writer. You have already been writing for years! Tell me what kind of topics or subjects you have in mind."

"As a single parent, I want to write something that can help other single fathers or mothers understand that single parenting isn't as challenging as it may seem," I shared. "A few years ago, I had someone called 'Annie' who helped me cross that bridge. It would be meaningful if I could be that 'Annie' for even one person struggling with single parenting." I revealed more insights about my intention to write the book, fueled by a desire to support and guide others in similar situations.

"Okay, you've already taken the first step by showing that you desire to write," Nataly affirmed. "Now, let's turn that desire into action. If you want to write a book but are unsure about the content, let's start with some research. We can look into potential publishers, explore different marketing methods, and even visit a bookstore to discover various genres and styles. I'll also share with you the motivational podcast I'm currently listening to and provide information on female entrepreneurship networking."

Nataly listed a range of practical steps I could take to get started. "Remember, small actions can lead to greater inspiration. Nothing will happen if you don't start, and your dream will remain just a collection of words." Nataly's encouragement motivated me to delve deeper into what kind of book I wanted to write and its purpose. "I've always enjoyed listening to your stories. You have a gift for inspiring and uplifting others. You have enough valuable content to share with the world, from your dating experiences to navigating single parenting. These are precious experiences that can resonate with so many people."

Her words fueled my determination to begin this writing journey and share my experiences with others. With Nataly's support and guidance, I started to believe that I could turn my dream into a reality and make a positive impact through my words.

I excused myself and went to the restroom. As I washed my hands, I noticed a quote underneath the mirror: "If you are searching for that one person who will change your life, take a look in the mirror." The words struck a chord, reminding me of the power and potential that lies within myself. It served as a gentle reminder that I can shape my destiny and create the changes I desire in my life.

We continued our afternoon by strolling through the elegant old town, enjoying getting lost, and exploring various boutique shops. While the clothes and accessories caught our eye, I observed Nataly's approach to each shop we visited. At the end of our interaction, she would confidently hand out her new name card as a proactive real estate agent. It wasn't just about the transaction or the items purchased; it was about the bold steps she took to make people aware of her new job and create potential opportunities for her future. Her actions spoke volumes about her determination and her commitment to making progress, no matter how small, toward her goals.

Little did I know that my encounter with Nataly would leave me brimming with inspiration. As soon as I arrived home that afternoon, I couldn't contain my excitement and reached for my trusty gratitude journal. It was the sixty-eighth day of my one-hundred-day gratitude journey, a practice I had established last year to counter the weight of negative self-talk during my divorce process. Little by little, throughout the journey, I had begun shedding the negative beliefs and limitations surrounding wealth, forging a vibrant and positive connection with the Universe.

Nataly's action plan brilliantly showcased that merely wishing for money or envisioning a better financial life falls short. Reaching our goals requires inspired and consistent action. Setting clear intentions and financial objectives, crafting a meticulous plan, and taking practical steps to increase income, reduce debt, or enhance financial literacy are paramount. Prioritization is vital, but remember, once the objectives and goals are in place, it is crucial to ground yourself in the present moment. That was one of the most significant *aha* moments—success thrives in the "now," only with our full presence.

I felt a newfound sense of empowerment and clarity as I continued to write in my gratitude journal, expressing appreciation for the guidance I received from Nataly and the growing awareness of the importance of taking actionable steps toward my goals. The energy and encouragement Nataly radiated during our conversation ignited an inferno within me. It propelled me to take that pivotal first step toward breathing life into my writing aspirations. It was a transformative moment, an awakening. As I settled in front of my computer, opening Microsoft Word, each keystroke became a brushstroke, artfully crafting the inaugural paragraph of this book. There were moments of typing, deleting, and retyping, but with every stroke, the words flowed effortlessly from my fingertips. It was as if Nataly's words had unlocked a hidden reservoir of creativity within me—a wellspring of inspiration waiting to be unleashed.

Before that very afternoon, I had only entertained the idea of writing a book, but after that lunch, I returned home and began crafting the first chapter of this book I had long dreamed of writing. Nataly's words of encouragement unlocked a wellspring of creativity and determination within me, propelling me forward on this exhilarating writing journey. Once again, this experience was a powerful reminder of the importance of surrounding yourself with the right people to grow and thrive.

The key question was, "What do I really want?" Every choice you make will move you in that direction. When you do that, the force of life will rise up to meet you. The Universe is abundant. Embrace the idea that there is more than enough money and wealth available for everyone and that we deserve a prosperous financial life. Living with this mindset helps open individuals up to receiving the abundance that the Universe has to offer. Nataly played a pivotal role in catalyzing this transformation within me. She propelled my focus from "I understand the concept" to "I got it! I trusted the Universe and leaped."

Summer Is Approaching

"Oh my God! It's scorching hot," I exclaimed as I arrived at Silan restaurant in Barcelona, craving Israeli cuisine. "Am I the only one feeling this heat?" I asked, walking toward Maddy and giving her a big hug.

"I knew you would be melting. We chose a shaded spot. This temperature is just perfect for me," Victoria replied, walking around the table and embracing me with a hug.

It was a warm late spring day, with summer just around the corner. The temperature outside was thirty degrees Celsius. Over the past year, some heatwaves reached up to forty degrees Celsius. Coming from the tropical weather of Taiwan, I felt a bit embarrassed to admit that I struggled to cope with the heat. Anything above twenty-five degrees felt uncomfortable to me. The summers in Barcelona over the past few years have always driven me crazy, especially when trying to sleep with higher nighttime temperatures that increase wakefulness. There's a saying that you can add more clothes in winter, but only so much you can take off in summer.

Additionally, compared to the USA and Taiwan, approximately 90 percent of households have some form of air-conditioning, while in Spain, only about 10 percent of homes are air-conditioned. Primarily, air conditioning is considered highly inefficient; it is expensive to install and operate. It is not cost-effective, and typically, in Barcelona's mild climate, it is beneficial for only a few weeks each summer. Most households, including mine, rely on fans. However, as much as I agree and would like to practice a sustainable living style, it becomes unbearable during those few weeks of heat waves without air conditioning. In my pre-Barcelona life, cool air was always a necessity, or I would say, part of many people's lives.

On the other hand, Victoria is from Lithuania, which has a much cooler climate, and I don't understand how she stands the heat! She loves the sun and enjoys the sensation of warmth on her skin. If we were sitting on a terrace, I would definitely choose the shady side, most likely wearing my Boston Strong cap and sunglasses, while Victoria would be more than happy to sit on the sunny side where the sun shines directly onto her face. She would relish every minute of it, appreciating the climate with style.

As we settled down, I asked Victoria how the ladies had been doing over the past week. "Weren't you supposed to go to Berlin for a job?"

"No, it didn't work out in the end. It's been a quiet week, but I'll be shooting in Madrid next week," Victoria shared.

"Speaking of Berlin," I eagerly chimed in, wanting to share a story, "I was talking to my friend Madoka, who lives in Berlin, and she told me about her struggles to get a visa. Then, during a parenting playdate group two days ago, I noticed there was a parent from Berlin. I debated whether I should ask him if he had any possible contacts to help Madoka. But before I could make up my mind, the playdate was over. I usually don't engage in conversations with fathers at school to avoid any misunderstandings. That's probably why it took me so long to draft out a proper phrase to ask something like this."

"Me too," Maddy confirmed, nodding as another mother.

"So I went home and translated my mental message into text, trying to make it as neutral as possible. I double- and triple-checked to ensure it didn't sound too crazy to ask for visa networking help from someone I didn't know," I continued, with both Maddy and Victoria listening attentively. "Guess what! He didn't reply at all. I don't understand how people can just do that! Wouldn't it be better to simply say, 'No, I can't help,' rather than giving the silent treatment?"

"Yes, it happens in my line of work too. There are people who have a nice interaction with you but then completely disappear once you reach out with a friendly catch-up message," Victoria added.

"It's almost a daily occurrence in the real estate industry," Maddy sighed.

"Now, there's another playdate group this weekend. I'm having this dilemma about whether I should pretend I never sent that text and just ease out, or walk up to him and confront if he received my message, insisting on an answer," I said.

"No! I would just pretend nothing happened and focus on the kids' party. I would feel so uncomfortable confronting him for an answer if it was already turned down silently," Victoria suggested.

"Yes! I would totally walk up to him and ask. Otherwise, it would look even more suspicious, like you were intentionally trying to do something with that man. Hey, whatever, just ask. He should be mature enough to turn down politely if he doesn't want to help," Maddy once again confirmed her fearless manner.

"I think I'll try again! I asked myself, Should I be the crazy mom who asks for this kind of help or be the friend who has a chance for resources but doesn't attempt to reach out?" I paused momentarily before continuing, "I'd rather be the crazy mom." Laughter erupted as we all started to feel more settled in.

"How are your kids? When does summer vacation start for them? My kids' summer vacation will begin in two weeks, and we'll be getting ready to head back to Taiwan for almost two months this summer. I have decided not to sign them up for any camp or daycare, thinking it would be nice to spend more time with family instead, especially since it has been so many years since our last reunion. It could be a testament to my patience, temperament, and zen space for six weeks of 24/7 time together though! I might need to steal some emotional management techniques my kids are learning at school to help me get through it," I said, changing the topic jokingly.

"Oh my, I feel you. Kids nowadays are fortunate to learn about emotional management at school," Maddy remarked. "I don't recall learning about that while growing up in Sweden. No one ever delved into dissecting emotions and explaining the differences between anger, disappointment, being upset, feeling worried, being terrified, and so on. They even practice breathing exercises in one of their sessions. How about you guys? What was it like for you growing up?"

"No way," I quickly responded with a hint of humor. "In my culture, as an Asian, we were trained to down-regulate emotional processing. We were told to suppress our emotions. Most of the time, people didn't even know they were unhappy. I think most people can't even define emotions like frustration, anger, sadness, rage, or irritation. We live in a constantly moving society, seeking comfort through efficient services and the material world, where happiness is believed to lie."

"I grew up during the Soviet Union era," Victoria added. "We were taught to keep everything inside. In theory, emotions didn't exist."

Victoria's answers never ceased to amaze me. My understanding of the Soviet Union was pretty much limited to what I learned from my world history book in high school. My poor knowledge of history from class didn't really help until I started to travel and discover firsthand, either at historical sites or through direct conversations with people. Whenever Victoria described her childhood in Lithuania, it evoked a mysteriously interesting feeling within me. Her stories painted a vivid picture of a world I had only read about, adding depth and nuance to my understanding of history. I realized that during a two-hour lunch with these ladies, I could learn more about Sweden or Lithuania than in a semester sitting in the history or geography classroom.

"Oh, you won't believe what my older daughter asked me out of nowhere last night," I exclaimed. "She said, 'Mama, if I drink water, will my teeth grow bigger?' It surprised me that a six-year-old would ask such a question, showing self-awareness about her front teeth gap. With much surprise, my motherhood instinct kicked in immediately, and I reassured her, 'You are beautiful just the way you are, and your teeth are wonderful. Even if you don't like something, we can always consult a dentist, but I'm sure your teeth are healthy.'"

Maddy jumped in, sharing her own parenting experience. "My daughter refuses to eat her dinner lately because she doesn't want to grow taller. As the tallest girl in her class, she thinks she's too big."

"My girl is an introvert and sensitive. She usually keeps her feelings inside and doesn't disclose much, asking for space. I feel like I need to read some parenting books because I'm not sure how to handle this kind of situation."

"My kid is the same; she doesn't like to talk too much about her feelings," Maddy added.

"Maybe we need your help with some well-rounded astrology readings, Victoria. Please break down the sun, moon, and rising for us!" I said half-jokingly. We all laughed together, recognizing the unique challenges of parenting and the importance of nurturing our children's self-esteem and promoting body positivity.

It was a reminder that seeking support from friends and exploring different approaches can be valuable in navigating these situations.

"What are your plans for this summer?" It's a common question that people ask one another around late springtime. In Europe, many people take their August off for days to weeks for vacation. Again, it is not something I was accustomed to in my previous experiences in the USA, Taiwan, or Brazil. Summer vacation is truly a European thing, where there is a significant migration going on—Spanish people heading out while tourists from countries like Germany or France come in to enjoy the Spanish beaches and sun.

"I'll be going to Portugal," Maddy said excitedly.

"I'll be heading to Lithuania to see my family for two weeks," Victoria replied.

After living in Barcelona for a few years, I have come to appreciate their approach to living. They work hard and play hard; many love to travel and take time off for themselves and their families. Work isn't everything and definitely not the most important aspect of life that should take up most of their time. According to the locals' explanation, August is just too hot to work! Under the Spanish influence, I don't even understand how I used to work sixty hours a week, starting on Sunday evening, with only two to three weeks of vacation a year. Yet, I still felt guilty about taking vacations. I vividly remember one instance when I was scheduling time off with human resources, and under the description box, I simply put "vacation." Within a day, I was called into my boss's office and asked to explain what kind of vacation I was taking. I felt cornered to tell him why I needed the break, where I planned to go, and what to do. The culture was telling me, "Why are you taking time off? Other people are working hard. You will be replaced if you don't." It's refreshing to embrace a more balanced lifestyle that prioritizes rest and leisure.

I wrapped up my final lunch with the girls before heading back to Taiwan. Of course, I knew we would see each other in two months, but it was just that ever since I moved to Barcelona, these girls were right there for me from the beginning, during the most complicated moments in my early Barcelona days. Our bond was created over time through several lunches and coffees. They have seen their families several times, while I have always stayed put in our beloved city of Barcelona. It was my first time seeing my family after all those years and challenging moments that I had experienced. I definitely felt a sense of closing a significant chapter with enormous gratitude for having them by my side. I was happy and fully supported by them in reaching this milestone.

"Send us news from Taiwan! It feels so exotic to us. It's a different world, a different time zone." We embraced each other with tight hugs. It was a bit emotional because I knew they were the tribe the Universe had sent to me, holding me tight and propelling me forward, helping me laugh, teaching me about Barcelona, and providing guidance and direction. They were indeed my safe harbor of female wisdom where I could always park my soul without judgment, without feeling lost. They were my core and dear friends, and I knew in my heart that no words could express how lucky I felt.

Entering Rémi and Gigi's apartment, a bittersweet feeling enveloped the air. This would be our final gathering before we all prepared to bid farewell to Barcelona for the summer. Tina and Ben had their sights set on returning to Germany, while Kenan would soon be heading back to Turkey with his kids. Meanwhile, true to his adventurous spirit, Thomas would continue to wander the globe—cycling in Catalonia, embarking on El Camino Santiago for the second time and then journeying back to Belgium before going to Turkey with his daughter. Meanwhile, Rémi and Gigi planned to visit Turkey and Japan, setting off their exciting adventures.

I was the first to arrive, and it was also my first time visiting their apartment. I took in every meticulous detail of its minimalist Nordic design. Indoor and outdoor plants adorned every corner, breathing life into the space. The air circulation within the apartment was so comfortable that I didn't feel the heat. The terrace beckoned, seemingly ready to welcome the gathering of guests. I had intentionally prepared a matcha cake roll to celebrate the couple's upcoming Japan adventures. Embodying the true American spirit, Tina arrived at the party with six bottles of wine, bringing her high energy and adding a touch of excitement and anticipation to the gathering. The food was neatly laid out on the kitchen counter, ready to be served!

As the temperature continued to rise relentlessly, signaling the imminent arrival of summer, sipping a glass of cool white wine seemed like a perfect option to start.

"You must be excited to go home after all these years?" Thomas asked me.

"Yes, but I'm still trying to gather myself. I am excited, but I'm feeling emotional at the same time. After all, it has been years without seeing them. In addition to all the marriage dramas I have experienced, from my family's point of view, I had to handle everything alone. I wasn't sure how I would deal with their emotions. But I just wanted to stay present and true to my feelings. I didn't want to be like the old me who always tried to be perfect and showed nothing but that everything was alright. If I feel like crying, I think I will. The truth is, I'm happy now, and my life couldn't be better. I am appreciative of everything I am experiencing at the moment. But these past few years, I have gone through quite a bit and needed to stay strong to be the mother of my children. I knew I couldn't slack off and needed to hold onto my life tightly with a strong mind. Therefore, if I feel like letting go a bit to relax and let my family take over, I will allow myself to be vulnerable and accept all the love and support they offer without pretending I'm completely strong," I explained. "I come from an extremely traditional Taiwanese family. My father can give me a poker face, say nothing, no hug, no 'How are you?' but at the same time, he's feeling a tsunami inside his heart," I added, recalling the complexity of emotions that could arise in traditional family dynamics.

During our discussions about expressing love in our respective cultures, it became apparent that regardless of our diverse backgrounds, many of us were raised in a generation where openly expressing love and affection was not the norm. This wasn't just true for Taiwanese culture.

Thomas shared an amusing story to lighten the conversation. "I remember an Argentinean friend who finally mustered the courage to say, 'I love you,' to her father," he recounted. "There was no immediate response, and she thought it didn't go well. But two days later, the father simply replied, 'I reciprocate.'" We burst into laughter, understanding the complexities of expressing love in navigating this aspect of our lives.

Time flew by in the blink of an eye as we spent nearly six hours completing the lunch, thoroughly enjoying their company and the delectable French food they had prepared. It was a delightful culinary experience, and amidst our conversations, I discovered an interesting cultural difference. In France, it is customary to serve cheese after the meat, while in Spain, cheese is typically enjoyed before the meat.

"In Belgium, cheese is treated as an appetizer and just before dessert," Thomas added. It was a fascinating insight into the diverse culinary traditions of these countries.

"Are you excited about Japan?" I asked the host. "Just to prepare you ahead, Japan itself is essentially a collective society. The society is tightly organized and structured. In my opinion, Japan has the world's highest service standards out of all the countries I have visited. They are extremely respectful! Enjoy the customer service to the fullest. Trust me, as a European, you guys will be amazed by it."

"Yes! We are so excited. I've done so much research and was told that Japanese people do not speak English well enough to understand native English accurately. Is that true?" Gigi asked with excitement.

"I would say that's mostly true. Using Google Translate can be helpful, and it's important to speak slowly and use short sentences. Japanese people will listen attentively for sure. I have had to use Google Translate to order food in Kyoto, especially outside tourist regions," I said, comforting the couple and setting their expectations.

"Alright, we will ensure our SIM card works to use Google Translate!" Gigi said, taking notes. "How about shopping? I would like to buy a new camera."

"Check out Bic Camera for electronic products. You should also try entering the Don Quijote store, where you'll be overwhelmed by shelves filled to the max with goods. Both shops will make you feel like you're on an adventure full of surprises. Many Don Quijote stores, especially the ones on major shopping streets, are open 24/7 to cater to the shopping needs of travelers at any time. Don't forget to bring your passport because you can do your tax return directly in-store," I shared, providing as much information as possible.

"The summer heat does concern me a bit," Rémi said. "Actually, typhoons could worry me as well. I experienced one in Hong Kong when I went to Indonesia under typhoon conditions. My heart was pumping out of my chest," he added with a hint of anxiety.

"It will be hot, but most places have air-conditioning. If you are flying from the inland toward the Pacific Ocean, I guess that typhoons should impact less, as they have a greater impact on the ocean side. Don't worry, if the conditions are not good for flying, the airline company won't risk it," I explained with my best-educated guess.

"We don't like Disneyland roller coaster rides," Rémi said again, nailing it with humor.

"Oh, one more thing, you will be greeted with a Toto electric toilet. The toilet culture is a thing! I loved it. There's music playing, water spraying, and a heated toilet seat. The Japanese always take convenience into account in everyday life, and the Privacy button is no different. This is used to mask any unpleasant noises when using the toilet. It will play a flushing sound, a song, or some kind of ambient noise for a short while before shutting off automatically. You can adjust the volume with the plus and minus sign buttons above the word Volume. I wish I had this kind of toilet on my overnight dates with men so I could go to the toilet in the morning without stress," I said, laughing as I showed them a panel of basic buttons on this electric Toto toilet, all written in Japanese with a few simple icons.

"We need to watch a YouTube toilet guide or get a PhD to help us through," Rémi chimed in with his humor.

"How is your visa status going?" I asked. Ben and Tina had been dealing with this ongoing visa issue forever.

"To get me legit in Europe as an American, we will first need to get married in Germany and then move our residence to Spain. After that, we will apply for a freelancer visa. I will need to spend this summer working on these steps since my current visa is expiring very soon," Tina explained with ease and organization, knowing how the complicated and lengthy process works as an expat. Her solution-oriented mindset was evident in her approach to handling the visa situation.

"Wedding! Wedding! Wedding!" Kenan chanted. "We need a wedding; there are too many divorcees here!" he jokingly added, adding a lighthearted touch to the conversation.

Over the years, our bond has deepened as we have spent more time together, sipping beer, hanging out at one another's apartments, or attending festivals. Within this particular tribe of single parents and members of the LGBTQ+ community living in Spain as expats, we share a common trait of often being categorized as a minority within society. However, in the company of these beautiful individuals, we have forged our own majority, where we find solace and a genuine understanding of each other's unique paths.

Despite the challenges we encounter, our shared experiences have brought us together, creating a supportive community where we can wholeheartedly embrace our identities and celebrate the richness of our diversity. Together, we have nurtured an environment of acceptance and empathy, empowering us to navigate our respective journeys with compassion and resilience.

In this close-knit circle, we find comfort and strength in one another's company, knowing that we are not alone in the paths we tread. The understanding and acceptance we share create a safe space where we can freely express ourselves as a family. Our bond transcends the limitations of societal labels, uniting us as a supportive community that celebrates the richness of our diverse backgrounds and experiences.

"The next time we meet, in September, we'll be asking each other about our plans for Christmas," Rémi concluded our final meeting before we departed for the summer.

Chapter 5:
A Gift from the Universe

"Flow with whatever is happening
and let your mind be free. Stay centered
by accepting whatever you are doing. This is the ultimate."

- Zhuangzi

"Hello, Bella Hsin! How are you?" It was a surprise message from Antonello. "I will be going back to Italy this summer as usual. It would be nice if we could make time to meet."

It'd been almost a year since I last conversed with Antonello, an ambitious Italian man who had adopted San Francisco as his American home. He effortlessly spoke American English, his Italian accent barely discernible. He carried a resolute work ethic and an ambitious entrepreneurial spirit. Before venturing into the realm of entrepreneurship, he had embraced the life of an athlete as a footballer and swimmer, and he worked hard to complete his MBA, embodying the virtues of discipline and perseverance.

The specifics of our initial encounter elude my memory, yet Antonello's presence gained prominence during the COVID-19 pandemic. Like numerous others confined within our home walls, we sought a sense of companionship through a constant stream of online and offline activities, longing for something to fill the void. It was via Instagram that Antonello's presence became more conspicuous. I had observed his status as a long-time follower of mine, consistently displaying his appreciation through likes on my posts. However, we had never engaged in any substantial interaction. Or perhaps I was the one who initially started following him; the details escape me, though it's not of great significance.

Speaking personally, the concept of meeting people online remained entirely foreign to me. I had grown accustomed to the conventional, organic approach to dating before my marriage. When it came to initiating conversations online, I always preferred adopting a cautious and distanced tone. I would never take the initiative to begin a conversation in the digital realm. After all, how could I truly trust the person concealed behind the screen? It was a world where virtual interactions could easily mask one's true intentions or identity, leaving me hesitant to fully embrace this new avenue of connection.

In the early stages of our interactions, my responses to Antonello's engagement were simple and modest, mere tokens of gratitude or a quick string of emojis. I wanted to acknowledge his support for my digital endeavors, but I couldn't bring myself to engage in deeper conversation. He was, after all, an enigmatic presence—an unfamiliar figure lurking behind the pixels of a screen. There was a certain allure in keeping him at a distance, a mysterious entity whose intentions remained hidden in the digital domain.

But persistent and undeterred, Antonello continued to venture further into my world. His interactions grew bolder, evolving from fleeting reactions to genuine questions and personal narratives. It was as if he was peeling back the layers of his own story, sharing fragments of his life with me. Nevertheless, I maintained an air of reservation, responding with curt yet polite messages, careful not to reveal too much of myself. The words of Maya Angelou echoed in my mind: "When people show you who they are, believe them the first time." Despite Antonello's seemingly genuine and sincere online persona, I couldn't wholly relinquish my skepticism.

"How did you manage to settle in the USA? As an expatriate who once resided there, I understand the challenges of securing a residential visa. And yet, there you are, holding an American passport."

"I won the green card lottery," Antonello replied, causing me to pause and contemplate the authenticity of his statement.

Months drifted by, punctuated by this delicate dance of distant connection. Antonello's messages arrived with consistency and regularity through my online interactions. Around 6:00 p.m. each day, I could anticipate his appearance on my screen. However, our interactions were not intense exchanges held before the monitor; they were more of greetings and slow updates on our days. Even so, I remained cautious about divulging too much of my personal life. At times, I would even candidly question why he invested time in me through the screen when I did not intend to fly to San Francisco to meet him or pursue any form of relationship.

Interestingly, instead of deterring him from the connections, it did the opposite. Slowly and unconsciously, I discovered a certain comfort in the familiarity of his presence, even though it lingered within the bounds of digital anonymity. The rhythm of our exchanges crafted a delicate equilibrium, a fragile thread that connected us across time and space.

Then, during one exceptional week, the messages abruptly ceased.

"Where is Antonello?" I thought. Without hesitation, I grabbed my phone and typed out a message, extending my virtual hand toward Antonello for the first time. It was a decisive moment that revealed the extent to which I had become enraptured by this digital persona, even without realizing it. The simple act of reaching out to him was a testament to the magnetic pull he had exerted on my thoughts, drawing me deeper into the enchanting realm of our online connection.

What sets Antonello apart, and what truly captivates me, is his sweetness. His words carry a gentle melody, a symphony of serene and charming sentiments that consistently bring a smile to my face. In those fleeting moments of reading his daily messages, my spirits were lifted by his endearing expressions—a treasure seamlessly woven into the fabric of our connection. Most days, I would be hypnotized by his poetic prose within the virtual realm. In my reality, however, two kids would clamor for my attention, their voices repeatedly calling out, "Mama." Amidst the chaos, I would dart in and out of the kitchen, attending to chores and preparing for our daily routine. I suppose Antonello's text messages gave me a brief moment of tranquility, akin to reading a fairy-tale story, even while juggling the demands of those I hold dearly.

Having lived in the States during my twenties, I understood the concept of the American dream. This shared perspective broadened the horizons of our conversations, bridging the gap between our experiences as individuals who had departed our respective home countries to live abroad. We delved into subjects that resonated with both of us—unique challenges and rewards encountered by foreigners in America set against the backdrop of the familiarity of European life. These discussions erected a sturdy foundation for our connection, allowing our conversations to glide effortlessly and enabling us to plumb into the depths of our shared experiences.

While navigating the intricacies of our online bond, I was also fascinated by the amalgamation of cultures within Antonello. He embodied the American dream while remaining firmly rooted in his affection for Italy. This unique blend of identities wove a narrative that progressed with each conversation we shared. It was much like my own journey; having lived abroad across various cities for numerous years, I no longer felt solely Taiwanese. However, my connection to Taiwanese cultural perspectives still lingered in certain aspects. Together, we explored the tapestry of our interconnected lives, embracing the similarities and differences that enriched and deepened our connection. Before I could fully comprehend it, our conversations began to flow more freely, evolving into exchanges of substantial length, as if writing slow, intimate letters rather than instant text messages. The connection between us silently grew stronger and closer with each passing day.

In one such conversation, Antonello shared a snippet of his past. "I lived in Spain before," he revealed, his words laced with a hint of nostalgia. His mention of this vibrant city awakened memories of his time there, accompanied by a beautiful Valenciana girlfriend, cycling through the streets and relishing in the charm that Valencia exuded.

There was an undeniable charm in Antonello's storytelling approach, consistently infused with confidence. The deliberate selection of his words to frame his sentences had a way of conjuring vivid images in my mind. I could nearly envision him—a dashing Italian figure—pedaling his bike with a carefree spirit, navigating the sun-kissed lanes of The Turia Park alongside his exotic companion, enveloped in laughter. The very idea ignited a surge of adventure and romance within me.

"I think she still has my bike," he added with a hint of amusement, punctuating his story with a touch of wistfulness. It was a playful remark that revealed a glimpse of the person he once was, a person intricately tied to the memories and connections he had formed along his journey.

My imagination started to run wild, conjuring an idyllic tableau where I cycled alongside this charismatic, attractive Italian man. His athletic build and golden skin tone exuded an irresistible allure under the sun's golden rays. Our bicycles navigated through picturesque Italian landscapes, every pedal stroke ushering in new adventures. The Italian breeze caressed my face, while the scent of Italy permeated my senses. Guided by his expertise, we went on a culinary journey, savoring the delights of authentic Italian cuisine. The flavors danced on my taste buds as we indulged in delectable dishes, accompanied by the finest Italian wines and prosecco, creating a symphony of tastes and aromas that awakened my sexual senses.

As the night went on, passion ignited like wildfire—body against body, lips pressed upon lips—leaving us entwined in moments of intimacy that transcended mere physical connection. From the bed to the table, and from the couch to the bed once more, our bodies moved in a harmonious rhythm, embodying desire and pleasure intertwined. I drifted asleep on his shoulder, surrounded in the embrace of his wrapped-around arm. With the first rays of morning light, I would awaken to the sight of my Italian lover, his left hand holding onto mine as he gently kissed my forehead. Moments later, he would lovingly hand me a cup of cappuccino, a gesture of care and tenderness that spoke volumes about our connection.

Such vivid scenarios danced wildly in the recesses of my imagination. Even if it was just a daydream, I was totally entertained by the idea and seriously thought, "It would be really nice to experience something like this." If the Universe were urging me to remain optimistic and manifest my desires, I would take charge of my own narrative and get to the bottom of my Italian dream!

Months flew by, and our connection thrived with each passing day. Our conversations were filled with a vibrant energy, resonating with a shared excitement and anticipation.

"I look forward to the day I embrace you in person." As the summer season drew near, my romantic Italian began to express his desire to meet me in Milano, his words carrying an undeniable passion.

Within the framework of our online connection, making things work required mutual effort from both of us. We dedicated time to each other through video chats and text messages, navigating the challenge posed by our significant time zone differences. While he began his day, gearing up for work in the morning, I was engaged in the evening routine—preparing dinner, showering my kids, reading bedtime stories, and ensuring they were ready for sleep. During his evenings, he would be occupied with work, describing himself as "spreading himself too thin," while I juggled the responsibilities of preparing for school and starting our day, all while attending to my children's needs.

Antonello ingeniously discovered pockets of time to connect with me. Whether cycling to his weekly soccer game or finding interludes during our weekends, he skillfully created moments for us. Remarkably, these moments often were when I wasn't occupied with parenting tasks, mainly when the kids were with their father. This allowed our conversations to flow naturally. Of course, there were instances when we scheduled phone conversations, only for me to find myself too exhausted to stay awake as the time approached, while he likely wrestled with his busy schedule. Ultimately, It requires two to tango, and mastering the intricate steps takes hours of practice. It was the collective effort that sustained us through these months.

One element of our unconventional relationship that intrigued me was the space we willingly gave one another, a result of the physical distance that initially separated us. With the time zone difference at play, there was no need to worry about adjusting expectations for message timing or length. We embraced the freedom that distance afforded, understanding that our conversations would happen organically without pressure for immediate responses. Within this virtual realm, the idea of a concrete future seemed nebulous and uncertain. It was as if the very distance itself carved out a void where discussions about tomorrow held no urgency, rendering discussions of commitment unnecessary. Instead, we centered our attention on cherishing the present, relishing the transient moments of connection that transcended time and space constraints.

Meanwhile, my life in Barcelona continued progressing, with a deep appreciation for mindful living and pursuing my passions. Yet a presence lingered, a virtual companion who seemed to be by my side, attentively listening to my thoughts and experiences. It was a peculiar dynamic, existing in a world where physical proximity was absent, but emotional closeness thrived. I found comfort in this unique and low-maintenance relationship, treasuring the space and freedom it offered. Having Antonello as my virtual confidant, I reveled in the joy of sharing my life, unencumbered by the weight of expectations or the need for concrete plans. In this delicate dance of distance and intimacy, our connection flourished.

The Sexting

With Antonello's suggestion of meeting each other, a latent desire to meet him in person surfaced within me for the first time. His proposition of a summer rendezvous lingered in my thoughts for weeks, ushering in waves of contemplation that washed over me repeatedly. The question of whether I needed to address the nature of our relationship had not arisen previously in our interactions, which had primarily remained flirtatious and lighthearted within the confines of online communication. The notion of commitment or the level of seriousness in our connection had not appeared pertinent or necessary in our dynamic. While the prospect of meeting him face-to-face ignited excitement, an array of doubts continued to cloud my mind, and I remained uncertain about the answer.

The idea of encountering someone in person whom I had come to know solely online stirred a flurry of thoughts and concerns. In my opinion, journeying to Milano to meet Antonello, essentially still a stranger, held no certainties or guarantees. It marked a significant leap outside my comfort zone, a step that evoked both hesitation and doubt. Yet, beneath the surface, an undeniable sense of curiosity and longing stirred, leading me to repeatedly question myself: "Should I seize the opportunity to meet him in person?" I engaged in aligning my thoughts with my feelings, endeavoring to find harmony before taking any decisive action.

In my contemplation, I grappled with the notion of security. Was it reasonable to anticipate a sense of safety and familiarity when meeting someone for the first time? What kind of expectation am I setting for myself here? The answer eluded me; it was a moment to explore whether I was willing to embrace uncertainty and let go of preconceived notions.

Leaving Antonello's invitation hanging in the air, I chose not to provide a definitive response. There was still ample time—a month, to be exact—before I needed to decide. I allowed myself the space to think, to delve deeper into my thoughts, and to feel, seeking to understand my emotions and find clarity amidst the swirling uncertainties, because I knew something was missing that prevented me from making up my mind.

During this month, the intensity of our connection grew exponentially. The words we exchanged carried a new level of heat and passion, weaving a web of desire and anticipation. I vividly recall a particular night when Antonello painted a romantic scene through our chat, his words igniting a flame within me. He described himself drawing closer, his breath mingling with mine as he tenderly kissed me. With each word that appeared on my screen, it was a story that promised an exploration of sensual pleasures.

"I want to meet you in person," Antonello declared, his text carrying a mix of longing and anticipation. "When that day arrives, I will gently wrap my fingers around your waist, pulling you closer to me. At that moment, I will feel the warmth of your breath against my skin, synchronizing with the rhythm of your heartbeats."

"My eyes will gaze into yours as we stand there in silence, without a single movement," I texted back.

"I let my hand move slowly, caressing your neck, trailing down to your shoulder, and gently making its way to the side of your breast. Continuing further, my fingers trace your waist until they finally rest on the edge of your skirt," Antonello continued, his expression of imagination retaining its romantic essence.

I could sense my body growing warmer, my heartbeat quickening its pace. The desire to continue surged within me, yet a nervous hesitation held me back.

"It's time to sleep. Good night!" I responded swiftly, abruptly retreating from the conversation.

I knew in my heart what might come next, and while a part of me was intrigued, I was not yet ready to delve into those uncharted waters—sexting—a territory so foreign to me that it gripped me with fear and uncertainty. My instinct led me to terminate the conversation swiftly.

As I surrendered to slumber that night, a mixture of curiosity and conflicting emotions left me feeling overwhelmed. Even though it wasn't conveyed through videos or images, just text alone, I was still uncertain whether it was a prudent idea—or perhaps even appropriate. I knew for sure that I didn't want my daughter to send her sexy pictures to anyone! In the tranquil solitude of my room, I began delving into the depths of online research, seeking validation and understanding. I entered questions such as, "Is sexting normal?" "Is sexting appropriate?" and, "What are common practices in sexting?" The search results inundated my screen, presenting a plethora of opinions and perspectives. Amidst the sea of information, I longed for reassurance. I plunged further, scrolling through forums, reading articles, and absorbing the firsthand accounts shared by others. With every click and search, I inched closer to unraveling the mysteries of sexting.

Within the depths of the online world, I realized that the answers I sought were not readily available. Ultimately, the decision would rest with me, for there was fundamentally nothing wrong with sexting, and it was within my power to discern what felt genuine and appropriate for me. It hinged on whether the person I engaged with made me feel comfortable to explore that aspect of myself. The choice was mine; no one could pass judgment or make decisions on my behalf.

I set aside my phone, allowing the screen's glow to dim, and turned inward, seeking solace within my intuition and inner voice.

"Bella Hsin!" Antonello's cheerful voice greeted me again a few days later, as usual, transcending the miles separating us. It was a typical San Francisco morning for him, and he extended his warm salutation before starting his day's endeavors.

"I just returned from the playground with the kids," I began to share the details of my day with him.

"I am looking forward to seeing you this summer in Milano! If you can make it," Antonello brought up the subject again.

"Yes, it would be nice to meet in person. What would you like to do if I come?"

"Many things! I would take you to my apartment immediately after picking you up from the airport, walk you through the door, gently push you against it, pin your hand above your head, and start kissing you. I desire to feel your body close to mine, to indulge in the scent of your skin."

"Where would your other hand be?"

"Gliding all over your body, trailing down your neck, and playing with your nipple. I would then guide you slowly to the bed we'll share for a few nights. As I gazed into your eyes, our kisses would continue, and my hand would move down to your skirt. I'd gently spread your legs with my hand, sliding my fingers between them and exploring your depths. Allowing you the pleasure of the first round."

"I close my eyes, fully embracing the moment, my left hand cupping your face, our lips still locked together. My right hand gradually moves down to your waist, undoing your belt buckle and unbuttoning your jeans. Once they're loosened, my right hand would continue slipping into your underwear, exploring your contours, holding and massaging you."

"I remove your panties, skirt, top, and everything. Observing and feeling every part of your body."

"And I also remove every fabric you wear on your body. Touching every inch I can."

Our conversation continued without pause, with every word exchanged feeling vividly tangible, igniting an escalating desire that grew increasingly intense. The arousal was undeniable. My imagination ventured into unexplored fantasies, carrying me to new heights of sensation and marking a new intensity threshold.

As the summer "potential meet-up" drew nearer, Antonello mentioned that he had already booked his ticket back to Milano. However, he quickly added that his visit would be packed with commitments to meet friends and family. This would mark his first time visiting family post-COVID, leaving me feeling that I might not be his top priority, even just a few days. As a "global mover" who has spent much of my life living away from my hometown, I understood the busy schedules that often accompany homecomings. Yet, deep down, I yearned for a gesture from Antonello—a sign that he was willing to carve out dedicated time to be with me, even if it meant rearranging his plans. I longed for the romance and the invitation to be present in our interactions.

Above all, I didn't want to feel like I was simply fitting into his busy schedule by flying over. It was vital for me to feel that he understood the effort I was making to visit him and that he was willing to put in his effort to spend time with me. It shouldn't be a situation where his original plan was that we both arrived in Milano on the same day, mainly because he was eager to see me within his tight schedule, while I would come before he even reached Milano. Furthermore, he had to leave for Puglia in the morning, where his family resides, before my afternoon flight took off back to Barcelona. Additionally, I was reasonably sure he might be tired after a long flight and need time to adjust to jet lag in the first few days.

Antonello possessed a unique personality that enchanted me from the moment we started chatting. He shared his ambitious journey as a professional basketball player, recounting his courageous leap to fly to America on his own. He passionately described his humble beginnings as a waiter in an Italian restaurant and his gradual ascent from waiter to entrepreneur, providing consultancy to Italian restaurants in San Francisco. I admired his resilience and determination.

However, despite my admiration for his accomplishments, a recurring theme consistently emerged throughout our conversations. He often portrayed himself as perfect and flawless. While I valued the space, freedom, and intimacy we shared, something just didn't sit right with me. I've always held onto a personal motto since my early years: "When in doubt, don't move."

The standard that I would like to set for effort in meeting a man, as well as my insecurities, sparked an internal mental dialogue that steered me in a different direction. Instead of eagerly embracing the idea of meeting Antonello in Italy, booking my tickets, and making my "fairy-tale dream in Italy" come true, I was contemplating the opposite path.

After a few days of wavering, I reached a resolute conclusion: we were simply online chat friends, akin to pen pals from a bygone era. There was no real future awaiting us; deep down, I didn't desire one either. It seemed wiser not to begin something that held no promise. And so, after a few more days of contemplation and internal debate, I finally mustered the courage to convey my decision to Antonello: "I won't be able to make it to Milano this year. I hope you have a fantastic summer with your family." It was a message fueled by a mixture of self-preservation.

In making this choice, I sought to honor my worth and prioritize my emotional well-being. I recognized that if our connection were to blossom into something meaningful, it would require enormous effort and investment from both parties. The dynamics of our relationship felt imbalanced, and I couldn't shake the feeling that I deserved more than being an afterthought in someone's busy schedule.

Instead, I packed my bags for Switzerland that summer—fulfilling my travel dream!

Dreaming of Switzerland

Antonello and I spent the entire summer without speaking, even though he was just a two-hour flight away. Our conversations dwindled to almost nothing after I made the decision not to go to Milano. While I did miss him, I found comfort in maintaining my distance. I preferred not to rush into meeting him. It became apparent that we weren't quite ready for that step.

Surrounded by the breathtaking landscapes of the majestic Swiss Alps, I allowed the mountains to wash away any lingering thoughts and worries. Standing atop the Eiger Trail, I found solace in the serenity and tranquility of the moment. It was a powerful affirmation that I had made the right decision by listening to myself and following my intuition.

Instead of succumbing to the fear of missing out or trying to force a connection that wasn't meant to be and diving into the arms of this Italian character I had invented, I let go and surrendered to the flow of my journey. This newfound sense of freedom and self-assurance was a profound lesson for me. In the past, I might have found myself clinging to a situation, desperately trying to make it work even when doubts were gnawing at me from within. This approach also extended to my marriage and career, which had damaged my well-being over the years.

But this time, I opted for a different path. I let go of any attachments and fully embraced my solitary journey, free from resentment or regret. It was a liberating experience, understanding that I was honoring my needs and remaining true to myself.

As I trekked through the alpine trails, from the Eiger to the Gelmersee circular hike, each step became a symbolic affirmation of my personal growth and resilience. I stood in awe of the natural world's beauty, realizing that as nature evolves and changes, so does our life's journey. There was no need for me to hurry or push anything. In those quiet moments amidst the grandeur of the Swiss Alps, I discovered a deep sense of peace and contentment. I realized that I didn't need to chase after opportunities or force situations to happen. By trusting in myself and allowing life to occur naturally, I opened myself up to genuine connections and meaningful experiences. The Universe has its way of presenting what's best for me. The right relationships and experiences will naturally come to me in due time, effortlessly and authentically. And right now, it was the dream of Switzerland, a dream I had longed for for decades.

As I continued my hike through the Swiss Alps, I carried this newfound wisdom with me, feeling both at ease and tense amidst the towering peaks surrounding me. Every step required my full attention, a lesson in being present with each footfall. I confronted my fear of heights, realizing that the Swiss way taught me the value of taking deliberate, mindful steps forward, rewarded with irreplaceable views before my eyes. Two particular instances stand out: as I continued to walk carefully, placing each step mindfully, I inadvertently landed my sneaker next to two rocks stacked upon one another. My feet touched the ground first, and as I looked down, I realized I was less than an inch away from a snake's body! While my heart raced, I chose to continue marching forward with bravery. During another part of the hike, I encountered a narrow path that required me to hold onto a metal string affixed to the wall without falling down the cliff. This threadbare trail supported hikers as they traversed this challenging section. Once again, I confronted my fear head-on. The mountains and the stunning lake became my silent companions, reflecting the strength and resilience that had always been within me. With each step, I embraced the freedom to be true to myself, follow my path, and confront my fears, knowing that I have the capacity to navigate them.

The experience of choosing Switzerland over Italy taught me the significance of tuning into my inner voice, trusting my instincts, and embracing the serenity of solitude. The Universe answered my dream, the one that will fall into place at the right time. It marked a profound shift in my mindset. I learned to appreciate my self-worth, to establish the standards I desired for myself in relationships, and to discover fulfillment within rather than seek it externally.

One year had passed since Switzerland. In the middle of summer, out of the blue, I received a phone call from Antonello on a warm day while he was in Milano, making his way back to San Francisco after his annual summer break. We spent two hours catching up, eagerly sharing the stories and experiences that had unfolded in our lives over the past year. There was a comforting familiarity in our conversation, a sense of connection that drew me back to the memory of that winsome Italian.

During these two hours, something was noticeably different. It resonated in his tone and his shared stories, which became more grounded and realistic. He opened up about his vulnerabilities, revealing some of his challenges and the personal struggles he was encountering. The stress he had endured had led him to lose around 10 kg in weight. He expressed feeling lost and needing a new direction, so he had taken his time in Italy for some soul-searching.

During our conversation, I saw the other true side of Antonello. This was the side of him that was reaching out for support—a pair of attentive ears and the attention of someone who could listen without judgment and offer care. It wasn't the same Antonello who always seemed highly confident and almost perfect, the one who had previously left me skeptical about the character he had portrayed in the virtual world.

"We live abroad alone, without the immediate support of family. It's crucial to be especially mindful of the people you choose to surround yourself with. Protect yourself from toxic individuals. Even though I haven't been around much this past year, please know I'm always here if you need someone to listen. At the very least, this is something I can offer," I told Antonello empathetically, understanding the significance of being selective in the relationships we cultivate in our lives, based on my own experiences (especially considering the complexities of an ex-husband) and the effort I'd put into decluttering my relationships.

"We should definitely meet in person, darling Hsin. I truly believe we should seize the opportunity to make it happen," Antonello reiterated by the end of our conversation.

While I could somewhat relate to his sentiment and valued his persistence, in my heart, I harbored a private awareness that such a day might never materialize. Nonetheless, I responded with grace and optimism, understanding the potential allure of manifesting an Italian fairy-tale story. The prospect brought a sense of delight, imagining its possibility under the right circumstances, at the right moment, and in the right location.

Embracing the Uncharted

Another year had gone by, and I held my phone, reading Antonello's text: "Bella Hsin! How are you? I will be going back to Italy this summer as usual. It would be nice if we could make time to meet."

This time, Antonello's invitation carried a distinct tone. He proposed Puglia or any other location I wished to go. It felt almost as if the Universe had relayed my preference for Puglia over Milano to him, and he had taken careful note to ensure my comfort and anticipation for our rendezvous. He presented multiple options thoughtfully, assuring me of his flexibility and willingness to accommodate my co-parenting schedule, all in pursuit of aligning with my desired location and dates, just to be able to meet me for a few days. This refreshing shift ignited a new sense of possibility within me.

Could this be the moment I had been manifesting? The instance where my Italian fairy-tale story would at last transition from a mere fantasy to a tangible reality? It certainly appeared so. Antonello's willingness to prioritize our time, to acknowledge my needs and desires, made me contemplate that perhaps, just maybe, this was the right time for us to come together.

As I contemplated his invitation, I felt a sense of anticipation building up inside me. Puglia, with its charming landscapes and rich cultural heritage, a place I had never been, beckoned me with its allure. It was as if the Universe had conspired to bring me to this particular place, at this specific time, with this attractive Italian man to show me around!

I smiled to myself, thinking about the possible adventure that awaited me. I began to be convinced that perhaps it was time to let myself off the hook and treat myself to some doses of Italian romance. I'd been focusing on doing the "right" thing and the "responsible" thing; perhaps Puglia was where the opportunity had landed for me to step out of the box, unwind, and let loose.

Deep within me, a sense of contentment stirred as I contemplated how Antonello had persisted for three consecutive years, despite the knowledge that our future together seemed uncertain and the prospects for a long-term future were hazy. It was heartening to feel how he clung to that desire to meet me in person, a longing he was steadfast in transforming into reality, regardless of the paths our individual lives might take.

In a world where practicality often takes precedence, Antonello could have easily invited someone already in Italy or chosen another person from San Francisco. He had numerous options at his disposal. Yet he chose to extend the invitation to a woman who had done little more than engage in a few months of daily texting and turned down his offer. Antonello's persistent invitations had shifted from skepticism to possibility and eventually to a resounding, "Let's do it!" It was both refreshing and intriguing. I truly appreciated that he consistently embraced the potential of our meeting, believing that our experiences were worth pursuing for the sheer sake of exploration and the opportunity to create cherished memories. It spoke volumes about his character and determination to give us a chance, without any expectations, to finally see each other face-to-face.

I mean, let's be honest here. The wild thoughts of me riding bicycles alongside a sexy Italian and savoring the heavenly taste of a perfectly crafted cappuccino still danced in my mind. It was like a rom-com playing out in my head, and I couldn't resist the allure of making those daydreams a reality.

Sure, it may have seemed like a whimsical fantasy, but why not chase after it? Life is too short to ignore those quirky desires that tickle your imagination. Who knows, maybe I'd find myself pedaling through the picturesque streets of Italy, wind in my hair, and a goofy grin on my face. And that cappuccino? It would be more than just a cup of coffee; it would be a decadent blend of caffeine and possibility.

So, with determination and a pinch of naivety, I made up my mind. I would embrace the adventure, spontaneity, and chance to create a memory that would make my friends raise their eyebrows in disbelief.

Because, really, what's the harm in letting your fantasies take flight? Sometimes, it's those crazy, outlandish manifestations that lead us to the most unexpected and extraordinary story. And if riding bicycles with an Italian charmer and indulging in cappuccino bliss was on my bucket list, then, dammit, I was going to check those boxes with a flourish.

"I'm going to leap! I should. Why not?" I thought to myself. When stepping out of my comfort zone regarding casual relationships, Antonello was the one who truly put me to the test.

With a glimmer of excitement in my eyes and a skip in my step, I responded to Antonello's invitation, expressing my willingness to meet him in Puglia, and proposed a few possible dates that worked for me. One month later, I was clicking that magical Book Now button and securing my ticket to Italy. I decided to take on the invitation from the Universe and let the journey flow, allowing myself to experience where this path would lead for Antonello and me, to let the story continue.

The thought of going to Puglia triggered a mixture of emotions within me: curiosity, excitement, and a touch of apprehension. It was as if a door had been gently nudged open, revealing a glimpse of a myriad of possibilities. We found ourselves at the juncture where both of us were willing to step into uncharted territory, explore the boundaries of our connection, and see what could develop without the weight of expectations. As I pondered the significance of this evolving journey, I prompted myself to approach it with an open heart and mind. The allure wasn't solely in the outcome, but in the very act of exploration and the wisdom I would gain along the way. The tale of Antonello and I experienced unforeseen twists and turns, defying conventional reasoning. Yet perhaps therein lay the essence of life's most profound encounters—embracing the unknown, savoring the enigma, and uncovering the extraordinary within the ordinary.

"Is there anything I can do to make our trip unforgettable?" I texted Antonello.

"Just bring yourself and the desire to relax," he replied. "I will finalize the details."

I had made a wish to the Universe to have a beautiful Italian man showing me Italy, but I didn't expect it to be so off the hook in such an unexpected way. I mean, what details? I had no clue about anything.

To be honest, I didn't know Antonello very well. Our previous conversations were in-depth but also brief exchanges from a few years ago. I didn't want to create an imaginary version of him in my mind, setting myself up for potential disappointment. Instead, I wanted to embrace the adventure and get to know him in person without overthinking. Beyond finally meeting face-to-face, I wanted to discover who he truly was, his style, mannerisms, and likes and dislikes.

"How is your Puglia plan coming along?" Victoria asked at one of our regular lunches.

"Other than booking my flight, everything else remains unknown. I have no idea where that Italian guy is going to take me. I have never met him and don't know where I'm staying. He sent some sample links to the places he planned to book. Look at this beautiful place with a Jacuzzi and all that," I said, showing Victoria and Maddy the links.

"I watched *Judge Judy* in my college years, and I always remember she said that when something sounds too good to be true, it usually is too good to be true. But it's okay! I will go without any expectations as if the Universe wants me to sit back, relax, and let the plan flow without trying to control everything like I normally do. If it turns out to be something weird, I will still enjoy my time," I added.

"Life is like that! You have been a single mom who needed to control almost every aspect of your life to keep your girls going. Sometimes, you just forget that you deserve it! It's not like you met this guy just last week; it has been three years since you guys opened up the conversation. The invitation was not the first time either. You deserve to have someone doing everything for you. It's a present from the Universe. Just show up and have a good time! Trust that everything will be alright." Victoria's positivity is always there for me.

"Are you still planning to go to Puglia?" Days later, I met Kenan during one of our single-parent tribe gang-up sessions. "Yes, I am. Apart from booking the flight tickets, I'm pretty much clueless! What if it's a no-show?" I questioned Kenan.

"You know the guy, right?"

"Well, kind of."

"Italians are famous for being sweet talkers. Not sure how much you can trust them," Rémi added with a smirky smile jokingly.

"Hey, if it's a no-show, just find another hotel at the airport. You will still have a great time. Who knows, you might even meet some-one else there!" Kenan offered a solution with a positive mindset.

"Yes, I'll still enjoy the trip, even if it's a no-show. I'll call you if that happens!" I told Kenan, needing to feel he would stand by if anything went wrong.

"Hey, if the Italian plan doesn't work out, Ben and I will find you a verified German guy with a sweetheart in Bodensee when you visit us at the end of August! Enjoy Italy. A German is on the way! Let's see who makes you believe in love again!" Tina chimed in with a big laugh, being supportive as usual.

My trip to Puglia, being with Antonello, was a journey of finding comfort in not knowing, letting things flow, and having faith that they would flow naturally.

The Italian

"On board, see you in about two hours," I texted Antonello, partly testing the waters to see if this would be a potential no-show. However, Antonello responded quickly, bringing a sense of relief.

As my flight arrived at Bari airport on time, I scanned the surroundings, searching for a familiar face—the face I had only seen through a screen.

"Where should we meet?" I patiently awaited his reply while questions swirled in my mind. "What should be the opening line when he shows up? Should we hug? Shake hands? One cheek or both?" My heart raced, unsure if the anticipation of meeting him or the worry of a potential no-show caused such nervousness.

The flight was scheduled to arrive at 15:40, and it was only 15:46. Reminding myself to be patient, I tried to calm my racing thoughts as I continued scanning the airport.

"Got stuck in more traffic than usual. I'll be there shortly. Hang tight," he messaged.

"Oh, thank goodness he finally replied." I breathed a sigh of relief, reassured that the thought of a no-show was no longer looming over me.

As I navigated my way to the drop-off and pick-up area, my nerves continued to flutter as the minutes drew nearer to the impending encounter. Amidst the anticipation, I attempted to enjoy myself fully in the moment, savoring the realization that this was what it felt like to meet someone in person after connecting online for such a long time. It was a novel experience, and I loved the excitement it brought.

My eyes remained vigilant, scanning each passing car. All of a sudden, I caught sight of this strikingly handsome Italian man, standing tall at 185 cm with his golden skin. I have to agree with Elizabeth Gilbert from *Eat Pray Love* when she spoke about the undeniable charm of Italian men. That is exactly what it is!

We embraced each other with a warm and tight hug. It was evident that Antonello knew how to charm someone at the right moment and in the right way. As he looked into my eyes, he swiftly complimented me, and as he held my hands, it felt as though we had known each other for a while. I didn't have to do anything or have the chance to decide what I needed to do. And there he was, holding my hand, walking toward his car. Despite not exchanging many words in the past years, the connection we had built virtually still lingered between us.

The hour-long ride from Bari airport to Locorotondo was accompanied by a multitude of questions swirling in my mind. As Antonello explained things to me, I was amused and trying to grasp the reality of the situation entirely. The Italian man I had known virtually for all these years was now physically right in front of me, and I was still in the process of absorbing it all.

"May I touch you? I'm still trying to wrap my head around the fact that this is real," I said, my excitement palpable. Unable to resist my curiosity, I reached out and gently touched his hand, arm, and face, as if needing to physically confirm that this virtual relationship had indeed transitioned into reality.

There was something hypnotizing about Antonello, not only in his charismatic face but also in the timbre of his voice, his actual voice, sounding next to me. I was immediately drawn to him, and my gaze fixed on him while he was driving. I reached out to touch him while listening intently to his stories. I looked forward to the opportunity to uncover his inner beauty in the days that lay ahead.

The car ride to Locorotondo seemed to whisk by in a mere blink of an eye, as if time itself was enchanted by the journey. As we ventured deeper into the narrow streets of the town, my eye beheld the mesmerizing sight of the unique Trulli architecture that adorned the landscape. The cylindrical structures with conical roofs, crafted from stone slabs and adorned with decorative pinnacles, stood as majestic symbols of the town's charm and heritage. The absence of mortar in their construction, achieved through the dry stone technique, only added to the allure and craftsmanship of these remarkable buildings.

As we approached the apartment Antonello had arranged, I was greeted by an aura of utmost exclusivity and serenity. It was a truly exceptional location within Locorotondo, enveloped in an atmosphere of tranquility that welcomed us with open arms. Antonello carefully noted my preferences—he understood my inclination for peaceful environments over bustling city centers and touristy areas. He listened to my desire for a serene vacation rather than a lively bar-hopping experience. The apartment was nestled in this oasis of calm, a sanctuary adorned with a sprawling garden that captivated the senses. Within the embrace of nature, a Jacuzzi awaited, inviting us to unwind and surrender to the gentle caress of warm waters.

What made this scene even more enchanting was the backdrop of Locorotondo's historical center, casting its ethereal spell upon the entire setting. As I stood in awe, the old-world charm and timeless beauty of the town's architecture danced harmoniously with the natural serenity of the surrounding landscape. It was a tableau that stirred the heart and ignited a romantic ambiance, as if the very air whispered sweet secrets of passion and possibility.

The bedroom we were about to spend a few nights in exuded an elegant grace, further enhanced by a ceiling with a rounded dome that created a cozy and intimate atmosphere. Positioned right above the head side of the bed, a small wooden window, resembling something out of a Disney movie, allowed soft beams of light to filter in, casting a gentle glow upon the room. A modest metallic chandelier added to the enchantment, diffusing a warm radiance that embraced every corner of the space.

As we stood in the heart of the apartment, the air was saturated with a serene calmness, a tranquil stillness that embraced us. Our eyes locked in a silent exchange, carrying unspoken words and a depth of understanding. Antonello moved closer to me, his hands delicately cradling my cheeks and neck, his touch gentle yet persistent. A magnetic pull drew us together, and our lips met in a tender and passionate union. It was a kiss that ignited a symphony of emotions within me. In that exquisite moment, butterflies danced in my stomach, fluttering with an intoxicating blend of excitement and arousal. It was a profound instance of surrender, where time seemed to stand still, the world outside faded into insignificance, and we allowed ourselves to be thoroughly enchanted by the present.

The Inner Wholeness

"Shall we take a dip in the Jacuzzi?" Antonello suggested with a smile.

"Sure, why not?" I replied, realizing my only plan was to simply follow Antonello's lead. The fairy-tale story of a charming Italian was unfolding before me, allowing him to reveal every corner of his hometown of Puglia that he knew and wanted to share with me.

As we made our way toward the Jacuzzi on the small stone path, Antonello extended his elbow, silently offering support in case the stones became uncomfortable to walk on with my bare feet. Happily, I took hold of his arm, allowing him to guide me step by step to the other side of the path, ensuring my comfort and safety along the way.

We eased ourselves into the warm embrace of the Jacuzzi, and a sense of detachment from the outside world enveloped us, leaving only the two of us in that intimate moment. Our conversation effortlessly flowed, expanding from the origins of our online connection to our thoughts and feelings about finally meeting in person. Time seemed to stretch as we delved into a myriad of topics, engrossed in each other's words and thoughts. There was a comforting ease to our dialogue, a sense of trust and openness that allowed us to explore an endless array of conversations without fear of judgment or hesitation.

Our conversation led us to contemplate the concept of wholeness within human beings. We discussed how, as individuals, we inherently possess a state of completeness, and the idea of seeking another person to fill a void and make us whole is a romantic notion that ultimately misunderstands our true nature.

"I don't see myself as a puzzle seeking a missing piece. I'd rather consider myself a beautiful painting; if I invite someone into my life, they should act as a frame that enhances it. They should bring value to my life instead of completing a part that I felt was missing," I expressed.

"The belief in needing someone else to complete us often arises from a sense of incompleteness or lack within ourselves," Antonello explained, resonating deeply with me.

I nodded in agreement, eager to delve further into the topic. "This belief is rooted in an overidentification with the ego, which is a false sense of identity created by the mind's thoughts and judgments," I added, elaborating on his point.

"The ego perpetuates the illusion that we are separate entities, disconnected from the world and from one another," Antonello continued, delving deeper into the conversation. I listened attentively, intrigued by his insights.

"It's crucial to acknowledge and connect with our inner selves in the present moment of consciousness," I shared, underscoring the importance of being fully present.

"It's through awakening and self-awareness, independent from the external circumstances or relationship, that we can genuinely experience true fulfillment and wholeness," Antonello concluded, his words carrying profound wisdom. Our words flowed like a harmonious symphony, each thought complementing the other with a shared understanding.

We both acknowledged that only by being fully present in the here and now, we could experience a profound sense of unity with ourselves, others, and the world. This conversation had set the tone for the days to come.

The weather was just right—neither too hot nor too cold—as we immersed ourselves in the soothing waters of the Jacuzzi. With every passing moment, we shared our stories, dreams, and aspirations; our conversations flowed effortlessly. The Jacuzzi became more than a vessel of warm water; it was a sacred space that added a new depth to our connection.

Our voices carried nuances, intonations, and subtle inflections that conveyed emotions impossible to capture through typing alone. The person before us was more than just a digital presence; it was a living, breathing soul. It was a dance of verbal exchange, where the rhythm of our words mirrored the rhythm of our thoughts. It was as if we had each other's minds. In this intimate setting, with each passing moment, we learned more about each other. With the backdrop of Locorotondo's historical center behind us, enveloped by endless olive trees and verdant greenery, the scene still felt like a dream at that very moment, akin to a scene from a movie.

After indulging in the cocoon of the Jacuzzi, we retreated to the privacy of our space for a rejuvenating shower that turned into a series of intimate moments. The gentle patter of the shower's touch became a rhythm of desire, a symphony of closeness that enveloped us. In this sacred space, the water droplets became celestial messengers, flowing over our bodies as if whispering secrets of passion and affection. Our hands, tender and deliberate, communicated volumes through the delicate language of touch. We took turns cleansing and cherishing one another, exploring and bestowing pleasure upon each other.

Locorotondo

Antonello, always the gentleman, clasped my hand, and together, we set off on a leisurely stroll toward the historic center of Locorotondo, ready for a delightful dinner. The streets welcomed us with quaint charm, lined with ancient buildings that whispered stories of the town's rich history. The slight uphill path didn't deter us from conversing; we kept talking while catching our breath, walking hand in hand, savoring each step. As we strolled side by side, the soft cadence of our footsteps mingled with the distant echoes of children playing and the tantalizing aromas of Italian cuisine wafting from nearby trattorias.

As we approached the outskirts of Locorotondo town center, the ancient stone buildings stood tall and proud, their weathered facades adorned with intricate details that told stories of generations past. Each step we took transported us to a bygone era, where time moved at a different pace. To our right-hand side, we spotted a park that offered a breathtaking view of the Locorotondo skyline, casting a mesmerizing array of colors across the horizon.

We stood there in tranquil silence, taking in the beauty of the moment. The sky morphed into a vibrant canvas, with orange, pink, and purple hues adorning a breathtaking backdrop. The sun gracefully descended beyond the horizon, leaving behind a trail of soft rays that danced across the evening sky, casting a gentle, warm glow over Locorotondo. As the sun bid its farewell to the day and the sky transitioned into twilight's embrace, my heart swelled with deep appreciation and wonder. At that very moment, I truly began to believe the fairy-tale story I had manifested had indeed started.

We continued our journey through the beautiful streets of Locorotondo, where the town's unique charm materialized before our eyes—the narrow streets adorned with cobblestones meandered through the enchanting surroundings. Old stone buildings stood tall on either side, their facades telling tales of centuries past. The tantalizing aromas of Italian cuisine filled the air, teasing our senses and awakening our appetites. Locorotondo revealed its culinary treasures to us, presenting a plethora of options that made our decision all the more delightful yet challenging. Amid the quaint alleys and hidden corners, we explored with shared excitement. Antonello's firm grasp on my hand conveyed a sense of assurance and connection, as if he were guiding me through the streets of Locorotondo and this enchanting chapter of our story. In that delightful uncertainty, we found joy and a sense of adventure.

As we continued searching for the perfect dinner spot, we stumbled upon a small restaurant within the maze of streets. It was adorned with a simple table under a canopy of twinkling lights. Delicate decorations hung overhead, casting a gentle glow and creating an intimate ambiance. The table was draped in a crisp white tablecloth and adorned with flickering candles that danced to the rhythm of the evening breeze. Antonello's hand, still securely holding mine, guided us to our seats at the table. I entrusted Antonello with the entire arrangement for dinner, as I wanted to understand his tastes and preferences and the nuances of typical Italian dinner fare. It was an opportunity for me to dive into his culinary world.

Our meal commenced with a delightful offering of olives and *taralli*. Taralli, a traditional Puglian treat, is a small, crispy bread dough ring that is typically infused with the rich flavors of olive oil. It is a beloved snack or accompaniment to meals in the region. Taralli comes in various sizes and flavors, ranging from the miniature, bite-sized versions we enjoyed to larger varieties known as *taralli giganti*. These larger taralli are often enjoyed as a satisfying bread alternative as a savory snack.

Our evening began with the delightful clinking of two glasses, each filled to the brim with the classic Italian spritz. Despite my multiple visits to Italy over the years, it was my first time experiencing a spritz! Curiosity danced on my taste buds as I took that inaugural sip of the effervescent cocktail. The delicate bitterness of the Aperol mingled in perfect harmony with Prosecco, while a subtle hint of zesty orange contributed a refreshing twist. With its well-balanced and invigorating notes, the drink captured the essence of Italian *aperitivo* culture. It was a delightful introduction to the pleasures of the evening.

Seated at a cozy restaurant in the company of Antonello, our conversation delved into the complexities of relationships and the interplay between ego and obsession. As we exchanged our thoughts, I recounted moments when my feelings had become entangled in a web of obsession and how my ego had taken control. With a sense of vulnerability, I opened up about my past encounters, specifically recalling my interactions with Stefan. I explained how my stubborn mind had led me down a path of painful experiences spanning fifteen years. My ego had driven me to fixate on certain outcomes, causing me to lose sight of aligning my thoughts and actions in the present moment. Within this toxic cycle, I was stuck with Stefan, a person I had never been in a relationship with. I just couldn't let go of this name for a long time. I realized that my obsession wasn't about Stefan as a person but more about my inability to accept that my ego had been guiding my path.

In this candid exchange, I laid bare the struggles many of us face in navigating relationships, the delicate balance between our desires, and the need to surrender to the organic flow of life. I shared how my ego-driven pursuits had created unnecessary tension and stifled the potential for authentic connection.

As the words flowed between us, Antonello listened attentively, his gaze fixed upon me with a sense of understanding and empathy. In return, he shared a personal story that shed light on the dangers of such entanglements. Antonello recounted an encounter with a single mother who had entered his life and gradually drained his energy.

"She initially gave me complete attention, like the missing piece I needed. And I reciprocated with my full attention. But then, over time, she started pulling back, offering only around 30 percent of what she used to give, while asking for extra efforts from me. My ego took control of the situation. I forcefully tried to make her return that original 100 percent because that's what I was used to receiving and believed I deserved. Instead of recognizing that moving on could break the pattern, I kept giving and giving," Antonello candidly revealed.

He continued, describing how his ego's dominance led him to persist in engaging with her toxic behaviors. Despite realizing the damage it was causing to his well-being, he was caught in a cycle of succumbing to her negativity. She mentally and emotionally mistreated him, fully aware that he was ensnared in this detrimental pattern. He couldn't come to terms with the fact that he hadn't achieved what was desired, and continued to desperately engage in these harmful dynamics, trying to obtain what he wanted.

As he narrated his experiences, I felt a profound connection and a sense of gratitude for his willingness to open up. These vulnerabilities we both expressed helped us create a stronger bond, rooted in our common human experiences. These anecdotes underscored our shared humanity, reminding us that we all journey through life as individuals. Our conversation served as a testament to the strength of self-reflection and the boundless potential for personal transformation.

The waiter presented us with a delightful appetizer platter, an assortment of antipasti snacks featuring slices of ham and various cheeses. As the platter arrived, I immediately saw the two exquisite oval-shaped mozzarella balls positioned among the other delicacies. Their appearance was fascinating, promising a creamy and flavorful experience. I couldn't wait to take the first bite of it.

Once more, Antonello showcased his charming nature by elegantly serving food on my plate. Being a single mother, I often find myself in the giver role, shouldering the responsibility of being the sole provider, which at times can be pretty overwhelming. Thus, Antonello's small yet thoughtful gesture of serving me resonated deeply with me. Despite its simplicity, it held great significance in allowing me to feel cared for, offering me a glimpse of the joy of being nurtured by someone else.

Concluding our delightful dinner, we proceeded with our stroll through the streets of the historic center, taking in all it had to offer. Once again, Antonello's hand held mine with a reassuring grip. Walking slightly behind him at a thirty-degree angle, I took the opportunity to admire his broad shoulders, tousled hair, and impressive height. Lightheartedly, I playfully contemplated if I might be suspended in a dream. It wasn't as though I was experiencing a Hollywood-style love-at-first-sight scene; it felt like this entire "virtual meeting" was unfolding by its flow. Whether it be friendship, a relationship, or a unique situation, it guided me to experience, perceive, and engage with life beyond the ordinary.

As we meandered through the narrow streets, we encountered fleeting glimpses of everyday life in Locorotondo. Passing under ancient archways, we caught sight of two young boys fully engrossed in their football game. Turning left, we came upon an Italian grandmother seated gracefully on a single black couch, reading her book, positioned strategically next to a small, round coffee table just outside her front door. I marveled at how she managed to place the couch in that exact spot. With the gentle evening breeze caressing her face, she appeared to savor a moment of serene solitude amidst the peaceful ambiance that enveloped her.

Antonello's voice interrupted my thoughts, pulling me back to the present moment as we walked toward the main gate. "Do you want ice cream?" he asked with a mischievous smile. I chuckled at his correction. "No, excuse me! It's gelato."

We made our way to a classic gelateria, entered the shop, and began selecting our flavors. I thoughtfully chose, "Stracciatella . . . Mmmmmm, and lemon!" As I looked up, I noticed two Italian men exchanging amused glances and couldn't help but burst into laughter.

"Your pairing is quite interesting," Antonello remarked, joining in the laughter.

"I'm sorry for changing my mind last time after saying I would meet you in Milano. While I found the concept of receiving attention without the pressure of putting too much effort into it quite appealing, I had a lot of insecurities lingering in my mind when it came to meeting in person. I wasn't certain if I truly wanted to pursue this path. At that time, it simply didn't feel right. There were a few reasons for my hesitation. First, I was unfamiliar with the world of online connections. Second, I had recently emerged from a broken relationship and was still in the process of healing. Third, you were also going through the tail end of your previous relationship. I wasn't sure if the whole situation was worth starting a new story, even though the idea of Milano with an Italian was tempting. It simply didn't feel like the right time back then, but now, in the third year, when you asked if I was open to the idea of meeting, I started to believe that you were serious about it," I explained, sharing my feelings with him while we were making our way back to the *trullo*.

"I believe there's already a level of trust that has been established between us, and I knew we would definitely meet one day.

I was always serious about it. I wanted to meet you in person!" he replied as we settled into the *trullo*.

Our gazes locked, and Antonello moved toward me with a gentle yet resolute stride. The air was charged with anticipation as he drew closer, and his touch ignited a spark as his hands found their place on my face, drawing me nearer. The warmth of his breath against my lips sent shivers down my spine. In that moment, time seemed to pause, and our lips finally met in a fervent embrace. The world around us faded, giving way to a rush of sensations and desires intertwining. In that intimate connection, we surrendered to the enchantment of the night. Our bodies moved in synchrony, every touch sparking a fire within us. With Antonello above me, I could feel the weight of his presence, his every breath harmonizing with mine. Within that sacred moment, we became lost in the rapture of our union, our souls entwined in a passionate dance. The room resonated with whispered words of affection and sighs of pleasure, creating a symphony that echoed through the night.

As I drifted into a tranquil slumber, Antonello's hand delicately held in mine, "This was all real." I closed my eyes with the final thought of the day.

Alberobello

Waking up to a beam of light filtering through the small wooden window above our heads, I observed as Antonello rose silently. He proceeded to attend to his morning routine, brushing his teeth and fastening his watch. Returning to bed, he leaned down to plant a gentle kiss on me, finding me still in the process of rousing myself from sleep. With one eye open, I beheld the sight of a handsome man before me, a morning treat that was akin to a delightful piece of candy.

As a single mom, as much as I adore my kids, this wasn't my usual wake-up call. My morning routine typically involves a swift awakening, getting myself ready, and slipping into my trusty motherhood sweatpants and T-shirt. Then, it's the process of rousing my kids, which can range from going smoothly to being a bit of a struggle. Two rounds of tooth brushing, taming unruly hair, and repeatedly saying, "Girls, have your breakfast. Come on, eat your breakfast. We're going to be late for school!" My background music is usually the sound of kids running around, with the chorus of, "Mama, Mama," repeating at least ten times in a minute, to exaggerate slightly. Tranquility rarely finds its way into my mornings; they're all about action.

"I'll brew you a cup of coffee," Antonello offered as I leisurely headed to the bathroom to prepare myself for the day.

As I emerged from the bathroom, a cup of Italian espresso was already waiting for me on the table, complete with a spoon and a neatly placed bag of sugar by its side. Everything was thoughtfully prepared and ready. The notion of a beautiful Italian man making coffee was a piece of the story I had envisioned in my manifestation. The Universe seemed to be gifting me "presents" at every turn. Oh my, on the second day in Puglia, I was still in awe of the sweetness of this fairy tale occurring before me.

We settled down at the rectangular wooden table that could accommodate six people, positioned in the center of the living room, facing each other. Antonello, already seated and waiting for me, set aside his laptop. He brought his cup of espresso closer, his smile radiating warmth as he focused his attention on us.

Over the span of an hour, while we relished our espressos, Antonello playfully dipped a small spoonful of Nutella into his coffee. "Mmm, the Marocchino definitely tastes better in Italy," he remarked with a satisfied smile.

I was intrigued. "I always thought that Nutella originated in Belgium or the Netherlands because it's so widely available in tourist areas and even at the airports."

Antonello's response was swift and certain. "No, Nutella is actually from Italy! It's manufactured by the Italian company Ferrero." Once again, I was enriched by his insightful tidbits of information.

"Before I settled in Barcelona, San Francisco was one of the cities I had contemplated moving to," I shared. "However, what deterred me from choosing it as my destination was primarily the widespread availability of guns in the United States. If I were alone, like two decades ago, living in the States, I might not have been as concerned. I've always appreciated the American way of life. But when you have kids, certain aspects start to weigh on your mind a bit more. Still, I can't deny that San Francisco is a stunning place to live."

Antonello continued elaborating on his feelings for San Francisco as he shared stories of his life as a daily biker in the city. With evident pride, he showcased his eye-catching red bicycle, which served as his primary mode of transportation. He emphasized how his strong legs enabled him to conquer the city's hills effortlessly. Moreover, he took the opportunity to delve into the intriguing phenomenon of fog formation around the Golden Gate Bridge in San Francisco.

"It is primarily influenced by the unique geography and meteorological conditions of the region," Antonello explained. "While it is not accurate to say that the bridge itself 'creates' fog, its presence can enhance the formation and movement of fog in the area. The bridge spans the entrance to San Francisco Bay, connecting the Pacific Ocean to the inland areas. This region features a deep and narrow coastal valley, and the bridge acts as a channel for cool marine air to flow into the bay. The topography, including the coastal hills and the constricted passage through the Golden Gate, plays a significant role in fog formation."

I listened attentively as he continued, "The Pacific Ocean and San Francisco Bay have different temperature characteristics, with the ocean generally being cooler and the bay slightly warmer. This temperature difference between the cool marine air and the relatively warmer air over the bay creates a boundary known as a *thermal inversion*."

"I agree with you that San Francisco is indeed a beautiful city. Funny how even as I talk about it here, I'm already missing it, and I've only been away for a week," he chuckled. "Alright, let's wrap up the science lesson," he said with a smile. "We should head out and perhaps dip in the sea today."

Sliding into the car and gearing up to drive, he stowed away his GPS, saying, "I'd rather trust my instincts for orientation." As he leaned his elbow on the storage compartment between our seats, his hand resting confidently on the gear shift, I delicately slipped my left hand into the space between his elbow and arm. Meanwhile, my left elbow found a resting spot, and I lightly hooked my arm around his, allowing me to gently touch his hand occasionally without exerting any pressure.

I had intentionally refrained from conducting any research prior to my journey to Puglia, not even casually scrolling through a few Instagram reel recommendations. That's how much I desired this trip to be characterized by its sense of the unknown and the unexpected. Upon our arrival in Alberobello, we were welcomed by a picturesque vista. This quaint town is famed for its distinct trulli houses, scattered across the landscape like enchanting fairy-tale abodes.

"It's still before 11:00 a.m. How about a cappuccino?" Antonello suggested, taking a glance at his watch.

"Oh, that's a good point! I nearly forgot that cappuccino is traditionally considered a morning drink in Italy," I acknowledged with a nod.

"Absolutely," Antonello chimed in. "When I worked in a restaurant, if a customer asked for a cappuccino after breakfast hours, I would jokingly reply in my mind that we were all out."

We sat at a quaint coffee shop and requested two cups of cappuccino. As we waited, time seemed to stretch out, almost teasingly slow. After forty-five minutes had passed, we couldn't help but share a lighthearted chuckle about how this experience embodied a genuinely Italian approach. We playfully speculated that perhaps the coffee beans were being handpicked in Guatemala right after we placed our order. This humorous exchange brought out our more accustomed American perspective on efficiency and timing.

Alberobello, a quaint town nestled in the enchanting region of Puglia, instantly beguiles its visitors with its distinctive architecture. It was June, and the tourist crowds hadn't yet swelled during that time of the year. As we leisurely strolled through the town's narrow streets, we were greeted by the iconic trulli houses that define its character. The trulli houses were built using a traditional dry stone technique, with walls constructed without mortar. The result was a labyrinth of interconnecting alleys and stairways winding through the town. It felt like stepping into a whimsical maze, with each turn revealing a new cluster of these adorable structures. These unique structures, boasting conical roofs and whitewashed exteriors, appeared straight out of a storybook.

"Alberobello means 'Beautiful Tree,' and these buildings called trulli originate from the Greek word *tholos*, meaning 'dome,'" Antonello explained as we explored the area.

"Trullo is the singular form, and trulli is the plural form, just like *vino* and *vini*, as you taught me last night, right?" I inquired, trying to pick up a bit of the local language wherever I travel.

"That's right!" Antonello gave me a fist bump, and we both burst into laughter together.

The whitewashed facades of the trulli houses added to the town's charm, creating a sense of purity and serenity. The sunlight reflected off the gleaming walls, casting a soft glow on the cobblestone streets below. It was as if the entire town had been immersed in a palette of whites, forming a visually stunning contrast against the azure sky.

As we ascended the stone steps, we marveled at the intricate details that adorned the trulli houses. Some featured vibrant symbols and patterns painted with meticulous care, contributing a whimsical touch to their overall aesthetic. This attention to detail highlighted the town's rich history and cultural heritage.

"The windows of the trulli are quite small, yet I'm astonished by how much light manages to filter through," I remarked as we attentively explored our surroundings, drawing from my observations at the *Trullo* where we stayed in Locorotondo.

"Trulli structures have unique architectural features that contribute to creating a comfortable indoor environment—the thick stone walls of the trulli help to regulate temperature by providing insulation. During the hot summer months, the stone walls keep the interior cool by preventing heat from entering. Conversely, the stone walls retain heat in winter, helping to keep the interior warmer. This natural insulation property of trulli structures has been appreciated for centuries and continues to be one of their remarkable characteristics." I felt educated, as Antonello explained.

"Sounds a bit like an igloo concept to me. Can you translate that for me?" I asked Antonello as we walked past a bench with Italian writing, "Se fai del bene DIMENTICALO, Se fai del male RICORDALO. Se fai le polpette DIMMELO."

"If you do good, forget about it. If you do harm, remember it. If you make meatballs, let me know," he translated with a smile. We shared a laugh, finding the humor in the translation. "So, if you do something good, don't dwell on it, but if you do something wrong, be prepared to have it brought up in every conversation! And oh, by the way, if you make some delicious meatballs, don't forget to invite me over for dinner!"

We strolled through the streets of Alberobello's Rione Monti district, engrossed in every intricate detail and corner of the town. The *Trulli* stood proudly against the backdrop of a clear blue sky adorned with fluffy white clouds. The front of the white-washed buildings matched the white cobblestone streets, while various plants and flowers in full bloom added a vibrant touch to the picturesque scene. It felt like we had stepped into a living painting, where every detail was thoughtfully crafted to create a mesmerizing atmosphere. The unique dwellings boasted conical roofs adorned with lime-painted symbols, further enhancing their mystical allure. The designs varied, encompassing symbols representing the sun, moon, love hearts, and other motifs with hints of the pagan. These symbols held religious significance for some and carried astrological meanings for others. The purpose of these trulli symbols was to safeguard against malevolent spirits and usher in good fortune for the town's inhabitants.

"If life is a train, I would consider myself the captain. There would only be first and second classes on my train. I don't reserve a room for acquaintances of the economy class, as time is too precious to invest in superficial connections." As we embraced the beauty around us, we paused at a corner, absorbing the surroundings while our conversation naturally delved into deeper topics. In sharing my perspective, I expressed myself openly.

"I like your analogy. In my case, if life were a train, I would be the ticket inspector, where all kinds of people mix without distinguished classes. If you have a ticket on my train, you are equally important in the collection," Antonello replied, offering a different viewpoint.

"I firmly believe in surrounding myself with the right people. If a relationship doesn't contribute positively to my self-esteem or takes me off track, I'm not hesitant to cut ties. Burning the bridge is my thing. I've learned this lesson through my marriage and how I used to manage my social circle. In the past, I used to distribute my energy, time, and efforts among everyone I knew, eventually leaving me drained and unfulfilled," I affirmed, underlining my approach.

Antonello considered my words, his expression serene. "I couldn't do that," he replied softly. "I believe in giving second chances and offering understanding. Sometimes, people make mistakes or go through difficult times, and they deserve a chance to redeem themselves. Forgiveness and compassion are important to me."

"The truth is, I experience a certain level of guilt when people attempt to rekindle a relationship with me. It's not that I don't believe in second chances, but there are times when I don't feel comfortable with the idea or simply feel overwhelmed at the prospect of reconnecting. In those moments, I understand the importance of honoring my feelings. It indicates that I'm either unprepared, not in need, or not interested in including that relationship in my journey. While I have forgiven what transpired that may have caused the rift, moving forward always comes with the understanding of not dwelling on the past. My preference is to forgive, acknowledge my past, and focus on the present to shape the future, rather than looking backward. Regarding my train classes, I have come to a point in my life where time is limited, especially being a single mom; my love is precious. Quality over quantity is more important."

As we walked side by side, Antonello's hand held onto mine, preventing me from slipping on the polished stone floor. Our conversation wove through the complexities of human relationships and our differing approaches. Despite our contrasting viewpoints, we respected and cherished the opportunity to share our thoughts openly, knowing that it was through these conversations that our connection deepened.

With each step, we attentively explore the small details that could inspire us. Our gaze was drawn to a trullo adorned with a gracefully trailing jasmine plant, its delicate flowers releasing a sweet fragrance into the air. The vibrant green leaves provided a striking contrast against the whitewashed walls, creating a visual harmony that captured our attention. As we marveled at the beauty of the jasmine-clad trullo, our attention was then caught by another trullo adorned with a tangling vine of grapes along the rooftop, right above the door and window. We could see the promising sight of a few grapes, slowly ripening and ready for harvest in a few months to come. It demonstrated the cycle of nature's abundance, where the trullo became a canvas for the flourishing vine.

"Time for a spritz," Antonello announced.

We stumbled upon a small restaurant in the central square and settled comfortably at a square table, facing each other. "Why are you sitting so far away? Come closer," Antonello playfully teased, his words accompanied by a warm smile that invited me into his embrace. As I surveyed the surroundings, in the middle of the day, the area wasn't as crowded as the bustling tourist spots in Barcelona, allowing us to enjoy a more intimate and peaceful setting.

"Due spritz, acqua frizzante e un'insalata, per favore. Grazie," Antonello placed our order in Italian, and surprisingly, due to my limited Spanish knowledge, I could almost understand everything he said. His courteous demeanor extended to the waiter. "And may I know your name?" I genuinely appreciate it when someone takes the time to acknowledge and value the hard work of those in the service industry.

"Can I invite my sister and her boyfriend for dinner tonight?" Antonello asked, his voice filled with anticipation.

"Yes, of course. What time should we expect them?" I inquired.

"Nine thirty," Antonello responded. I chuckled inwardly, 9:30 p.m.? Oh my, the dinner time is reminiscent of the Spanish tradition.

After nearly an hour of waiting, our salad, made with fresh lettuce, juicy cherry tomatoes, and two mozzarella balls, was finally served. As time passed, I started feeling more European than Antonello. It seemed he had become "Americanized," accustomed to the efficiency of things in the United States. I even playfully teased him, asking, "Are you about to call the manager?" On the other hand, I realized that I was completely fine with the wait. In this instance, I fully embraced being "Spanishized," learning to take things at their own pace and go with the flow.

With a handsome Italian man beside me, I was in no rush!

"Where's your *dolce far niente*?" I said to Antonello, referring to the Italian concept of enjoying the sweetness of doing nothing.

Monopoli

Our journey continued to Monopoli, and once again, Antonello confidently declared, "No GPS, let's just go." I smiled at him, appreciating his sense of adventure and spontaneity. The notion of getting lost took on a poetic quality, signifying our willingness to trust our instincts and embrace the uncertainty that lay ahead. In my case, I was placing my trust in Antonello, allowing myself to stay in the present moment with him, regardless of what might happen. After all, some of the most remarkable experiences come to us when we relinquish the need for control and welcome the mystery of the unknown. Wasn't that the true purpose of this trip?

"Look, there's the church. It's probably the city center. That's one of the beauties of Italy and Spain as well. Churches often serve as landmarks, guiding us toward the heart of the town or city. They often symbolize the spiritual and cultural core of the community," Antonello explained as I looked up at him with admiration.

"There's something unique about Italian driving—they never seem to stop! Whether you're behind the wheel or walking on the street, you have to navigate smartly and assertively to make your way. It's as if waiting for someone to stop and let you pass isn't the norm on Italian streets," I commented, reflecting on my observations.

"Imagine you are driving in Rome!" Antonello added.

We parked the car and began walking on the street, with me slightly behind him. He extended his right hand, signaling his desire to hold mine. We strolled toward the city center, paying little attention to the specifics like street names. Antonello led me to a stunning bay with crystal-clear blue waters situated right at the entrance of the city center. This unfolding of events was utterly spontaneous, devoid of elaborate planning. We hadn't brought much beach gear—just a single towel to share and a small bag. Instead of opting for a spot in the crowded beach area, we ventured toward the rocky shoreline. After finding a vacant space, Antonello's excitement was palpable as he quickly removed his shirt, revealing his impressively toned and golden-tanned physique once again. With his handsome face and the athletic body he maintained through disciplined habits (I could go on endlessly about his physique), he appeared ready to plunge into the sea.

"Are you going in?" Antonello asked, a hint of excitement in his voice.

"Yes, but give me a moment," I replied, wanting to savor the atmosphere a little longer.

"Why wait?" he asked curiously.

"I just want to be here alone a little bit," I laughed, staring at him.

"Jeez, are we already fighting?" We both cackled at our playful exchange. Antonello approached the water, ready to take a refreshing swim.

I observed him swimming across the bay, his blue Speedo accentuating his well-defined physique, a hint of gray hair elegantly mingling with his dark locks. His hands moved rhythmically as he swam across the bay. He looked remarkably fit! (My mind was in overdrive.) I couldn't help but conclude that the charm of Italian men is on par with the beauty of French women.

Shortly after taking my time observing the surroundings alone, I joined him in the refreshing sea waters of Monopoli. The temperature was still a bit cool, but the combination of the invigorating water and the warmth of the sun created a perfect balance.

I discovered "the spot" that I preferred—a large rock where the surface was comfortable for my feet, and another substantial rock behind me that I could lean against to relax while standing. Antonello swam toward me and positioned himself in front of me. The seawater rose to our tummies, creating a refreshing sensation, while the sun and warm rays embraced the upper parts of our bodies. I could sense his vigilant spirit. Glancing over my shoulder, I noticed our personal belongings placed just a short distance away, perched on the edge of two large rocks. They were situated less than fifty meters higher and slightly behind me. "I don't think anything will happen, but just in case," he mentioned cautiously.

"I don't think you'll have enough time to climb up and reach our belongings before someone steals our bag," I playfully challenged him.

"I can charge forward very fast," Antonello replied, with his confident demeanor.

I thought, "Yeah, he plays football every week and cycles daily. I guess I have to believe him." (Not that I had any other option.)

Having no clue how long we had been in the refreshing sea water, engrossed in our endless conversation, we also took notice of a hardworking local man diligently collecting some sort of seafood that resembled the shape of sea cucumbers. We stood there, captivated, for as long as he continued his work.

"What's your favorite color?" I asked, and we started exchanging some lighthearted dialogue to explore our likes and dislikes.

"Blue."

"And you?"

"Also blue."

"What's your preferred alcoholic drink?"

"Negroni."

"And you?"

"White wine."

"Have you dated an Asian woman before?"

"Yes, a Japanese-American. You're the first Taiwanese."

"Have you dated an Italian before?"

"Yes, a friend with benefits in my college years was Italian. But he was more of an American Italian! I'd say he was more American than Italian."

"Antonello, I'm grateful to be here and glad I took the chance to meet you. Thank you for spending all this time driving me around, explaining things, and sharing your Italian charm. I truly feel that this year of getting to know each other feels more like the right time and the right place than the previous years," I expressed, changing the topic.

"I agree. We're more aligned this time. As I mentioned before, I always believed we would meet, and I promised myself that I would come back to ask you again because I truly felt that we needed to make it happen, at least once. I'm also grateful to have you here with me," he replied sincerely, making me feel that the decision to come to Puglia was not just the right choice, but the perfect one!

Monopoli is a beautiful coastal town, and cities dot along the cliffs that stretch southeast below the main city of the region, Bari. As we walked inside the city center, whitewashed houses contrasted perfectly with the turquoise waters that crashed along the coast.

"What's the name of this town?" I asked.

"Monopoli," Antonello answered.

I repeated it, pronouncing it as "Monopoly" in English.

"No! It's Mo-no-po-li," Antonello corrected me, ensuring I got the *o* in a round lip shape, not an oval lip shape.

Monopoli boasts a rich history that dates back to its settlement in 500 BC. At the heart of the town's historic center stands the Monopoli Castle, also known as Castello di Carlo V. This splendid castle occupies a prime location, offering panoramic views of the Adriatic Sea and the charming streets of Monopoli. As we meandered through the surrounding area, we were enchanted by the narrow alleys, traditional whitewashed houses, and lively buildings adorned with delightful flowerpots.

On the opposite side of the castle's gate, a picturesque scene greeted us as we made our way through: small boats gently swaying in the tranquil port, some quietly docked. The castle stood tall and commanding, its stone walls, towers, and battlements exuding a sense of history and grandeur. It was a serene and enchanting sight, enhancing the allure of this coastal town.

The narrow streets of Monopoli are unique. As we leisurely strolled along these enchanting lanes, my gaze was often caught by the occasional large vases adorned with lively plants outside the houses, injecting a burst of natural beauty into the surroundings. Overhead, between the buildings, artistic decorations dangled gracefully, lending an authentic touch to the ambiance of Monopoli's historic center.

"I want *acqua frizzante*," I said, using the first Italian word I had learned since arrival. It meant sparkling water, and applying my language skills in this charming setting felt satisfying.

"It's pronounced a'cq'-ua as in not a'g'-ua," Antonello corrected my pronunciation, distinguishing between the Italian and Spanish.

Twenty minutes later, it felt like we had walked through the entire town, yet we couldn't find a single convenience store or supermarket in sight.

"I guess people here don't run errands," Antonello commented.

"There's something intriguing about the American way of approaching tasks. 'Running errands,' this phrase always makes me wonder, why can't they walk? In Chinese, when we want to express running errands, it's literally translated as 'doing house tasks.' We do the tasks, but we don't run. Even in Spanish, they use *hacer*, which means 'to do," It's interesting how the English language itself implies a sense of stress and time management,"

I replied, highlighting the cultural differences in language and expressing my observation.

"You're right. In Italy, we often prioritize a more relaxed and leisurely pace of life, much like the Spanish. We value taking the time to enjoy moments, savor meals, and engage in conversations. However, having been in San Francisco for ten years, I understand how the American approach may be perceived as efficient and task-oriented. Ultimately, life is about finding a balance that works for each individual," Antonello said. From wanting sparkling water to discussing running errands, our conversation shifted toward finding balance in life. I truly loved the way our conversation flowed and evolved.

"Speaking of savoring meals, when people insist on calling Chinese noodles 'pasta,' it annoys my soul," I said, injecting a hint of humor into the conversation.

"And when someone breaks the pasta before cooking, it breaks my heart," Antonello chimed in, again showcasing his poetic side.

About My Marriage

Getting ready for our 9:30 p.m. dinner with Antonello's sister and her boyfriend, Antonello and I made our way from the trullo toward the historic center of Locorotondo. We could feel a hint of tiredness settling in, as it had been a long day of walking and sunbathing. The refreshing shower rejuvenated my body, making me feel ready for bed even before dinner.

The evening breeze in Locorotondo was wonderfully refreshing, defying the expectations of a typical early summer night. Instead of the usual stifling heat and humidity, it carried a coolness that made the atmosphere feel more like a pleasant spring evening. As we made our way toward the outskirts of the historical center, Antonello, as always, took hold of my hand and suggested, "Spritz time! We have an hour of appetizers just for ourselves." We strolled along, passing by several restaurants with a few outdoor seating areas that offered panoramic views of the Puglia skyline.

So far, every spritz we had was accompanied by different types of olives and taralli.

"Do you miss your husband?" Antonello asked out of the blue.

"Oh, well, if I'm in the North Pole, my ex-husband is definitely in the South Pole. We're completely disconnected, no internet or anything," I replied, highlighting the distance and disconnection that defined my past marriage. "I've experienced much pain throughout that journey, and now I can barely look him in the eyes. But I'm glad he has a great relationship with my daughters. At least he's the most trustworthy weekend nanny I could have asked for! For me, that's enough." Sipping my spritz, I briefly touched upon the dynamics of my previous marriage, allowing Antonello to understand the situation.

"I noticed that you didn't talk much about your marriage situation when we were chatting," Antonello said.

"I didn't want to delve too deeply into my marriage situation earlier when we were chatting because it felt unfair to bring unnecessary drama or my stress into your life," I continued.

"Overall, it was my issue to deal with. However, my divorce was finalized earlier this year. It wasn't easy, and I had to take on every term he requested, but I knew the chapter had been closed. I've spent years healing, and while it wasn't a topic I could easily open up about, now I feel comfortable discussing it. You can ask me questions if you want." This was the first time we had a proper conversation about my broken marriage and relationship with my ex-husband. It was the story of how it all began and how it ultimately came to an end.

"When did you start realizing that you both had issues?" Antonello delved deeper.

"I realized it quite early on, even before we got married. I believed in my commitment to the relationship, and I saw fixing it as my path forward. The thought of leaving him never even crossed my mind," I explained.

"Did that also extend to the decision to have kids?" he inquired further.

"Yes! I quit my job, moved to a new apartment, changed our lifestyle, planned a wedding, and had our first child. All of these decisions were driven by the intention to repair our relationship and hoping for improvement," I said.

"How did you end up having a second child then? I've heard similar stories where people try to use children to fix their marriage," he said, intrigued by my determination.

"I knew I wanted two kids, but I didn't want to have two different fathers. When I decided to have my second child, it was a deliberate plan. I didn't want to enter into another long-term committed relationship and go through the process of the pregnancy race with someone new if I ended up getting divorced. So, in my case, having a second child was mainly because I needed his 'assistance' to achieve what I wanted. It might sound ridiculous, but that's the truth," I explained, elaborating on my intentions.

"Oh, that explains it! Have you been dating?" Antonello asked.

"I do date casually here and there. My only commitment is to the present hours I share with that person. There's no future planning, no merging of lives, and no moving into each other's homes. I want to be alone for now. Furthermore, falling in love has become a source of fear for me. I spent almost four years trying to mend my marriage issues and another four years coming to terms with the fact that the problems were much deeper, and I had to move on to rebuild my life. It was a painful journey that spanned eight to ten years in total. Now, even if I wanted to experience love as I did in my twenties, I'm uncertain about how to navigate those emotions," I admitted, baring my vulnerability in that moment. "I'm not sure if I'm afraid of new love or old pain."

"I stopped trying to label each dating experience I had; instead, I started viewing every encounter as a story to tell. Through the lessons from my marriage, I understood that it's not about labeling things as good or bad, but about stepping back from the situation and approaching it as an event that requires a solution. Moreover, a story like ours, where we spent a few beautiful days together without expectations and created a romantic narrative, feels more memorable and akin to fairy-tale moments. This is in contrast to having someone sleep next to me every day without a true understanding of what brings me happiness or the motivation to be with me," I explained, taking the opportunity to reiterate the reasons for our presence here.

Ten minutes before dinner, we made our way to Bina Ristorante di Puglia, a boutique dining establishment on the basement floor. The restaurant exuded a warm, cozy, and inviting ambiance. Antonello and I took a seat on a bench just outside the restaurant, patiently awaiting the arrival of his sister and her boyfriend. As we sat silently, our gaze shifted to the sky above, allowing us to savor a peaceful moment.

Upon entering Bina Ristorante, we were greeted by a charming sight—an elegant restaurant within the arched undercroft of an ancient building. As our party of four settled into seats, we perused the menu, which proudly showcased the culinary traditions of Puglia. The dishes offered a delightful blend of the region's fresh ingredients and distinct flavors. One particular item that caught my attention was the "Donkey Chops in Ragout with Bread Crust." I leaned in closer, doubting if I had read the word correctly.

Antonello noticed my curiosity and asked, "Is everything okay?"

I responded, pointing my finger at the word *donkey*, "Yeah, I just caught sight of 'donkey.' Is this meant metaphorically?"

"No, it's actually made with real donkey meat. In some parts of Italy, horse meat is also consumed. I understand it may sound shocking to you."

"Oh my, I need a glass of wine right now. I don't even want to imagine how it tastes," I quickly interjected, closing the conversation with amusement.

Antonello's sister, Mirabella, is an art teacher with flowing long hair. Her right cheek bears a captivating mole that, in my opinion, adds a touch of sexiness. Accompanied by her wide, beautiful smile, she dons stylish black plastic-framed glasses, exuding an air of sophistication.

Above all, it was a delightful experience to finally engage in authentic Italian conversation. Antonello's English had acquired an American flair, with barely a trace of an accent. However, I was irresistibly drawn to the endearing charm of Mirabella's careful pronunciation of each word and the thoughtfulness with which she posed her questions. Every now and then, Mirabella accompanied her verbal expression with the iconic Italian gesture of pinching her fingers, adding an expressive touch to her body language. I absolutely adored it!

"What do you call Antonello normally?" I asked Mirabella.

"Anton or Boo Boo," she answered while we all laughed lightly.

"You know Boo from *Monster and Co.*? It was derived from there," Antonello added, briefly explaining how the nickname came about. "Interestingly enough, your older daughter also bears a resemblance to Boo."

Oh, right. It was a surprise to hear Antonello casually bring it up like that. I wasn't actively hiding anything, but it simply wasn't a topic I expected to discuss. However, I was delighted to discover that he was so accepting of who I am and my daughters, and that he was willing to talk about it with his family openly. There was no sense of needing to conceal the fact that I am a single mom.

"Show them their picture. I have seen it before," Antonello added. It felt incredibly liberating to be in an environment without judgment.

After dinner, the four of us took a midnight stroll through the historic city, setting the stage for the first official Mandarin lesson between Antonello and me. He initiated the lesson by inquiring about the correct pronunciation of my full name. I had previously expressed my desire for him to stop calling me "Bella," suspecting that he used that term with everyone. It reminded me of how people in Spain are called "guapa," in Taiwan, anyone can be referred to as "mei-nu," meaning beauty!

For the rest of the night, our Mandarin lesson encompassed various topics, starting with the correct pronunciation of my name and extending to discussions about different types of alcohol and basic greetings. Eventually, our conversation shifted to a history lesson about Taiwan and the complex dynamics that have led to the tense situation with China. We delved into my family's approach to this issue and even touched upon my political stance in such a nuanced situation.

Cisternino

On the third day in Puglia, my darling Italian companion once again greeted me with a cup of espresso, placed enticingly on the table. We were in the same seats and positions as the morning before, with him across from me and our toes gently touching. We were ready to continue our casual morning chat before starting a day filled with exploration.

It had been three days, and I was quite amazed by the range of topics we could enjoy discussing with each other. Additionally, I found great pleasure in the moments of shared silence during our car rides, walks, and various other instances. Moreover, I consciously allowed myself to be in the flow of our interactions, letting things occur naturally without any sense of force. It had been an experience to embrace the present and allow things to happen organically.

After our morning coffee, he slipped into a casual white shirt. I walked over to him and instinctively buttoned it up, helping him fold the sleeves to his elbows. He paired the shirt with camel-colored khaki shorts. As for myself, I opted for a white T-shirt and a pair of blue denim shorts. I loved how we coincidentally matched!

We made our way out to Cisternino, a charming town in the province of Brindisi, Puglia, situated amidst Valle d'Itria, known for its rolling hills, vineyards, and olive groves. Cisternino has a long and fascinating history that dates back to ancient times. It was originally settled by the Messapians, an ancient

Italic tribe, and later became a Roman municipality. The town's name is believed to derive from the Latin word *cisternae*, meaning "cisterns," which were essential for collecting and storing rainwater during ancient times. Over the centuries, Cisternino has retained its medieval charm. The town's architecture reflects its historical past, showcasing Romanesque, Gothic, and Renaissance elements.

As we continued our exploration of Cisternino, I expressed, "Let's have a cup of coffee," I said.

Antonello, confirming again, said, "It's still before 11:00 a.m.," ensuring that we adhered to the traditional Italian coffee culture.

Within the first three minutes of entering this enchanting town, I felt an immediate connection that assured me it would hold a special place in my heart. As I strolled along, a staircase composed of seven smooth stones, each step adorned with vibrant hot-pink morning glory flowers, caught my eye. The flowers gracefully trailed from the first step of the staircase, winding their way up toward the magnificent arched door. The door stood as a tribute to the town's beauty, its grandeur heightened by the delicate embrace of the flourishing morning blossoms. The striking contrast between the vivid pink flowers and the pristine whitewashed walls created a picturesque scene that effortlessly drew me in.

Adjacent to this grand and elegant door, I noticed a boutique art gallery, adding to the artistic ambiance of the surroundings. The juxtaposition of architectural beauty and artistic expression seamlessly blended, creating a sense of sophistication.

The streets of Cisternino may have been narrower than any town we had visited earlier, but they possessed a unique charm. What struck me the most was the exquisite composition of the stairs and the lush greenery against the whitewashed wall. These authentic stone stairs gracefully led up to the entrance of a family door. Together, they created a harmonious display of simplicity and beauty that was simply mesmerizing. It was as if the town itself had been carefully curated, reminiscent of a picturesque painting come to life.

"These flowers are so beautiful and organized," I said casually, admiring every corner as much as possible.

"If you plant it at the right time and right place, it will grow," Antonello said.

I couldn't agree more with this sentiment. It felt like the perfect moment and location for our story to take a small leap forward.

In another corner, we came across a similar small, narrow alleyway adorned with two white staircases leading up to adjacent entrance doors, forming an elegant angle. The entire scene was bathed in pristine white, except for the vibrant plants that added pops of color. Even the plant containers were elegantly designed in white, seamlessly blending with the overall aesthetic. Directly beside the entrance of the stairs, a white bench invited visitors to pause and appreciate the beauty of the surroundings. Every element was perfectly placed. The authenticity and thoughtful arrangement of every detail made me fall in love with the town.

As we continued exploring the town, a street was decorated with hats hanging between the buildings. In the next corner, we saw quotes carved on a wooden board hanging above our heads.

"Se no credi in te stesso, troverai sempre un modo per non vincere," Antonello looked up and read, "meaning, if you don't believe in yourself, you will always find a way not to win."

Walking ten steps forward to the next wooden board, "Le persone che amano mangiare sonon sempre le migliori," Antonello continued. "People who love to eat are always the best."

"That's right! There's even a Chinese saying that 'Having a good appetite is a blessing.'"

Over the chat screen, I manifested this wildest dream of having a charming Italian man riding a bicycle with me a few years ago. And now, at this very moment, he was standing right next to me, not expecting anything from us but putting in all his effort to show me around and spend quality time. That, my friends, is truly a blessing.

Ostuni

Ostuni was our next stop, and I could sense a more touristy atmosphere in this town. The streets were bustling with activity, and a noticeable commercialized vibe was in the air. However, despite the increased tourist presence, Ostuni still held its charm and beauty.

Perched atop a hill, Ostuni captivates with its enchanting white-washed buildings, earning it the title "The White City." However, it did make me wonder why Ostuni specifically earned this name, especially when many other towns also seemed to have a coordinated effort by the government to paint their buildings white!

As we wandered through its streets, it was noticeable that there were more shops, souvenir stores, and elegant lounges within this town. Even electric passenger motor tricycles were available to transport tourists around the town, providing an alternative to walking.

At the heart of Ostuni lies the impressive Cathedral of Santa Maria Assunta, a striking example of Gothic and Romanesque architecture. "How did ancient people manage to construct something so sophisticated? Were those decorations on the top built as a single piece?" I wondered to myself while observing the intricate details.

Antonello and I ascended to the highest point of the town, where a breathtaking panorama materialized before us. Olive groves and vineyards stretched out in every direction, creating a tapestry of lush greenery. In the distance, the Adriatic Sea shimmered under the sun, its crystal-clear waters glistening.

A sense of awe washed over me as I stood there, taking in the magnificent view. I turned to Antonello and expressed my admiration. "You're incredibly fortunate to have been born in this place. Living here is a privilege, surrounded by such natural beauty, the serene simplicity that defines this region," I remarked, my words filled with genuine appreciation.

"Yes, I am. I was also surprised to discover so much green space in Puglia," he responded. The expansiveness of the landscape, the vibrant colors, and the peacefulness of the scene stirred a profound sense of gratitude in him. Retrieving his phone, we prepared to capture a candid selfie moment.

"I want *acqua frizzante*," I said, requesting a search for water.

"Let's leave this spot and find a different place to have a drink," Antonello suggested, and I instantly understood his reasoning. Drinking at this bistro might come with a hefty price tag.

"You're right," I replied, fully aware of the potential expenses. "Let's keep moving."

I must confess that while Ostuni is undeniably a unique place, it didn't quite capture the top spot in my favorites. This was largely due to the influx of tourists and the realization that some of the so-called "Instagram-worthy" spots had been commercially influenced, compromising the authentic atmosphere. Antonello mentioned that he was considering accommodations in this region before we ultimately settled on our exclusive Trullo in Locorotondo.

"Thank goodness he didn't. That would have made my peaceful vacation with my beautiful Italian a bit too crowded," I thought, keeping my little secret.

"The advertising has now reached the American audience! Social media's influence has taken over; what used to be a quiet place is now flooded with tourists during peak holiday times. It's a good thing we didn't stay here," Antonello said, almost as if he was echoing my thoughts.

In search of my *acqua frizzante*, we ended up randomly selecting a seafood restaurant on the outskirts of the city center. The restaurant offered a comprehensive array of seafood options, showcasing fresh catches displayed in refrigerated cases before being brought to the dining table. It was the establishment where you approached the counter and picked your seafood, and they would weigh and prepare it to your liking. Opting to sit outside on the covered veranda, we indulged in a delightful spread of lightly fried and roasted seafood dishes, each bursting with excellent flavors. We relished fresh mussels, tuna, squid, and raw fish, all accompanied by a glass of white wine and conversation.

"Ever since I adopted a lighter diet in Barcelona, I haven't been preparing meat regularly unless my kids specifically request it. Our family's—meaning the two kids and myself—food preferences lean more toward seafood and vegetable-based dishes. Aside from my morning coffee, sparkling water is my primary choice of beverage. I typically reserve a glass or two of wine for social occasions on weekends," I shared a glimpse into my lifestyle.

"On my side, I had started a no-carb diet, which means eliminating almost all carbs and encouraging intakes of fat and protein. This diet may boost weight loss, heart health, and blood sugar control."

"Why? You seem very fit," I inquired about Antonello's preference.

Antonello passionately delved into the biological processes and how they can impact health. As he spoke, he smoothly transitioned from discussing gluten to glucose. While I might have gradually lost track of the technical details somewhere along the way, my attention was drawn to his presence, admiring his handsome features. (I just couldn't resist!) Even though I wasn't fully following what he explained, it resonated with me like sweet music. I wondered, "What is this gorgeous, seductive man doing here, explaining intricate scientific concepts to a single mom?"

"It would have made a lot more sense for you to spend time with someone else who can provide immediate physical affection in San Francisco and plan a future that you desire," I said, inadvertently changing the topic as the words in my mind slipped out.

Antonello appeared momentarily puzzled but swiftly grasped my train of thought, redirecting the conversation. "I wanted to meet you, and I've always believed we should give ourselves a chance. I'm here without any particular expectations. And up until this point, everything has unfolded so seamlessly," he explained.

"I could write a book about expectations. When you engage in something without anticipating anything in return, it's an act of love. But the moment you attach a desired outcome, it becomes an expectation, resembling a business transaction," Antonello elaborated, sharing his perspective.

"Other than expectation, attachment can be a toxic ingredient in relationships, too," I continued, expressing my point of view. "It harks back to our previous discussions in the Jacuzzi the first day about being content with ourselves and comfortable with being alone. "When someone becomes attached, they seek the other half to fill a perceived void and create a sense of security and comfort."

"Indeed, attachment can lead to dependency and expectations that may weigh down a relationship," Antonello continued. "Trust is an essential ingredient in any connection. Without trust, doubts and insecurities can arise, and a sense of freedom is compromised. Trust fosters open communication, mutual respect, and the liberty to be oneself. I don't believe in the concept of the Universe, but what I'm saying here seems to contradict myself. But I love it! Trust that opportunities will naturally occur without force. Just like us!" Antonello reached out his hand to mine and signaled to move on to our next stop.

Final Stop: Polignano a Mare

As we arrived in Polignano a Mare, Antonello guided me to a mesmerizing viewpoint overlooking Cala Porto. Standing high up on the bridge, we were greeted by a breathtaking scene of the beach and the iconic Red Bull Cliff Diving stage. He shared some interesting insights, "Since 2009, the Italian round of Red Bull Cliff Diving has taken place here, attracting numerous tourists to this picturesque town." His words shed light on the commercial significance of this stunning location, adding an intriguing layer to its beauty.

We could see the azure waters below from our vantage point, glistening under the warm Mediterranean sun. The stage for the cliff diving competition stood tall and vibrant, ready to host the daring acrobats who would leap into the depths with grace and precision.

"At its core, Red Bull may not be a unique product. The market is saturated with energy drinks. However, what sets them apart is their powerful marketing team," I explained to Antonello, drawing from my past experience working in a marketing agency. "Their ability to combine creativity, athleticism, and a daring approach to action sports differentiates them from other brands."

He continued, "This is a perfect example of a brand that possesses such strength that it can elevate the economic value of a city. Since Red Bull cliff diving came to this town, Polignano a Mare became an instantly recognized vacation spot worldwide."

As we made our way toward the center of Polignano a Mare, it was evident that the town attracted more tourists than the other towns we had visited in the past few days, including Ostuni. The bustling streets, upbeat music, and lively atmosphere indicated its popularity.

Walking through the narrow alleys and streets, bustling with people strolling in and out, we soon arrived at a breathtaking viewpoint overlooking the cliffs and houses perched precariously on the cliffside. The view was simply mesmerizing, I must say. The rugged cliffs stood tall against the backdrop of the sparkling turquoise waters below. It was a sight that seemed almost surreal. Due to the crowd, we had to take turns and navigate our way to secure a viewing spot.

Antonello stood tall behind me, enveloping me in his embrace as we leaned against the security bar, gazing out at the expanse of the sea. In that moment, it felt like we were characters in a scene from a movie, where time stood still, and magic filled the air. Amidst the crowd, we focused solely on each other, not minding the people around us taking selfies or family photos. The sight of the houses clinging to the cliffs, seemingly defying gravity, added a touch of awe and romance to the experience. It was like the town held onto its history and traditions, standing strong against the crashing waves below. In that serene and cinematic moment, with Antonello behind me, I felt deeply grateful for all these extraordinary experiences over the days.

The Universe had been so kind to me, giving me everything and more than I could have asked for.

"Our afternoon spritz time has arrived," Antonello said with a smile.

As we enjoyed our afternoon spritz, I took a moment to express my heartfelt thoughts. "I just want you to be happy and move on with your life," I told Antonello. "I won't be texting you constantly because I believe it's important for both of us to be fully present in our own lives. Let's spend time with the people physically with us and not rely on our phones to prove our connection." These words came from a place of sincerity, emphasizing the significance of authentic, in-person interactions and prioritizing genuine relationships over virtual ones.

"I know there were times when you tried to derail me from this relationship, but I couldn't ignore the connection we had. I wanted to believe that stories like ours can happen. They may be rare, but they do exist," Antonello expressed his faith in our unique bond. "I agree that we don't need to be physically next to each other or hover over each other's backs. As you said, no labeling is needed as well. I know we are close to each other no matter where we are in the world."

"I appreciate the experiences we have shared, and I am genuinely happy to have an Italian man like you be a part of this beautiful story we're creating." As the evening progressed, I felt that our time together was coming to a close. Knowing that closure was not too far ahead was a bittersweet feeling.

Up until this point, defining our relationship hadn't been a pressing matter. It had always been crystal clear that Antonello and I shared a connection that defied traditional labels. While he resided in San Francisco and I had firmly established roots in Barcelona, I had no intention of uprooting or making major changes for a man. My children would always be my top priority, and I was currently content with the casual nature of my relationships. Moreover, I was happy to have reached a level of maturity where I could handle situations like this without getting caught up in the whirlwind of "falling in love," as I might have done in my younger years. I'd come to appreciate the importance of living in the present moment.

That said, I was thankful for the time I'd spent with Antonello and our unique connection. Each chapter we open in life must eventually come to a close, and I was glad I could navigate this situation with clarity and wisdom. It was a testament to my personal growth and understanding that not every connection needed to fit into a predefined box or follow a predetermined path.

On our final evening stroll from the old town of Locorotondo back to the trullo, Antonello and I walked hand in hand, enjoying each other's closeness for the last time. As we walked, Antonello directed my attention to the night sky. We looked up and marveled at the stars, with him pointing out the familiar constellation of the Big Dipper. He counted the seven stars that formed its shape and then shifted his finger slightly toward the northeast, indicating the bright star known as Polaris. It was a magical moment, standing beneath the vast expanse of the night sky, connected not only to each other but also to the wonders of the Universe.

We spent our final night together, him lying on top of me, on our bed, underneath the dome of the Trullo architecture. It wasn't in the bathroom, at the dining table, or on the couch. It was a simple, intimate night where we gazed into each other's eyes, cherishing the moment, with this beautiful man telling me, "You are in my heart no matter where you go and what you do." Every minute I spent in Puglia felt like I had stolen an episode from a movie scene. The Universe sent me a dosage of Italian charm that I would not imagine to be in my reality.

But what adds an enchanting touch to this story is that neither of us came with any expectations. We entered this union simply to be present with each other, to savor every moment before us, and to engage in meaningful conversations. Even though this was just a temporary dream spanning a few days, it was genuinely nourishing for my soul to be in the company of someone so poetic, someone who resonated with the same humor and lightheartedness.

"My star, ready to board soon, thanks again for these few days and for sharing your life with me. I am feeling super spoiled. Good luck with your adventure. Whatever you do, I'm on your side, and you will have a special place in my heart. Take care and kisses." This was my final message to Antonello.

"Thank you for spending time with me. It was great to share these days together. Let's stay in touch. We will see each other again, shen shen." Antonello's message made me giggle. It seemed like he wanted to see me again, and he found a way to address me instead of using the usual "Bella."

Without a hint of heaviness, after four days of living in this enchanting, movie-like setting, it was time to return home. My reality awaited me, along with the unresolved sleep issues that plagued me throughout the trip. Three nights without a restful sleep in a foreign place, alongside a foreign man—it was clear that it was time to go home and be with my girls. This lingering feeling of "one day too many" had reached its limit. Enough was enough. Mama had gotten a total dosage of Italian charm, and staying one extra day could lead to what Victoria referred to as the Spanish saying "empalagoso," meaning "sickly sweet."

While I was still trying to settle back into Barcelona for the remainder of the day, I was still savoring every beautiful moment we had created in the past few days. It took time to get myself together. However, instead of feeling saddened by our parting, I embraced the longing for someone and focused on appreciating the story that had taken place. It was all too dreamy.

The following morning, I woke up to the sound of my two kids' voices saying, "Mama, I want chocolate milk." The aroma of cappuccino from an Italian man may no longer linger in the air, but seeing my girls' beautiful smiles brought me immense joy.

"Next time, before you do something like this, please let us know first! We should have a safe word, like 'Pineapple,'" Ofek told me after I shared my Italy experience with him and Zohar during the playdate the day after my Italy trip. His immediate feedback grounded me, made me laugh, and made me feel like I was truly back home with my Barcelona family.

That's a Wrap

Summer had arrived in full force, bringing with it sweltering heat that engulfed the air. The excited laughter of children filled the streets as they reveled in their newfound freedom from school. It was a few days before our long-awaited trip back to Taiwan, a place I hadn't visited in years.

As the departure date drew near, I felt a mix of emotions. The anticipation of returning to my homeland after such a long time was overwhelming. So much had changed since I last set foot on Taiwanese soil.

I had a profound sense that as I journeyed back to Taiwan, I was not only revisiting my past and childhood but also bringing along a glimpse of my future self. It was as if I was carrying the wisdom and growth that had shaped me into who I am today.

In my younger years, I often consumed myself with worries about being judged and the constant need to prove myself to others. Those insecurities and fears profoundly influenced my thoughts and actions, shaping my perception of the world around me.

But as I prepared to take this Taiwan trip, I held the intention to present my homeland with a new attitude and a stronger mind. I wanted to showcase the growth and self-acceptance I had cultivated over the years. It was an opportunity to demonstrate that I no longer needed external validation to define my worth.

Above all, I have come to realize that there is no shame or problem in being a single mother and being myself. In fact, it has been an extraordinary journey that I will cherish for the rest of my life. Each person I have encountered, from the unconventional Catalan musician who fell outside my usual dating preferences to the principled and disciplined tall man from the Netherlands, has played a significant role in my personal growth.

Each of these individuals, representing different tribes and backgrounds, has contributed to my journey in unique and invaluable ways. They have pushed me to new heights and helped me become the person I am today. Their diverse perspectives, experiences, and qualities have enriched my life beyond measure, and I wouldn't trade any of them for anything in the world.

As I brought this chapter of my story to a close, I was entwined with a charming Italian man. It feels like the perfect culmination, the icing on the cake of my journey so far. The experiences, the lessons, and the love I have encountered have all led me to this point, and it feels better than perfect.

As I reflect on my path, I am filled with gratitude for the people who have joined me on this remarkable adventure. They have taught me the importance of embracing life's unexpected twists and turns and shown me that love and connection can transcend boundaries and stereotypes.

Being a single mother has not hindered my ability to create meaningful connections and build a life filled with love, joy, and growth. It has only added depth and richness to my story. I am proud of the woman I have become, and I am excited for the future that lies ahead.

The night before our flight back to Taiwan, we revisited an old favorite, *The Little Prince,* during our customary bedtime storytelling. Although we had read this enchanting tale together before, we always found new insights and revelations.

In the story of *The Little Prince*, the essence of simplicity is exalted, and the significance of essential things in life is emphasized. The Prince's rejection of material possessions is a powerful reminder of the transformative power of appreciating life's simplest wonders. Whether it be the delicate petals of a flower or the sketch of a sheep, the Prince showed us the beauty in appreciating the small and precious moments.

Throughout the story, the Prince encounters various characters who are fixated on the past or consumed by the future, such as the geographer and the businessman. In contrast, the Prince treasures each encounter with the fox, the rose, and the narrator, immersing himself fully in those precious moments. This teaches us the importance of living fully in the present, free from distractions and preoccupations.

The Little Prince also unveils the ephemeral nature of the rose and the transient existence of the stars, mirroring our understanding and acceptance of impermanence. The Prince embodies non-attachment as he gracefully lets go of his physical body and returns to his asteroid, symbolizing the freedom of releasing attachments.

In his exploration, the Prince personifies innocence and curiosity, asking simple yet profound questions and seeking understanding with childlike purity. This simple story serves as a gentle reminder for us to approach life with a sense of wonder, shedding preconceived notions and judgments and embracing each moment with a fresh and open mind.

Each character that the Prince encounters challenges conventional perspectives and societal norms, encouraging us to reflect on who is essential and valuable in our lives. Through this mindful process, we can rise above rigid dualities and cultivate a more expansive and inclusive view of the world.

And so, I switched off the light, symbolizing the end of one chapter and the beginning of another. It was time for us to board our flight back to Taiwan, a journey that held immense significance, as it marked our return after our time in Barcelona and the challenges posed by the COVID pandemic. This voyage represented an opportunity for me to weave together the threads of my past with the person I had become.

A mixture of excitement and anticipation filled my heart as I contemplated the transformative power of time and distance. Over the past four years, on this voyage of self-discovery, gaining a deeper understanding of who I aspired to be, I have learned to perceive the world not just with my mind, but with my heart. I have allowed myself to take time to process the inner journey of the heart and have become the scientist of my own spiritual experiences. It has led me to understand the significance of being in the flow, where things are neither inherently good nor bad, but simply part of a larger story.

Self-awareness has been the key to this transformation. It involves attentively observing the world within and around me and using that information to determine whether adjustments are needed in my consciousness, behavior, thoughts, or actions. This process has allowed me to gain insight into my internal world and pay attention to the external world. Through this ongoing practice, I am on a journey of self-discovery, uncovering the depths of my true identity.

Through the practice of manifesting positivity, we can witness the magic that transpires when we hold steadfast beliefs. The Universe is abundant, and it rewards those who pay attention to the subtle signs and synchronicities that guide us along our journey. By aligning our thoughts, intentions, and actions with positivity and gratitude, we open ourselves to a world of infinite possibilities and experiences.

I create a harmonious, energetic environment by consciously practicing the law of vibration and surrounding myself with the right people. When we align ourselves with positive, like-minded individuals, we elevate our vibration and attract positivity into our lives. Through this intentional cultivation of supportive relationships, we can experience personal growth, fulfillment, and a more profound connection with the Universe. Everything you need to know you have learned through your journey.

When it comes to love, by its very definition, it entails a willingness to give without expecting anything in return. In the context of my casual relationships, where I'm constantly measuring whether I am getting back what I am giving and wondering if it is all worth it, aren't we all seeking someone who can reignite our belief in love unconditionally? Every story may have its unique beginning and end, but there is always the potential for more. Love has a way of developing and evolving beyond what we initially perceive.

With a heart overflowing with gratitude and anticipation, I venture forth once again!

Acknowledgments

I would like to express my heartfelt gratitude to all those who have played a significant role in shaping my journey. To protect their privacy, I decided to change the names of the individuals I encountered along the way. It is important to emphasize that during our interactions, none of these individuals were aware of the thoughts and emotions that filled my mind. None of us could have anticipated that these experiences would become a part of my book, not even me.

I am immensely grateful for all the individuals who have crossed my path, whether they were aware of the role they played or not, whether they are mentioned in this book or not. Every interaction, no matter how small or seemingly insignificant, has contributed to shaping the person I have become and taught me valuable lessons. It is with profound appreciation that I reflect upon the connections forged and the impact they have had on the story of my life.

Last but not least, I want to give enormous thanks to my parents and brothers from the bottom of my heart. Growing up in a traditional Taiwanese family, the eldest is often burdened with the responsibility of holding the family structure together. We are seen as the backbone of the family simply because we are older. We are expected to stay close to home, near our family members. Not only did I fail to fulfill that role, but I also decided to leave my promising corporate job, and instead, I chose to become a writer, a path that isn't accepted easily in traditional ways. I am always aware of how difficult and emotional this has been for my parents to accept, and perhaps they are still in the process of accepting that I am not following the "safe" and "stable" path they desired for me. Despite limited communication over the years, I have always known that they have my back. I am appreciative of their unspoken understanding. I also want to express my gratitude to my brother for assuming the role of the eldest, which allowed me the freedom to pursue my passions and live in the place I desired. It was through his and my parents' unconditional and tremendous support that I can complete my book today.

Author Bio

Hsin Chen is an author, proud mother, seasoned marketing specialist, and the visionary founder of *Nanani World*. With her rich multicultural background that spans eight cities, five countries, and four continents, Hsin draws on her incredible personal odyssey to offer unique perspectives and profound insights in both the corporate world and beyond.

Hsin's remarkable journey of self-transformation began in 2019 when she relocated to the vibrant city of Barcelona with her two young children. As the author of her memoir *Venturing Forth*, she aims to share her story, inspiring readers to overcome their own life challenges and dare to dream of a better future. Hsin's inspirational story has earned her recognition in esteemed media outlets including Business Insider, Bloomberg, and Yahoo.

Through her innovative wellness business, *Nanani World*, Hsin aims to provide single parents with a sanctuary where they can cultivate self-love, mindfulness, and holistic well-being. Her fervent advocacy for women's empowerment drives her to share her wisdom, illuminating paths to self-discovery and encouraging her clients to cherish life's simple joys with their children. For more information, or to book her services, visit www.nanani.world

Printed in the USA
CPSIA information can be obtained
at www.ICGtesting.com
LVHW011448161023
761176LV00009B/26